magazines

Media Industries

David Sumner,
General Editor

Vol. 2

PETER LANG
New York • Washington, D.C./Baltimore • Bern
Frankfurt am Main • Berlin • Brussels • Vienna • Oxford

David E. Sumner
and Shirrel Rhoades

magazines

A Complete Guide to the Industry

PETER LANG
New York • Washington, D.C./Baltimore • Bern
Frankfurt am Main • Berlin • Brussels • Vienna • Oxford

Library of Congress Cataloging-in-Publication Data

Sumner, David E.
Magazines: a complete guide to the industry / David E. Sumner, Shirrel Rhoades.
p. cm. — (Media industries; v. 2)
Includes bibliographical references and index.
1. Periodicals. 2. Periodicals—Publishing.
I. Rhoades, Shirrel. II. Title. III. Series.
PN4832.S86 070.5'72—dc22 2006017769
ISBN 0-8204-8835-6 (hard cover)
ISBN 0-8204-7617-X (paper back)
ISSN 1550-1043

Bibliographic information published by **Die Deutsche Bibliothek**.
Die Deutsche Bibliothek lists this publication in the "Deutsche
Nationalbibliografie"; detailed bibliographic data is available
on the Internet at http://dnb.ddb.de/.

Cover design by Lisa Barfield

The paper in this book meets the guidelines for permanence and durability
of the Committee on Production Guidelines for Book Longevity
of the Council of Library Resources.

Contents

Preface

In October 2003, I was at an out-of-town convention when I received a cell phone call from Damon Zucca, an editor with Peter Lang USA in New York City. He wanted to know if I would be interested in editing a series of books on media industries and writing a book about the magazine industry for that series. Of course, I said yes. I told him I couldn't start right away, however, since I still had considerable work to do on the magazine-writing textbook I was working on at the time.

While flattered to be asked to write a book about the magazine industry, I wasn't sure how qualified I was. My knowledge of the magazine industry came from thirty years of freelance magazine writing and fifteen years of teaching and doing research in the field. Shortly after I began working on this book in early 2005, I was introduced to Shirrel Rhoades by a mutual friend—John Robinson, former president and chief executive officer of Dynamic Resources Group, Inc. in Berne, Indiana. When I learned about Shirrel's extensive background in magazine management and publishing, I knew I had found the perfect match for this book. I asked Shirrel to coauthor the book, and he immediately agreed.

It was a real "small world" story, since both Shirrel and I had attended Stetson University in Florida as undergraduates—he had graduated five years earlier than I.

We both spent most of our careers in magazine journalism—even though neither of us majored in journalism. Stetson, although a fine liberal arts university, still doesn't have a journalism major.

I wish to thank many others who contributed to this book. In August 2005, I spent a week in New York interviewing Nina Link, president of the Magazine Publishers of America; Scott Crystal, publisher of *TV Guide;* magazine designers J. C. Suares and Walter Bernard; Joe Treen, former editor with *Discover* and *People* magazines; John Squires and Ned Desmond, executives with Time, Inc., magazines; Jackie Leo, editor-in-chief of *Reader's Digest;* and Victor Navasky, a publisher and director of the magazine program at Columbia University. I did telephone interviews with Dick Stolley, the founding editor of *People Weekly;* Hal Karp, a contributing editor for *Reader's Digest;* Whitney Sielaff, publisher of *National Jeweler;* and Stewart Ramser, the founding publisher of *Texas Music.* I also wish to thank the Magazine Publishers of America, International Federation of the Periodical Press (FIPP) in London, and Veronis Suhler Stevenson Investment Bankers in New York for giving me numerous reports and research publications without charge. I thank all current and former students in my magazine-management classes, with whom and upon whom many of the ideas in this book have been formed and tested.

The list could go on, and there are those whom I am sure I missed. The story has a sad twist, however, since our mutual friend John Robinson died of cancer a few months before this book went to press. Because of his accomplishments at Indiana's largest magazine publisher and his commitment to journalism education at Ball State University, the department honored him posthumously with its annual Indiana Journalism Award in April 2006. Shirrel and I dedicate this book to his memory and the example he set for his employees and friends in moral character and managerial leadership.

David E. Sumner
March 2006

Why Magazines Are Special

Introduction

One of the twenty-first century's newest **magazines** is *Self-Defense for Women*. The magazine's purpose statement says that it "covers all aspects of self-defense, from keeping in shape to techniques on keeping assailants at bay. As long as violence is a part of our society the need to curb violence will always be an important skill needed to survive in the dog-eat-dog world in which we live." *Self Defense for Women* was one of 1,004 new magazines launched in 2004 according to *Samir Husni's Guide to New Consumer Magazines*.

Many times since the twentieth century began, skeptics have predicted the decline of magazines. First, after World War I, when automobiles first became popular and inexpensive, some people felt that the time people spent driving would cut into magazine reading and hurt the magazine business. Second, when commercial radio stations flourished in the 1920s, some thought radio would steal all the advertising from magazines as people stopped reading them. Third, the Golden Age of movies during the 1930s again convinced the skeptics that magazines had a dim future as the public became fascinated with the new medium. Fourth, television's introduction and its mushrooming growth in the 1950s again made people wonder whether magazines could survive. The demise of such icons as the *Saturday Evening Post*, *Look*, and *Life* in the late 1960s convinced many that magazines were doomed.[1] Finally, the introduction of the Internet during the 1990s again brought out the "death of print" chorus to sing its eulogy to magazines.

Yet during the twentieth century, the number of magazines grew five-fold, from three thousand to more than eighteen thousand. Ad revenue grew almost every consecutive year even when adjusted for inflation. On average, every household purchases six different magazines annually, and the average American spent more time reading magazines at the end of the century than he or she did at the beginning.[2]

The power of magazines stems from the personal identity conveyed not only by their content, but by their total package of color, design, and editorial tone of voice. Magazines are the most intimate form of media because they can establish a relationship with their readers unequalled by newspapers, television, or radio stations. A magazine sometimes becomes a friend and an integral part of the reader's personal and professional life.

"Magazines occupy a unique place in consumers' hearts because they're portable, and they're tactile. People allow them into their homes as trusted companions on a weekly or monthly basis," said Scott Crystal, publisher of *TV Guide*, in an interview. "The nature of magazines is totally unique because it engages the reader with the editorial product and a relationship that the editor starts to build over time. And that relationship is different than just turning on a television set where all of it comes blasting right into your home. So it is different, it is personal and it has, therefore, a more involving and engaging nature," he said.[3]

The beauty of magazines is the emotion and passion that you can pour into reading them. Catherine Black, president of Hearst Magazines, said in a television interview, "At the end of the day, think about where you read your magazines: in bed at night or on an airplane or any place where you are feeling good. You are engaged in it. You are entertained by it."[4] On the same program, Jack Kliger, president of Hachette Filipacchi Media USA, said, "Reading is still the number one leisure activity among most Americans. And it's always among the top three of how people like to relax. I don't think that's going to change."

Researchers at Northwestern University conducted a "Reader Experience Study" for the Magazine Publishers Association.[5] When they asked people why they read magazines, the subjects' answers each tended to follow one of two different themes. One was the "It makes me smarter" answer, illustrated by the following quotations:

"The magazine stimulates my thinking about things."

"It updates me on things I try to keep up with."

"I get ideas from the magazine."

"I remember at least some things I have read in the magazine for a long time."

The other type of response coming from magazine readers was the "It's

Table 1: Number of Magazines Published by Country (2003 data—latest available)

Country	Consumer Magazines	Business-to-Business Magazines	Total
United States	6,234	5,078	11,312
United Kingdom	3,229	5,108	8,337
Germany	2,300	3,623	5,923
Japan	2,524	1,846	4,370
France	2,904	1,200	4,104
Italy	782	2,000	2,782
Brazil	2,296	150	2,446
Czech Republic	1,010	1,250	2,260
Finland	284	1,834	2,118
Australia	780	870	1,650
Canada	1,032	525	1,557
South Africa	515	580	1,095
Mexico	1,081	5	1,086
Netherlands	152	887	1,039
Spain	634	300	934
Argentina	685	67	752
Sweden	182	321	503
Israel	102	341	443
Denmark	91	337	428
Turkey	126	300	426
Ireland	330	34	364
Norway	83	240	323
Malaysia	192	47	239
Lebanon	51	26	77
United Arab Emirates	34	8	42
Saudi Arabia	26	11	37

Note: Some directories mentioned in this book list more than eighteen thousand U.S. magazines. This total includes organizational magazines, academic publications, and free-distribution tourism or travel magazines not included in this table. Source for this table: World Magazine Trends. 2004-2005 (London: FIPP/ZenithOptimedia, 2005).

my personal recreation" answer. Here are some answers that fall into that category:

"The magazine takes my mind off other things that are going on."

"Reading this magazine is a bit of a luxury for me . . . It's a treat."

"My goal is to relax with the magazine."

"Reading this magazine is my time alone."

Regardless of content, all successful magazines begin with an idea—a concept about a particular type of information that people are willing to pay for. The word *magazine* originated with the French *magazin*, which means "storehouse." A magazine is, therefore, a "storehouse" of information. Here's a definition of a magazine: *a regularly published periodical offering specific editorial content to a clearly defined audience with common interests that advertisers or a sponsoring organization want to reach.* (Magazines are sometimes referred to as "books" by people in the industry. "We're closing the book," the advertising director says as he cuts off the issue's sales activity and locks in the number of ad pages sold. Don't be confused; we're still talking about magazines.)

Differences between Magazines and Newspapers

How do magazines differ from newspapers? Besides obvious differences in design and appearance, they have less obvious differences in content and production techniques:

- Newspaper writing aims to please a local geographic audience with a broad range of ages, interests, and educational and socioeconomic backgrounds. Newspapers focus on reporting local and national news. Magazines aim their content at a narrow target audience with specific interests and demographic characteristics. Although a magazine may appeal to a narrow set of reader interests, members of its audience may live anywhere the world.
- Newspapers employ large staffs of reporters and a few editors. Magazines employ large staffs of editors and few full-time writers. Most magazines rely on freelance writers for most of their stories. One reason is that magazine editors want content from writers throughout the country who reflect the geographic diversity of their audience.
- Newspaper feature writing is generally detached and objective. The personality of the writer remains hidden. Magazine writers have more freedom than newspaper writers to display viewpoint, voice, tone, and style in their writing.
- Newspaper writing requires daily or weekly deadlines; magazine writing has monthly deadlines except in the case of a few weeklies and quarterlies. That means readers expect more complexity, analysis, originality, depth, and accuracy from magazines.

Ted Spiker, a journalism professor at the University of Florida and former senior editor for *Men's Health*, said:

> To me, working for a magazine feels like you're part of a sports team—in all the good ways. There's lots of game-planning in the form of brainstorming and big-picture discussion. There's lots of locker-room camaraderie in the form of laugh-your-butt-off creative meetings. There's lots of game-on-the-line pressure in the form of frantic closes. There's lots of team play in the form of col-

laboration. There's lots of competition in the form of rival magazines. And what I really like is that, in a way, you have a 10-game or 12-game season depending on how many issues you put out a year. It's not like you have 365 chances in a year the way you would at a newspaper, or maybe one chance a year in books. You have a dozen chances to do great, perfect, creative, reader-inspiring work—and that's a fun, motivating process to be a part of.[6]

Mousetrap Theory of Publishing

As Ralph Waldo Emerson said, "Build a better mousetrap and the world will beat a path unto your door." A magazine is simply a better mousetrap. On our trap, we place bait: interesting articles. This "cheese" is designed to attract a plump "mouse" called a reader. And there are "fat cats" called advertisers who want to get to those "mice."

That is the way a **consumer magazine** works: we create bait to attract a mouse to sell to a cat. Or, in plain language, a magazine's editorial content attracts specific readers whom certain advertisers want to reach with their messages.

Successful magazine publishing has been defined as a "three-legged stool," which depends on: (1) strong *editorial content*, which leads to (2) high *circulation*, which in turn attracts (3) *advertisers*. If any one leg of the stool is weak, it will topple over. With strong editorial content in a specific area of interest, a magazine attracts readers who are interested in this topic. But this isn't enough. A magazine must also attract a group of advertisers who sell products that these readers are interested in. Therefore, these magazines don't really sell "space" on their pages. They sell *access* to their readers with the information about products that will interest them.

For example, *Backpacker*, which calls itself "The outdoors at your doorstep," connects hikers and campers with the plethora of companies who sell shoes, clothing, camping and hiking gear, travel destinations, and health foods. *Bead World* connects manufacturers, retail outlets, and importers of beads with an audience of readers who enjoy the hobby of making beaded jewelry.

A strong magazine niche is a specific activity (golfing, fishing, boating, cigar smoking) with a reachable audience requiring much paraphernalia (clubs, rods, engines, humidors) that provides a strong base of endemic advertising.

Types and Number of Magazines

The three major American magazine directories—*Bacon's Magazine Directory*, the *National Directory of Magazines*, and *Gale Directory of Publications*—vary in the number of magazines they include. According to the *National Directory of Magazines*, there were 18,821 magazines in the United States in 2004. Of those, 7,188 were consumer titles. A consumer magazine is any magazine available to the general public through subscription or single-copy sales. These are the most popular magazines that most people read and know about. A **business-to-business magazine** seeks to help people in specific professions and occupations become more successful at their jobs. **Organizational magazines**, which could number up to four thousand in this country, include those published by civic and fraternal associations, corporations, religious organizations, and colleges and universities for their constituencies.

Consumer Magazines

The typical magazine that most people read is a "consumer magazine" because anyone with the money can purchase it at the newsstand or subscribe to it through the mail (or online). According to the Magazine Publishers of America, the major publishers association, the average single-copy price for a consumer magazine (in 2004) was $4.40 and the average subscription price was $25.93. About 38 percent of all magazines are purchased at supermarkets, followed by mass merchandisers (17 percent), bookstores (11 percent), drugstores (10 percent), convenience stores (7 percent), and terminals (6 percent).[7]

Business-to-Business Magazines

These magazines, sometimes called simply "trade" or "business" magazines, are service magazines whose main purpose is to provide information to workers in specific jobs, careers, and occupations. About five thousand "B-to-B" magazines are published in the United States. Some are paid subscriptions, while others are supported entirely by advertising and sent free to key executives and decision makers in various industries. Advertisers of products for specific industries and occupations are so eager to reach these key players that they're willing to pay the entire cost of publishing the magazine.

Organizational Magazines

Organizational magazines are published by companies for their employees or customers, universities for their alumni, denominations or religious organizations for their members, and special-interest and professional associations for their members. Because they're privately published, it's difficult to estimate the number of U.S. magazines in this group, but it could be as high as five thousand. Organizational magazines differ from consumer magazines because they are not sold in stores nor can the general public subscribe. They are published by their sponsoring organizations and generally sent free as a membership benefit.

Consumer Magazine Life Cycles

James B. Kobak, author of *How to Start a Magazine and Publish It Profitably*, likes to categorize magazines based on where they are in their life cycle. Some new titles are in their infancy, others are going through a fitful childhood, still others are growing into adolescence, then manhood and middle age—all the way to old age and eventual death. It's easy to identify them:

- A hot new title like *Every Day with Rachel Ray* is certainly in its infancy. The question always is, Will it survive? The TV cooking show personality is taking on Martha Stewart and other well-established competitors, a major challenge for a newborn.
- Launched in the late 1990s, *O* magazine is enjoying a robust childhood. Driven by the personality of TV diva Oprah Winfrey, the magazine has enjoyed an early success.
- *Martha Stewart Living* is entering its angst-ridden teens impacted by the trials and tribulations of its namesake.
- *Stuff* faces its young manhood. A cocky young Turk, it is among those so-called laddie magazines taking on an old-timer known as *Playboy*.
- *Boy's Life*—according to Kobak—has been experiencing an extended middle age since the 1970s.
- As the oldest monthly magazine in America, *Harper's* is dealing with old age. Can it remain relevant or will it eventually die? That depends on the editor's ability to maintain a relevant editorial discourse with its thought-leader readers.

Finally, many magazines do die. We can easily name those classic titles like *Look* and *Colliers* that have met their demise. Others—such as *Vanity Fair*—have been successfully reborn. Originally launched in 1860 as a humorous weekly, it failed a few years later. Condé Nast tried it again in 1914, and it became the gold standard for the so-called smart magazines throughout the 1920s and '30s. Falling victim to the Great Depression, it ceased publication in 1936. Then in the 1980s, Condé Nast relaunched it with much fanfare. Under the editorships of Tina Brown (1984–92) and E. Graydon Carter (since 1992), the magazine found new prestige, and increased circulation and revenue—indeed, the advertising in the magazine is so plentiful that one has to thumb many pages even to find the table of contents.

Taking the new *Vanity Fair* as an example of life cycles, Kobak places the magazine in its infancy in 1984, its childhood in 1987, its adolescence in 1990, its manhood in 1995. One could argue that it has now settled into a comfortable (and successful) middle age.

Unique Characteristics of Magazines

Are print magazines just another medium of delivering information? Or do they have some unique characteristics that distinguish them from competing forms of mass media, especially radio, television, newspapers, and the Internet? We will address that question by looking at four possible answers:

1   Magazines adapt content quickly to reflect changing lifestyles and social trends.
2   Readers develop a personal relationship with magazines they read regularly.
3   Social trends affect magazine success or failure in unexpected ways.
4   New technology pushes down cost of magazine publishing.

While all media benefit from these same characteristics to some degree, we believe none of them does so as well as magazines.

Magazines Adapt to Changing Lifestyles and Trends

The adaptability of magazines has enabled their survival and success. While magazines are an information-delivery system, their ability to provide specialized and practical information to targeted audiences helped magazines to survive. If one type of content isn't working, magazines can make minor or major changes.

Can magazines change, find a new lease on life? Yes—sometimes as something quite different. Magazines can even undergo a sex change. What would you say if we told you that *Cosmopolitan* used to be a *men's* magazine? There are many other examples. Magazines are constantly repositioning themselves (both subtly and not so subtly), undergoing redesigns, "refreshing" their editorial format. This sometimes comes as a deliberate response to market shifts; other times it the natural result of a change in editorship.

Reader's Digest morphed from its historical covers featuring its table of contents to today's more stylistic covers. In what *Reader's Digest*'s CEO Eric Schrier tagged "the Quiet Revolution," the magazine in 2001 was given the most far-ranging redesign in its history: a new, contemporary look that unified home-delivery and newsstand versions. The new cover treatment was adapted to all forty-eight global editions of the *Digest*.

What are typical signs?

Changing editors. When *Popular Mechanics* decided to get a new look, its longtime editor saw that as a logical time to hand over the reins to a new editorial leadership.

And when the men's marketplace started getting bombarded by the myriad of laddie magazines, *Playboy* began stealing away editors who could add more features to its venerable pages that were reminiscent of the "short takes" found in this new genre.

Consulting the strategists. Experts are called in to shape a new strategy. With the market shift in the late 1980s, Scholastic used positioning gurus Jack Trout and Al Reis to help plot a step-by-step transition from *Family Computing* to *Family & Home Office Computing* to finally simply *Home Office Computing*. This editorial adjustment followed a shifting marketplace.

Bringing in the makeover artists. Legendary designers like Roger Black, Walter Bernard, and Milton Glaser are often called in to give a magazine its new look. A one-time art director at *Rolling Stone*, Black has reshaped some of the world's most visible magazines, including *Newsweek*, *Reader's Digest*, *Esquire*, the *New York Times Magazine*, *The New Republic*, and *National Enquirer*. As he said, "I've designed more magazines than you'll ever read." What does a Black redesign cost? The number can range from $250,000 to $500,000 for a major magazine.

Why are publishers willing to pay it? Often for the same reason a movie star gets a facelift: to stave off the ravages of time, to prolong the life cycle. As Black has noted, "There is always some volatility at the time of a redesign. They don't call it a redesign because everything is going great."

Readers Develop a Relationship with Magazines

"People don't merely read consumer magazines; they have a close personal relationship with them," said Renetta McCann, chief executive officer for Starcom Worldwide. She told *Magazine World*, "Magazines offer benefits that are distinct among competing forms of media. In a world in which consumers increasingly seek control, magazines give it to them. They allow consumers to customize their reading experiences to suite their own taste. They determine where they read magazines; how and when they read magazines."

Magazines make no pretense to being "unbiased," and most even admit their "bias." Beginning with the abolitionist magazines in the nineteenth century, magazines have historically advocated social causes, political causes, and particular points of view. Two of the best-known liberal political-content magazines are *The Nation* and *The New Republic*, while two of the best-known conservative magazines are *National Review* and *The Weekly Standard*. "We are in business to make a point and not a profit," said Victor Navasky, publisher of *The Nation*.[8]

The Economist, a magazine about international affairs, has been published continuously since 1843. In 2005, it reached a circulation of 1 million, with readers in 201 countries. Its circulation director said in an article in *Magazine World*, "The viability comes from remaining true to one's readers by having strong and firm beliefs which either don't change or change only slowly over long periods of time."[9]

Social Trends Affect Magazine Success or Failure

An entrepreneur can develop a brilliant idea for a new magazine and execute it perfectly with unlimited financial backing. Yet the magazine can fail because of social trends over which he or she is helpless. At the same time, some magazine titles can ride the wave of success with almost anyone at the helm. For example, the 1980s saw many computer magazines launched with remarkable success in a short time. However, only the best survived the shakeout of the industry that came in 2000 and 2001 with a recession and glutted market.

Changing social trends generally help magazines because people need the specialized information magazines provide to pursue new leisure activities and social interests. For example, *Thrasher* magazine was launched in the early 1980s to serve the growing number of skateboarders. Because magazines aim specialized editorial products at specific audiences, shifts in the size or nature of their audiences can hasten their success or failure.

Magazines have a dependent relationship on social trends in three ways that can bring success or failure to certain types of magazines: (1) shifting age **demographics**; (2) changing social values, lifestyles, and interests; and (3) economic cycles of recession and prosperity. Prospective publishers and editors must study these trends as closely as they do their stylebooks and spreadsheets.

First, the changing size of some age groups in the population (called "age cohorts" by sociologists) is directly tied to the fate of magazines targeted at those age groups. An aging population has already given *AARP: The Magazine* the number-one circulation ranking among American magazines, with 22 million subscribers. The most highly sought-after age cohorts are the "baby boomers" born between 1946 and 1964.

The number of adults aged forty-five and older increased by 12 percent between 1999 and 2004 and was projected to grow another 11 percent in the next five years. In contrast, the number of adults aged eighteen to forty-four rose just 1.3 percent from 1999 and 2004 and was projected to grow less than 1 percent in the next five years.[10]

The number of births grew from 3.4 million in 1946 to 4.3 million in 1957, and stayed at over 4 million until 1964. Then it steadily declined to a low of 3.1 million in 1973. After that it steadily increased to 4.1 million in 1990, after which it began to decline again.

As a result, children and teenagers' magazines faced a difficult challenge in the 1980s with relatively few readers who were born in the early 1970s. Their circulation figures, however, improved in the 1990s. Circulations of lifestyle, leisure, and travel magazines grew in the 1990s as the baby boomers entered middle age with "empty nests" and more leisure time and money.

Second, changing social values and lifestyles affect magazine success and failure. Many magazine experts believe that television helped magazines grow because it introduced Americans to a broader range of interests. "As book publishers have learned that a successful movie spurs rather than harms book sales, so magazine publishers have been able to take advantage of television. Popularity of televised spectator sports has stimulated sales of sports magazines, and fast-breaking news on TV has created opportunities for deeper analysis and perspective in the newsweeklies," writes Benjamin Compaine.[11]

But trends that help magazines can also hurt them. The rise of television created the success of *TV Guide*, whose circulation was about the fifth highest among all magazines in the late 1980s. At first, the popularity of television created an insatiable demand for program listings and content. But by the 1990s, most Sunday newspapers included a television supplement. Cable and satellite television networks offered on-screen TV schedules and program guides. By 2005, the circulation of *TV Guide* had plummeted, and forcing the magazine into a major redesign and a reduction in its rate base.

"What we're doing is investing to make sure that the magazine or the brand remains strong and relevant," said *TV Guide* publisher Scott Crystal in an interview. "The magazine had to manifest itself differently into a full-sized, four-color magazine with richer and more robust editorial content. Our research has shown that is what our customers want—less listings and more feature content."[12] In late 2005 *TV Guide* was relaunched as a full-sized magazine, a major shift from its longtime digest format. And an important adjustment to its ink-on-paper business was providing programming information to cable TV systems.

Complex social pressures brought a decline in civic and fraternal participation in the 1980s and '90s. As a result, membership in popular organizations like Kiwanis, Elks, and Rotary clubs declined along with readership of their high-circulation magazines.

A joke making the rounds at *The Nation*, a left-leaning political magazine, after the 2000 election, went like this: "What's bad for the country is good for *The Nation*," according to publisher Victor Navasky. Since George Bush was elected president, the magazine's circulation more than doubled. *Mother Jones*, another liberal magazine, increased its circulation by 10,000, to 176,000. Two smaller left-leaning magazines, *American Prospect* and *In These Times*, also had healthy increases in 2001. The same phenomenon occurred with conservative magazines in the early 1990s after Bill Clinton was elected president. *The American Spectator* experienced a sevenfold circulation jump, and *National Review* grew 66 percent during the Clinton years. Another conservative magazine, *The Weekly Standard*, was launched in 1995 and grew to 65,000 readers by 2000.[13]

As more women began to move into the workplace during the 1970s, magazines such as *Working Woman* and *Working Mother* were launched to serve their needs. Such examples of trends influencing magazine popularity and content are numerous.

Third, economic shifts make an impact on magazines as well as other mass media. When sales and revenue decline among manufacturers, advertising budgets are always cut. But magazines feel the effects of recessions more than other media—and they recover later, according to Nina Link, president of the Magazine Publishers of America.

"Because our issues close so far in advance, we often feel it later, then we recover later. In August, for example, editors are working on their November issues. They're always set for the next three or four months. We feel it later and we recover after other media appear to be recovering. That's more of our cycle," said Link.[14]

Economic shifts that occurred within certain segments of the economy had a subtler impact—either positive or negative. More women in the workplace in the 1970s and 1980s brought new magazines such as *Working Mother* and *Working Woman* to serve their needs. But those same changes created a flat growth pattern among some women's magazines aimed at traditional homemakers. While the Great Depression of the 1930s brought the demise of major magazines, it also helped create the success of others. For example, Henry Luce (founder of *Time* magazine in 1923) started *Fortune* in 1930, which was an immediate and permanent success. The magazine offered concise and objective information about American business conditions to business leaders who needed that information. *Sylvia Porter's Personal Finance* flourished for a while, but then was ploughed under by the decline in money funds and the death of its namesake. Stronger magazines like *Money* survived the dip in advertising revenues.

New Technology Pushes down Cost of Magazine Publishing

Finally, new technology has probably helped the startup of new magazines more than it has benefited the establishment of new newspapers, radio, or television stations. As late as the 1980s, publishers needed a $25,000 typesetting machine to fulfill the same functions that a $500 computer can do for them today. Even with a $25,000 typesetter, magazine publishers still had to hire people to re-key the editorial material sent to them, do manual paste-up and layout, send film out for expensive color separations, and physically transport camera-ready copy to printers. Because of the stunning technological innovations of the 1990s—especially digital photography, layout, and design—the startup cost for launching a magazine has plummeted.

The only part of the production process that did not get cheaper or easier was mailing and delivery. For subscriptions, postal delivery costs continued to increase, and changed from an insignificant to significant percentage of total production costs. For newsstand sales, the national distribution network consolidated into four major companies that maintained an oligopoly in the single-copy delivery chain. This delivery system remains plagued with inefficiency, high costs, and barriers to entry for new magazine entrepreneurs.

Then came the Internet in the 1990s, which enabled publishers to launch online magazines that bypassed all of the delivery problems of print publications. Consumers resisted, however, when it came to paying for online-only subscriptions for magazines.

While only a few online magazines succeeded in attracting paying customers, most magazines found the Internet more of a friend than a foe. Despite being a competitor for leisure-time activities such as reading, it helped them attract new subscribers for their print publications while they used their sites to enhance customer service and strengthen relationships with existing subscribers. Chapter 10, "How Magazines Embraced the Internet," will explain these developments in more detail.

Now that you know a little bit about how the magazine industry works, let's look at a typical magazine and see how it works.

Questions for Further Thought

1   What social trends seem to be emerging that may create a need for new magazines to serve those fields of interest?

2   Since the number of Americans aged forty-five and older is growing, what kinds of new magazines might serve their interests? Tip: Don't just consider "retirement" magazines—think recreation, finance, fitness and health, and so on as areas of interest for older Americans.

3   How do college-age students think about the benefits and advantages of print-only magazines to online magazines? Are they losing interest in print-only magazines?

Shop Talk

Business-to-business magazine: A magazine published for members of a specific profession or occupation to help them do their jobs better or advance their careers.

Consumer magazine: A magazine available to the general public (consumers) through mail subscriptions or retail outlet sales.

Demographics: The specific characteristics that define a magazine's readership. Demographics include—but are not limited to—the readers' age distributions, occupational status, marital status, gender, race, and geographical breakdowns.

Magazine: A regularly published or updated periodical offering specific editorial content to a clearly defined audience with common interests that an advertiser or group of advertisers wants to reach.

Organizational magazine: A magazine published by a company, professional association, nonprofit organization, or religious group for its members, employees, or customers.

The People
Who Work
at Magazines

While people who "like to write" are attracted to magazine journalism, the positions involved in putting together a magazine involve a wide variety of skills. Publishers hiring a staff—or students considering a magazine career—should understand the differences among these skills.

Writing involves the ability to put together words and sentences in a logical and coherent way. Great writers know how to express great ideas in an entertaining and engaging style while using very few words. Most writers say that writing involves only about 20 percent of the work of putting together most magazine feature articles. Researching and reporting the material takes up the other 80 percent of the time.

Reporting involves finding good sources to interview, going out and interviewing them, and knowing how to locate the unique resources that make a story engaging and interesting. Some great reporters are poor writers and must depend heavily on editors to edit their material. Great reporters, however, know how to dig and dig to find the "scoops" and great stories that no one else can find.

Editing involves not only copy editing—fixing the words and sentences—but creating ideas, and crafting and shaping them in a way that will have the strongest appeal to readers. Editors have a clearer sense of who their readers are and what they like than do most of their writers. They recognize a great idea when it comes along and find the right writer to execute it.

"Good writers don't always make good editors. It's also true that not very good writers can be reasonably good editors," said Richard Stolley, founding editor of *People* and currently senior editorial adviser for Time Inc. "What we found when we were trying to convert writers into editors is that some people can control their own prose, but when it comes to doing something with someone else's they just freeze up. They are confident enough to do their own writing, but when it comes to editing someone else, their confidence just leaves."

Stolley also said that some journalists have reporting skills that are better than their writing ability. "At *People*, the reporting has always been absolutely critical. Even when the writing lacked something, the reporting was good. We stressed reporting more than we did writing. At the beginning, our stories were very simply told—just lay out the facts and hold back on adjectives and adverbs. Nothing is more interesting than reading simple facts simply presented," he said in a telephone interview.[1]

Characteristics of Great Editors

Biographies of the great editors in history reveal an uncanny ability to figure out what people are interested in reading about and deliver it month after month. Like any successful entrepreneur, they see a need and proceed to fill it with an innovative product. Because they love their readers, great editors connect with them emotionally and intellectually. People feel an emotional bond with their favorite magazines, and great editors create it. These editors have a voracious appetite for information and read everything from labels on cans to encyclopedias. But they also travel and converse with their readers. They see their readers not as social inferiors to whom they deliver information, but as friends with whom they carry on a conversation.

"A good magazine editor has to be a wordsmith, a good judge of talent, a good delegator," said Joe Treen, who has held senior editorial positions with *People* and *Discover* magazines.

> Editors have to see the big picture and the details at the same time. They have to have a strong affinity for the subject of their magazine. They have to be able to work with all the various departments in a magazine: art, photo, production, human resources, the printer, circulation, ad sales. They need to be curious, to be interested in the rest of the world. And I think they need to be uncompromising. They have to keep high standards and they can't let anyone (like advertisers) intrude on the vision of the magazine.[2]

"Editors deal with copy, deadlines, sources and more, but they may also spend time fact-checking, completing expense reports, work on next year's editorial calendar, meet with the marketing/sales department to discuss each issue's pagination according to the number of ad pages sold," said Nicole Voges, a special projects editor with *Modern Healthcare* in Chicago. "In general, while a reporter's focus is more short-term, an editor may be working on things months or years in advance," she said.[3]

According to John Mack Carter, editor emeritus for Hearst Magazines, "The job of a top editor includes more publishing vision, industry visibility, and vitality of ideas than blue-penciling skills."[4] Think of an editor's job like a funnel with a large scoop at one end and a small pointed hole at the other. The scoop end encompasses all of the available words and images in human experience, the Internet, and other published books, newspapers, and periodicals. The editors then siphon and distill that information into the relatively tiny quantity of content on the other end that most interests their readers.

Here are ten characteristics of great editors based on our years of experience in the publishing industry. If you want to become a successful editor, work on becoming:

1 Aggressive. Great editors create ideas for articles and find writers to execute them. They don't depend completely on volunteers or freelance submissions for ideas.

2 Sociable. Editors can't be shy or introverted. You have to learn to mix with readers and other staff members. Great editors develop strong relationships with their staff members and with their readers.

3 Perceptive. Editors develop a sense for what's interesting and what's not interesting. They know the public pulse. Read so widely that you develop a clear sense of what's news and what isn't, what's original and what's old stuff, what's interesting and what's boring.

4 Meticulous. Editors learn grammar, punctuation, and spelling. They care about the details because they know that if it's not right, some reader will always let them know.

5 Humble. A great editor knows when to admit mistakes and is always willing to print a correction in the next issue. One of the by-products of humility is a sense of humor because it helps you to laugh at your own mistakes.

6 Thick-skinned. Readers get mad about what you print and what you fail to print. If an editor never gets phone calls from angry readers, it's probably because that editor prints mostly boring stuff.

7 Decisive. Editors learn to say "no" to inappropriate material and those who would try to use and manipulate them. Discerning editors can withstand the pressure of these special interests and say "no" when necessary.

8 Technical-minded. Today's editors must love and use technology. You must also appreciate statistics and finance, and know how to use a spreadsheet. While writers can sometimes get away with disliking numbers or new technology, editors can't.

9 Courageous. Great editors know when to take risks in reporting and design, and when to avoid it. "Pushing the envelope" with controversial content can sometimes be tasteless and crude. Sometimes it can bring honors and accolades. Sensitive editors understand the difference.

10 Compassionate. Finally, editors love their readers and see them as peers and friends. Because they care about people, a great editor looks for content that will meet the intellectual, emotional, practical, and spiritual needs of their readers.

Great editors are also great marketers. They know that their job is to get people to read the magazine. So the selection of articles and other content in an issue must draw the reader in. And the editorial features on the magazine's cover—usually the editor's responsibility—must make buyers want to pick it up at the newsstand or open it up frequently enough to want to renew. Many editors' compensation packages include bonuses based on newsstand sales or renewal rates.

Other Staff Members

The **masthead**, which usually appears in the first few pages of a magazine, includes its mailing address, the names and titles of all staff members, the corporate **publisher** or owner, and other contact information. Some of the most common editorial titles seen on magazines include editor-in-chief, managing editor, editorial director, executive editor, associate editor, senior editor, articles editor, department editor, and editorial assistant.

All magazine editors serve one basic purpose: to plan the content, choose which articles to publish, help the writers choose the best possible angle, and ensure that writers do their job in the most interesting fashion with factual accuracy and proper grammar and punctuation. Precisely how magazines divvy up these duties among their editors varies. It depends on each magazine and the particular talents and skills of each editor. Duties also change as personnel at each magazine changes over time.

Some titles, however, have consistent job descriptions among different magazines. The publisher is the chief executive officer of a magazine. The person who holds this job oversees the editorial, advertising, circulation, and business departments of a magazine. Often the senior advertising executive gets this title because advertisers like to talk to the person at the top. And to make it even more confusing, the term *publisher* can also refer to the company that owns the magazine.

When Shirrel Rhoades was launching *Cricket: The Magazine for Children*, he met with the company's owner to discuss his title. He explained that his hands-on, day-to-day responsibility of managing the magazine would normally be called "publisher." The owner got a sad look on his face and said,

"But I thought I was the publisher." Rhoades was quite happy to accept the title of "general manager" to protect the feelings of the guy paying the bills.

The editor-in-chief (or some magazines simply use the title "editor") oversees the editorial department of a magazine. This job also involves some management and public relations duties for promoting the magazine. At a small magazine, the editor-in-chief does everything. As magazines grow, they add positions and divide up the work.

A **managing editor** supervises the work flow of editors, writers, and designers. The managing editor works with the printer and production staff to enforce deadlines and make sure the magazine gets to the printer on time.

An **editor-in-chief** with heavy management or public relations duties may assign another editor the title of editorial director to oversee all editorial content. Editors at high-circulation magazines receive heavy demands on their time for speaking engagements and public appearances. Other

Editors on Editing: Ted Spiker

"Writers only have to work with one person—their editor. But magazine editors have to manage all kinds of relationships. Take the senior editor, let's say. The senior editor has to work with a writer, coach the writing, and get the best work out of all of the writers. But the senior editor also has to be able to manage up (to sell and push for the stories he's working on to the top editors), manage down (to instruct interns or researchers), and manage across boundaries (to negotiate more space with art staff). Each relationship is a little bit different, and being good at it takes a lot more interpersonal ability than just simply having the tools of being a great writer or editor.

"I also think that editors have to find ways to balance individual performance and team concept since the editorial process is so collaborative. Editors need each other to brainstorm headlines, to tell each other honestly if a story sucks, to create original ideas. It's not that writers don't work well in a team; it's just that they tend to get their individual recognition (or criticism) because of the byline. So as an editor, when you make decisions or push ideas or criticize content, it always has to be about what makes sense for the overall quality of the magazine-and not about any one story or any one individual.

"I tell my students that the great editors are usually the ones who never touch a word. They coach. They inspire. They allow writers to retain their voice and style, but are able to instigate the changes that the story needs. While some of it simply comes down to individual personality, I think great editors have a skill for being able to tiptoe the line of criticism and motivation in the perfect balance, to get their writers from first draft to revision."

Ted Spiker, journalism professor at the University of Florida and former senior editor, Men's Health editors-in-chief may have to expend large amounts of time solving and dealing with personnel issues. Therefore, the editorial director can focus on the magazine's editorial content and relieve the editor-in-chief to perform other duties.

Associate editors or senior editors are responsible for planning and writing features in a specialty area (or department) and for all editorial work in that area. They supervise assistant editors, freelance writers, designers, and photographers. Amy Weingartner, editor of *Disney Adventures*, describes these as "the real workhorses of a magazine's editorial department."

The **copy editor** proofreads all articles and corrects the copy to ensure accurate punctuation, grammar, and spelling. Copy editors may also write titles, decks, and photo captions and do fact-checking. All editors may share the duties of writing articles, display text, titles, photo captions, and miscellaneous "blurbs."

An editorial assistant is the most common title for entry-level staff members. Editorial assistants serve as fact-checkers, copy editors, and **first readers** for **query letters** and perform general office work. All editors may do some writing of news, features, columns, or departments on a regular basis. Contributing editor is just another name for freelancers who are called on with regularity for their contributions to the magazines.

How Magazines Find Story Ideas

All articles begin with an idea. Most magazines get their ideas from a combination two sources: freelance writers and staff editors. Most editorial staffs meet weekly to plan for future issues. They discuss ideas for articles that originate among the editors as well as those that come from freelance writers.

Jacqueline Leo, editor-in-chief at *Reader's Digest*, describes the process this way: "We meet every week to review the proposals that are coming in from our contributing writers, outside freelancers, and ideas that our staff develops for stories. If we like an idea, we give it a green light. The green light means that what we have seen is a strong enough proposal that the next stage is giving an assignment letter to the writer."[5]

Originality is the most important criterion for a publishable idea. Magazines compete fiercely with each other and other media to be the first with the scoop.

No editor will accept rehashed content from the Internet or from competing magazines. Writers' guidelines for *The American Legion Magazine* say, "We will not accept just a warmed-over compilation of quotes and background material taken from other publications. Our authors must be willing to undertake firsthand research." As Leo said, "We never do secondary quotes at *Reader's Digest*. We might paraphrase a quote [from another magazine], but we'll give credit to the source."

David E. Sumner surveyed 135 professors who taught courses in magazine journalism asking them what writing mistakes they saw most often in their students' assignments. The four most commonly cited weaknesses among students were: (1) not reading widely enough to distinguish between original and unoriginal ideas; (2) choosing an angle that's too broad and poorly focused; (3) writing articles that do "too much 'telling' and not enough 'showing'"; and (4) conducting poor-quality or an insufficient number of interviews.[6]

"I am concerned about students' failure to take their feature stories beyond a dull recitation of facts and quotes," said one professor. Another professor replied, "The biggest overall problem I see from my students in all writing classes involves the amount of personal reading they do. They either read very little or not at all. If they do read, it's rarely outside of their highly focused interest."

Anyone wanting to write original articles for magazines, therefore, must love to read. Interviews with more than a dozen syndicated feature writers and columnists revealed that their number-one source for ideas was reading. Any magazine wanting to succeed in the marketplace can and must consistently publish original material.

As Charlie Brock, the founding editor of *Florida Time-Union's Sunday Magazine*, liked to say, "A great feature writer is one who brings a unique viewpoint."

Most consumer magazines rely on **freelance writers**. One reason for this is that choosing writers who come from around the country with differing ideas and social backgrounds results in more original content. Magazine editors want content to appeal to the interests of readers, who may live in all fifty states and dozens of foreign countries. Most consumer magazines are published in New York City, and their editors definitely do not want a content that reflects merely the interests of writers who live there.

Another reason that magazines rely heavily on freelance writers is economic: it's cheaper to pay thirty writers $1,000 each for their articles than to pay a $30,000 salary to one full-time writer to write thirty articles. A full-time staff member has the added expense of benefits that can reach 30 percent of salary. Staff members also require office space, equipment, and supervisory time.

Most magazines publish a set of writer's guidelines, either printed, online, or both. These guidelines explain in detail what types of articles they look for and what types they reject. Guidelines usually specify desired lengths and payment rates. Some magazines publish these guidelines on their websites, while others send them upon request to prospective writers who include a self-addressed, stamped envelope with their request. Some directories, such as *Writer's Market* and *Market Digest*, offer abbreviated guidelines from thousands of magazines to prospective writers.

Many small or regional magazines accept freelance articles, but can't afford to pay them except in contributor copies. Midsized magazines pay between $50 and $1,000 for feature articles. Large, national magazines pay writers $1 per word and more, which can amount to $5,000 to $10,000 for lengthy articles. The typical magazine feature, however, ranges from 1,000 to 2,000 words.

A freelance writer pitches an idea to an editor through a query letter. This type of letter proposes an idea to the magazine's editors. It shows the general thrust of the article, its angle or point, explains whom the writer plans to interview, and outlines its basic structure, content, and length. Popular consumer magazines receive thousands of query letters each month. Usually an **editorial assistant** or first reader scans the query letters and presents the best ideas to the editors for further consideration.

The only magazines that hire full-time writers—with some exceptions— are large, high-circulation national magazines. That includes the news-magazines and other weeklies such as *People* and *The New Yorker* with a need for consistently strong editorial content. The percentage of freelance content in magazines typically ranges from 20 to 100 percent. Most staff editors also write some articles in addition to their editing duties.

Understanding Your Strengths and Weaknesses

To help you decide on a magazine career, the Journalist's Self-Analysis Test below will help you understand your strengths and weaknesses. It will help publishers look for different skills in different positions in their hiring process. Different questions focus on skills required in writing, reporting, or editing. Some deal with the management duties of editors. There are no right or wrong answers, and no skills or traits are necessarily "good" or "bad."

The Journalist's Self-Analysis Test

You can use your writing skill in many different jobs and types of employers. This test will help you discover what type of writing, media or publishing job you will like the most.

Please answer the following questions with a 5, 4, 3, 2, or 1 based on this scale:

5 = I love doing this
4 = I like doing this
3 = I'm not sure I like doing this
2 = I don't think I like doing this
1 = I definitely don't enjoy doing this

_____ 1 Researching a topic in the library
_____ 2 Researching a topic on the Internet
_____ 3 Reading newspapers and magazines daily as part of my work
_____ 4 Reading books daily as part of my work
_____ 5 Dealing with numbers, charts, graphs, etc.
_____ 6 Thinking analytically about ideas
_____ 7 Coming up with original ideas
_____ 8 Writing about my ideas
_____ 9 Persuading others to accept my ideas
_____ 10 Editing and critiquing the writing of others
_____ 11 Persuading and encouraging others to do things
_____ 12 Teaching others how to do things
_____ 13 Taking my directions from someone in charge
_____ 14 Going out and interviewing strangers every day
_____ 15 Talking to the same group of people every day
_____ 16 Talking on the telephone with strangers
_____ 17 Working mainly alone with some supervision
_____ 18 Working mainly with a small group of people
_____ 19 Discussing plans and ideas in meetings with others
_____ 20 Working in an office building all day
_____ 21 Getting outdoors or driving places as part of my work
_____ 22 Figuring out what I have to do and doing it without being asked
_____ 23 Having clearly defined duties and responsibilities every day
_____ 24 Working in media for a for-profit business that produces products or services
_____ 25 Working for a for-profit company that publishes newspapers, magazines, or books
_____ 26 Working for a non-profit or educational organization that serves people
_____ 27 Working for a non-profit organization that promotes a special-interest (social cause, political, environmental, etc.)
_____ 28 Working for a religious organization
_____ 29 Seeing the tangible results of my work
_____ 30 Knowing that I have helped others without seeing the results
_____ 31 Working in a very large city (500,000 or more)
_____ 32 Working in a large city (100,000 to 500,000)
_____ 33 Working within a few hours' drive of my family
_____ 34 Working in another state or country
_____ 35 Getting a master's degree or Ph.D.
_____ 36 Teaching journalism or writing

Using the same 1–5 scale, evaluate how much you enjoy reading about these subjects.

_____ 37 Philosophy or religion
_____ 38 Science and medicine

_____	39 Business and law
_____	40 Biographies
_____	41 Health or fitness
_____	42 Travel/geography
_____	43 Computers or technology
_____	44 Social trends
_____	45 Politics

Circle and re-read all questions that you answered with a "4" or "5." Based on these answers, describe your ideal job—doing what, for whom, in what type of situation and where?

Describe two other types of writing or publishing jobs you think you would like.

Shop Talk

Copy editor: Proofreads all articles and corrects the copy to ensure accurate punctuation, grammar, and spelling. Copy editors may also write titles, decks, and photo captions and do fact-checking.

Editor-in-chief: Oversees the editorial department of a magazine. This job also involves some management and public relations duties for promoting the magazine. Some magazines simply use the title "editor" for the position.

Editorial assistant: The most common title for entry-level staff members. Editorial assistants serve as fact-checkers, copy editors, and first readers for query letters and perform general office work.

First reader: Large magazines receive thousands of unsolicited articles and query letters each month. They assign an editorial assistant or intern as first reader to choose a small number of the best ideas and forward them to the senior editorial staff for further review.

Freelance writer: A writer who doesn't work for any particular magazine, but writes and sells articles one at a time to those magazines willing to purchase them.

Managing editor: Supervises the work flow of editors, writers, and designers. The managing editor works with the printer and production staff to enforce deadlines and make sure the magazine gets to the printer on time.

Masthead: The masthead, usually printed in the first few pages of a magazine, includes its mailing address, the names and titles of all staff members, the corporate publisher or owner, and other contact information.

Publisher: The chief executive officer of a magazine who oversees the editorial, advertising, circulation, and business departments. The term *publisher* can also refer to name of the company that owns the magazine.

Query letter: A letter from a freelance writer proposing a magazine article idea. It shows the general thrust of the article, its angle or point, explains whom the writer plans to interview, and outlines its basic structure, content, and length.

Writer's guidelines: Magazines publish these guidelines for prospective freelance writers specifying in detail what types of articles they want and don't want, desirable lengths, and specified payment rates. They also explain the submission procedure.

How Magazines Choose Their Content

The Content of Magazines

Richard Stolley, founding editor of *People*, has said, "The Three R's of magazines are the reader, the reader, and the reader." Publishing timely, readable, and interesting content in the magazine issue after issue, week after week, and month after month is the goal of any magazine editor's job. Magazines exist only because readers have interests. You can break almost every other rule of publishing as long as people buy the magazine and read it. The number-one rule of magazine editing, therefore, is simple: make it interesting.

The purpose of this chapter is to help you do that. It will help those involved in starting or editing a magazine to plan its content. Anyone who launches a new magazine or edits an existing magazine has to plan its editorial formula—the particular mix of news, features, and departments. A magazine exists only because its readers are interested in its specific field. The editor's job is to provide that particular mix.

James B. Kobak, author of *How to Start a Magazine and Publish It Profitably*, succinctly states what he calls "some very obvious basic truths about magazines":

- Each issue of a magazine is a consumer product with a short shelf life.
- People will read only what interests them.

- Most people do not really enjoy reading for its own sake. It is hard work for a great many, and there are many conflicting influences.
- The easier you make it, the more articles people will read.
- You must invite, lure, entice or even trick readers into reading.
- The editorial content has more to do with developing continuous readers—and renewals of subscriptions—than anything else.[1]

One requirement for a successful magazine is sustainable content. That means that the magazine must have a steady flow of information, news, trends, and developments from within the field of interest that it serves. While that sounds like an obvious point, some have missed it. Three magazines about houseplants, for example, were published for a couple of years in the 1980s: *House Plants and Porch Gardens*, *Plants Alive*, and *Popular Gardening Indoors*. All eventually failed. "The only explanation was that there simply was not enough subject matter to keep interest up. After you have told readers not to over-water and to talk to their plants, there really isn't much more anyone wants to know," said Kobak.[2]

Newspaper articles begin with an event, but magazine pieces begin with an idea. Therefore, the continuing creation of new ideas and content is critically important. The staff's job also involves packaging them in a way that attracts and keeps the readers' attention. Packaging means making sure each article is only as long as it needs to be—and no longer. It means ensuring that each article has an attractive lead paragraph and that its key points are clear and easy to understand. It means working with photographers and designers to create artwork that enhances each article's attractiveness and readability.

Packaging involves the artwork and design, but only to an extent. As Kobak said, "Artwork is useful only if it helps reading and understanding. Otherwise, it is not only useless, it is actually inhibiting to the reader."[3]

Any magazine has only three types of articles: news, departments, and features. Each of those types, however, contains many variations and divisions within itself. We will look at each one separately.

News Articles

Every magazine should have a news section. No matter how specialized the niche, every area of special interest generates news of interest to its readers. The news articles may be the primary reason some subscribers subscribe. They need not be long. One-paragraph "briefs" are sometimes the first part of a magazine that readers turn to.

Even the *History Channel Magazine* has a news section. Its "Gazette" section features brief news articles about new museums, historical stamp releases, or other events of special interest to history lovers. *Ms.* publishes news sections titled "Dispatches National" and "Dispatches Global" containing short news briefs from around the country and world. Readers also want to know what key leaders in their industry or area of interest are doing. For example, *Rolling Stone* publishes its "Random Notes" page with photos and celebrity gossip. These "people pages" are also very popular among readers.

Departments

Every magazine relies on its departments to maintain a consistent flow of information to its readers. Most magazines contain about a dozen departments. Samir Husni, author of *Launch Your Own Magazine*, describes them this way: "Departments are the skeleton that holds the publication together. You may change your weight, you may change your percentage of fat, you may change your hairstyle, but your bones will remain the same."[4]

Here are some of the most common departments found in many different types of magazines.

Editor's Column

The editor's (or publisher's) column is an important component of creating the magazine's personality and relationship with its readers. The most common mistake editors make in their columns is repeating the table of contents. The editor shouldn't use this valuable space to duplicate what readers can find elsewhere. Neither are readers interested in the reason that the editor chose certain writers for particular assignments. The best columns reveal the editor's personality, sense of humor, vision for the magazine, experiences in communicating with readers, or even admission of mistakes when necessary.

Letters to the Editor

Publishing letters helps a magazine create a personal relationship with its readers. They encourage reader loyalty and—consequently—high renewal rates. Many readers of some magazines turn to the letters before they read any other section of the magazine. It's a good idea to publish a box in each issue encouraging readers to write and telling them how and where to send letters to the editor. Include editorial guidelines, such as length and content restrictions. Establish a reasonable word limit, such as 250 words, that gives readers enough space to speak their minds. Publish both critical and complimentary letters about the magazine's content.

Columnists

The most useful magazine columnists provide expert information to readers in the area of interest that the magazine serves. A question-and-answer or "ask the expert" column is one of the most popular at many magazines and an excellent way to encourage interaction with readers. For example, nutritionist Liz Applegate writes a monthly food and health column for *Runner's World*.

The most boring columnist is one who tries to entertain readers by writing about personal or family experiences. Humor or entertainment columnists should be limited in number, because writers capable of writing this type of column with consistent quality are rare.

Calendar of Events

A "calendar" page is another popular department in many magazines. Readers want to know what events are coming up in their fields of interest. B-to-B magazines feature trade shows and conferences, while entertainment magazines feature concerts and performances by popular entertainers. *Runner's World* features a two-month calendar of upcoming key races throughout the country. *Ebony* publishes "Travel Guide," which highlights upcoming performances and special events of interest to African Americans.

Reviews

Every area of interest served by magazines has new books or products that its readers may be interested in knowing about. Entertainment magazines publish reviews of new CDs and DVDs. The basic purpose of a review is to help the reader understand the new book or product and make a decision about whether to purchase it. For example, *Popular Science* publishes a department called "The Goods," which offers brief reviews of new gadgets and electronic devices. *Ebony* publishes "Ebony Bookshelf," with brief reviews of books of special interest to its readers.

Reader's Column

Many magazines encourage readers to submit personal opinions or essays through a guest column. Probably the best-known example is *Newsweek's* "My Turn" column. *Backyard Living*, a magazine for gardeners and do-it-yourselfers, has an entertaining page called "Backyard Blunders." It encourages readers to submit stories about a "blunder in your backyard that left you a bit red-faced, but you can laugh about now." The *History Channel Magazine* has two departments for reader contributions. For its "Heroes" page, readers submit profiles and stories about their heroes in history. For its "History Alive" page, readers tell stories about ancestors or other historical figures with whom they had a personal connection. *Reader's Digest* is famous for its reader-contributed anecdotes in "Life in These United States" and "Humor in Uniform." The reader feedback page is an excellent way of encouraging interaction and building relationships with readers.

Features

Newspaper editors use the term *feature* broadly to describe any article that isn't a news story. Within magazines, it encompasses a large of variety of story types whose boundaries overlap.

Profiles and Interviews

Profiles and interviews with interesting people and key leaders in any field are crucial for magazines. You typically see three types of interviews in magazines: profiles, expert-information interviews, and question-and-answer interviews. The profile focuses on the *person* interviewed. It's a mini-biography highlighting unusual or interesting aspects of a person's life or career. The expert-information interview focuses on what a person *knows* that will be of service to readers. The person interviewed may be dull or unknown, but possesses knowledge with a strong reader interest. The question-and-answer interview offers a series of questions followed by the subject's directly quoted answers. The Q&A offers a different way of structuring the content of an interview. The Q&A requires more time and concentration to read. Therefore, it works best with highly articulate celebrities or experts whom readers really want to know about.

Despite the old joke about guys saying they "only read *Playboy* for the articles," one of its most popular features is the "Playboy Interview." And the late Andy Warhol built an entire magazine around the concept: *Interview Magazine.*

Service and Information

Service journalism provides useful, practical information to readers that they can apply to their everyday lives. B-to-B magazines have a heavy focus on service journalism, with articles that help readers succeed in their chosen careers. Consumer service articles focus on information such as personal finance, shopping, health, leisure and recreation, career preparation, and education. A "how-to" is one type of service article that offers specific steps to follow. Some service articles provide readers with useful information but don't prescribe specific how-to steps. Both types give readers information designed to help them raise their families, do their jobs, stay healthy, live longer, and so on.

For example, the January 2005 issue of *Southern Living* published an article titled "Easygoing Houseplants: You Don't Need a Green Thumb to Grow These Beauties," which profiled four types of attractive and easy-to-grow houseplants. *Backpacker* published a service feature on "America's 10 Hardest Day Hikes." It tells its readers where these trails are located, along with their length, elevation, and other factors that make them challenging.

Readers are always looking for new ways to save, spend, make, and invest money. If you have a creative approach for saving money on taxes, making money in your spare time, or finding bargains in unusual places, then you will find markets for your material.

And there's an entire category of magazines known as "women's service magazines." These include such familiar titles as *Ladies' Home Journal*, *Redbook*, and *Good Housekeeping*. When Shirrel Rhoades was an executive with *Redbook*, he found that the two most compelling cover topics were dieting and saving time. Thus practically every cover carried some blurb on losing weight or doing things more efficiently.

Trends and Issues

A trend is a social phenomenon with quantifiable dimensions such as growth or decline, acceleration or slowing, or increase or decrease. An issue is a sometimes-controversial development that people have different opinions about. Every field of interest served by magazines has its trends and issues. These types of articles require interviews with several expert sources who give different opinions about the issue or trend. These stories neither focus on a single person nor rely on a single interview. They help readers understand what, why, and how these things happen. They report on issues in any field of human interest, recreation, or endeavor. Most important, they explain how these developments affect readers. One variation on this type of article is the round-up, so called because the writer "rounds up" and interviews several sources to present a variety of opinions and views.

For example, the April 2005 issue of *Scientific American* published a lengthy feature titled "Stopping Spam: What Can Be Done to Stem the Flood of Junk E-mail Messages?" Part trend, part issue analysis, and part service journalism, this in-depth feature explored causes behind the rising tide of spam e-mail and offered readers some practical ways to stop the flood. It included five sidebars and a list of suggested books and websites for further reading.[5]

Investigative Reporting

The basic purpose of investigative articles is to serve the public interest by uncovering wrongdoing among leaders in government, private companies, or nonprofit organizations. "Serving the public interest" distinguishes positive investigative reporting from "muckraking," which simply exposes personal wrongdoing or failings. Investigative articles stimulate needed reform in the company, organization, or government unit that they report on.

All editors secretly dream of delivering that prize story, the kind of hard-hitting piece of investigative journalism that has made movie reporters say, "I'm gonna bust this town wide open!" When Jackie Leo was editor of *Family Circle*, she veered from the magazine's tried-and-true editorial formula to publish an exposé of the notorious Love Canal. It won her magazine a National Magazine Award.

Seasonal and Calendar-Related Stories

Most magazines look for particular types of articles at special times of the year—Christmas, back-to-school, tax season, and so forth. A health magazine may write about colds and flu in its December issue or summer allergies in its June issue. Every Mother's Day and Father's Day produces an abundance of articles in most consumer magazines. Newsmagazines publish features on anniversaries of historic events such as the attack of Pearl Harbor, school desegregation, and the end of the Vietnam War. Every special-interest magazine has historic events within its field that readers will be interested in knowing about.

Real-Life Dramatic Stories

The real-life drama focuses on one person and a significant event or turning point in his or her life. In some cases, the focus may be on two or three people who encountered a dramatic experience together. A real-life story differs from a profile because it focuses on action while a profile focuses on personal interests, hobbies, or insight into the personality of the subject.

Motivational, Inspirational, and Self-Help

People need all kinds of encouragement simply to get through life. You don't have to write for a religious publication to write an inspirational article. Hundreds of magazines look for articles that provide motivation and inspiration toward success, career advancement, or finding meaning in life.

The Freelance Writing Process

A staff writer works for one particular magazine, while a freelance writer is one who writes for more than one magazine. Freelance writers sell their articles to any magazine that will accept and publish them. *Writer's Market* and *The Writer's Handbook* are resource books published annually and used by most freelance writers to locate markets for their articles. They contain listings of thousands of magazines that solicit freelance articles and tell what types of articles they are looking for, desirable lengths, payment rates, and other details. Most of these magazines acquire between 25 and 75 percent of their content from freelance writers.

Beginning freelance writers usually come up with an idea, do the research, do the interviews, write the article, and then look for a magazine to publish the article. Advanced and professional freelancers do it the other way around.

They start by choosing a group of magazines for which they wish to write. They study these magazines, study their content, and then develop creative ideas that will appeal to their editors. Once they come up with an idea for a particular magazine, they send a query letter to the editor. They don't begin the research or the interviewing until after they receive an assignment from the editor. This reverse process enables advanced writers to target specific ideas to specific magazines with a considerably higher success rate than beginning writers.

Publishing protocol requires that writers send an enclosed self-addressed stamped envelope (SASE) with their query letters, submissions, and any other correspondence with editors. You probably won't get a reply if you don't. Most editors feel overwhelmed with mail and e-mail, and some magazines get thousands of unsolicited queries and articles each month. More and more magazines, however, will accept e-mail queries and submissions from freelance writers. It's important for any prospective freelancer to carefully check the magazine's **writer's guidelines** to determine whether it requires e-mail or "snail mail" correspondence.

If an editor thinks a freelance writer has a good idea, the editor will sometimes assign it on speculation or "on spec." Translation: The editors have no obligation to buy the article if it isn't good enough. However, an "on spec" assignment gives the writer assurance that the editors will give the article serious consideration when it's finished. Beginning writers frequently receive their first assignments "on spec." After you gain experience and a reputation for dependable quality, editors will give you firm assignments based on query letters and sometimes even telephone conversations.

Any writer owns the copyright to his or her article as soon as it is written. No copyright registration is necessary for legal protection. When selling a freelance article, however, the writer gives up a portion of those rights, which may range from limited one-time use to full copyright ownership for the magazine. The legal aspects of copyright and the selling of rights are explained in chapter 13.

Hundreds of resources and websites are available to aspiring writers hoping to break into print. In fact, an entire industry has emerged to serve people who want to sell their words to newspapers and magazines. Products for would-be writers include reference books with names and addresses of publications; magazines and newsletters that offer tips on how and where to sell articles; workshops that offer how-to sessions on aspects of writing and marketing; newsletters that keep writers up to date on changes in the publishing industry; and writing-related websites that sponsor chat rooms where writers swap tips about potential markets. To get started, search for phrases like "freelance writing," "selling magazine articles," or "writer's resources" on Google or Yahoo and find lots of useful information.

The Editor's Challenge

A magazine's content is like any other consumer product. People look for bargains. They want to pay as little as possible for as much as possible. They will buy your magazine if they get original information at a reasonable price that is unavailable elsewhere. That's a formidable task with all the free information on the Internet, but great editors know where to find it and how to deliver it. Regardless of whether it's print, online, or broadcast, there will always be a need for great editors.

Questions for Further Thought

1   How do you read a magazine? Back to front? The table of contents first? Or do you just skim through the magazine for articles that jump out at you?

2   Which departments do you always read in your favorite magazines?

3   Do you read the letters to the editor in magazines? Why or why not?

4   Do you read any newsmagazines such as *Time, Newsweek,* or *U.S. News & World Report*? Why or why not?

Shop Talk

Department: Any section of a magazine that recurs in every issue. Most common departments include letters to the editor, columnists, reviews, and calendars of events.

Feature articles: A broad description of types of articles that can include interviews and profiles, news analysis, dramatic stories, service, how-to, and any others not categorized as a "news" or "department" article.

News: Current events and developments within the special field of interest served by a magazine. Every hobby or special interest has new developments that readers may be interested in.

On speculation: A tentative assignment given to a freelance writer, meaning that the editors will give the resulting article serious, priority consideration when it's completed and submitted but that they are not obligated to buy it.

How to Design
a Magazine

Just about anyone can design and lay out pages with the currently available software. "Unfortunately, just about anyone seems to be doing it," said James B. Kobak.[1] How many times have you encountered any of these difficulties when trying to read a magazine?

- Finding an article highlighted on the cover.
- Straining to read an article because of a confusing type style or dark background.
- Trouble finding the jump page on a "continued" article.
- Feeling frustrated because an article's content didn't live up to its title.
- Experiencing disappointment because the magazine just wasn't easy or fun to read.

Bad magazine design could have caused any of these problems. The purpose of magazine design is to pull the reader's attention into a magazine's content—not to call attention to itself. A person who wants to look at beautiful art should visit an art museum. A person who wants to read a good article opens a magazine. Good design should strengthen and enhance that reader's experience—not distract from it.

"Bad design is simply design that makes it harder to the reader," said Richard Stolley founding editor of *People*, in an interview. Bad magazine design distracts the reader, clutters up a page, confuses the reader, or makes reading more difficult. Good design makes reading a magazine easier. Bad design makes it harder.

Stolley went on to say that an editor doesn't necessarily need to possess design skills, but should be able to recognize bad design. "That's not always as easy as it sounds," he said. "Art directors get bored, so they want to experiment and do funny things to layouts, and that's where the editor simply has to resist. If you recognize good design, that's fine, but it's critical to recognize bad design and get rid of it as fast as possible and send the art director back to find something else."[2]

Walter Bernard is one of New York's best-known magazine designers. As a partner with Milton Glaser in WBMG, an editorial design and development company, he has helped redesign more than a hundred magazines and newspapers, including *New York Magazine, Time, Fortune*, the *Atlantic Monthly*, the *Washington Post*, and *Barron's*. "We consider ourselves an editorial design and development company in that we contribute to development of the total editorial package, not just the graphics," said Bernard in an interview. "It's not just about how to make the magazine look better. We feel that the way to deal with any kind of magazine problem is to help with 'added-value ideas' and then try to make them graphically appealing."[3]

Bernard's company was asked by new managing editor John Huey to redesign *Fortune* in 1998. After conducting anecdotal research, Bernard said, "Our assessment about *Fortune* was that readers felt the magazine was a necessary part of their lives, like a medicine taken regularly. Our goal was we want to create affection for the magazine. We wanted people to look forward to reading *Fortune*."

Recognizing that their readers' professional and social lives were often "intertwined," Bernard and Glaser worked with the editors to create more entertaining upfront and back-of-the-book sections. "We added features like humor, cartoons, quotes of the week, something about drinks, cars, and developed features called 'What's in Bill Gates's Wallet?' Based on John Huey's sense of the magazine, we wanted to inform and entertain."

The purpose of good magazine design is like that of a well-designed store. It tries to attract customers. The art director's job is to present the editorial content to readers in a way that makes them want to read it. The art director and design staff take the material that arrives from the editors and the advertising staff. They combine the editorial content and ad copy in ways that enhance the visual appeal of both. Their job is to ensure that readers spend time reading both the articles and the ads. As Milton Glaser sometimes said to clients, "You're wasting your money if you want us to only look at how the magazine's designed. We have to look at editorial, too."

Strong design focuses on the four general content areas of any magazine: the cover, the contents page, the departments, and the features. A well-designed cover entices the reader to pick up the magazine, while an attractive contents page helps the reader find the articles. Well-designed features and departments sustain the reader's involvement throughout the magazine.

The Cover

"The single-copy market is an impulse market," observes newsstand consultant Angelo Gandino. "The cover has to grab them."[4] The average consumer takes about five seconds to decide whether or not to buy a magazine, concluded a New York Times Magazine Group study. Consumers spend most, if not all, of that time glancing at the cover image and the cover lines. Because cover design is so critical to a magazine's success, we're devoting a whole chapter (chapter 5) to the subject. For now, let's move on to other parts of the magazine.

The Contents Page

Some readers use the contents page and others don't. Some bypass the contents page and flip through a magazine to find interesting articles. Others start reading from the back to the front. Nevertheless, it's essential that titles of articles on the contents page be similar to both the cover lines and the titles as they actually appear later in the magazine. Nothing frustrates readers more than picking up a magazine because of an enticing cover line and then being unable to locate that article. In many magazines, it's impossible to find the same words used for the same article on the cover lines, the contents page, the article itself, and the jump pages.

A recent design trend in contents pages is to highlight an article by using a small photo with an enlarged page number. That's fine if that page number also matches the title and description of the same article on that same contents page. A photo with a page number not referenced elsewhere on the contents pages will not make readers turn to that page.

James B. Kobak has this advice for designing contents pages:

- Make sure the type is large enough to be easily read.
- Make the descriptions of the articles understandable—and "not so cutesy that you have no idea what the piece will be about."
- Put the contents page in a fixed position in the magazine, preferably close to the front, like pages 3, 4, or 5.
- Follow a consistent pattern so that readers become familiar with it and can easily find the columns and departments they always read.
- While you follow a pattern, make sure you have a surprise for the reader every so often.[5]

Features

Unity of design means that the magazine looks as if it were designed by one person with one editorial purpose and one particular type of reader in mind. Such design unity helps create the "personality" of a magazine as much as its editorial content. To achieve this design unity, the editor and art director have to make three decisions before they create a single page.

Grid

The first decision is the grid plan. Think of grid like an architect's blueprints. The grid creates a consistent design standard for editors, designers, and photographers to follow. It establishes the number and width of columns per page, size of margins, and guidelines for photos, **cutlines**, white space, and information such as page numbers and department headings. A traditional magazine grid uses a two- or three-column format with standard margins of around half an inch. Features may use three columns, and departments two columns. Many excellent books go into much more detail about magazine grid design than we can here, but in short a grid is like a container into which you pour content. *New York* magazine designer Will Hopkins told a Stanford University publishing class, "It's difficult to carry water without a bucket, and it's difficult to carry content without a grid. It's a structural and visual aid that should be flexible, and not a straitjacket."[6]

Typography

The second decision is how to use typography—the visual component of words and text. As Bernard explained in an interview:

> Typography is a crucial tool in shaping a magazine's personality. A magazine can choose to be loud and bold, dignified and classic, modern and cool, trendy and funky, or even neutral—all through type design. There are now, of course, many typefaces available to enable a designer to achieve whatever design personality the publication needs. We make judgments based on each individual project, always with a goal to be readable and clear for starters.

The name of an individual typeface is its font, while style refers to numerous style variations such as bold, italic, bold italic, extra bold italic condensed, and so forth. Most magazine text appears in a serif font such as Times New Roman, Palatino, Baskerville, or Century. A serif font (like the one used in this book) has curving lines or "feet" at the top or bottom of letter strokes. Sans serif fonts (as the word *sans* implies) lack these curving lines and usually have a consistent width throughout their letter strokes. Some of the most popular sans serif typefaces are Helvetica, Arial, and Futura. Most typographical research says that serif is easier to read.

The lines of text should be consistently **justified** or **ragged right**. Design experts believe that ragged-right text is easier to read and results in a more "relaxed" feel, which is why you see it in many magazines.

Magazines can use different font for **display text** than they do for **body text**. Display text means the titles, subtitles, cutlines, ads, and the like. All other text, particularly in the body of the articles, is body text. A serif font is usually used in body text, while sans serif fonts can work in the larger display text.

There are thousands of fonts, and each communicates a distinct personality and feel. Some have a traditional, serious feel to them, while others convey an upbeat, contemporary mood. Editors and designers should choose a font that conveys the mood and tone consistent with their editorial content—and stick with it. It's fine to choose one font for the body text and another for the display text. Too many fonts, however, confuse the reader.

Marcella Hawley, the art director for *Victoria* magazine, judged a group of collegiate magazines in a 2004 student contest. She said, "Some magazines used too many different fonts in an effort to change the look from feature to feature. While it can be an interesting look, I think it makes the magazine somewhat disjointed and hard to follow in the long term, and from issue to issue—very confusing."[7]

Figure 4.1. Ten Design Tips

1 The principle of the unity of display means that the article's title, subtitle, and main illustration communicate one central message. The connections among these elements must be instantly obvious to the reader.

2 Every page must have one dominant image—not two or three. That image must support the main theme of the accompanying article.

3 Reverse type makes reading more difficult. If you use it, enlarge the text size or limit it to sidebars and one-page articles.

4 Never use a full page of solid type. Interrupt the text with at least one photo, illustration, or pull quote.

5 Tint blocks behind the text make it more difficult to read. Keep tint blocks lightly screened and limit them to sidebars and short features.

6 Use only one font for all articles and body text. Titles, captions, or other special features may use a second complementary font. Italics are harder to read and should be used only for emphasis in sidebars or small portions of text.

7 Use generous amounts of white space to give your magazine a relaxed, inviting feel. Cluttered pages give the magazine a "junky" feel (like tabloids).

8 Try to create a design balance and symmetry between facing pages even when their content doesn't come from the same article.

9 Print the magazine's name and date at the bottom of every page or on every other page. When an article gets photocopied, subsequent readers will always know its source.

10 Serif type styles (such as Times New Roman or Palatino) are easier to read than sans serif typestyles (such as Helvetica or Arial).

Design Elements

The third decision for the editor and designer is the design elements they will use throughout the magazine for departments, **folio**, **dingbats**, **cutlines**, and jump-page descriptions.

Departments. A department is a section of a magazine that appears in every issue. It includes such areas as letters to the editor and columnists. For the convenience of readers, both design and placement of departments should be consistent from month to month. For example, *Consumer Reports*'s popular department "Selling It" appears on the inside back cover of every monthly issue. The "Selling It" page reprints ridiculous or funny advertisements sent in by readers. It's one of the first pages many readers turn to— even before the table of contents.

Because readers love their favorite columnists and departments, magazines should make them easy to find in every issue. To do that, use a consistent color or logo for the department heading, as well as a consistent placement in the front, middle, or back of the magazine.

Folio. The information published at the top or bottom of every page that includes the page number, the date or month of the issue, and the title of the magazine is called the folio. The decreasing use of page numbers represents an unfortunate trend in magazine publishing. It occurs because some full-page advertisements come in at the last minute after remaining pagination has been set. Or these full-page advertisers don't want to damage the aesthetic appeal of their ad by inserting a page number. Whatever the reason, the lack of page numbers frustrates readers trying to find a particular page. The editor and designer should try to place a page number on every page.

The title and date of a magazine at the top or bottom of a page helps protect its copyright. Photocopying articles and passing them along to a few friends for noncommercial purposes doesn't usually violate copyright laws. Folio that includes the date and name of the magazine, however, will discourage subsequent plagiarism and illegal, commercial distribution of that information.

Jump-page description. When an article continues to the back section of the magazine, the jump page must be easy to find or you will lose the reader. The easiest way to achieve clarity is with key word indicators. That means choosing a key word that reflects the content of the article and saying something like "Please see HERO on page 34." On page 34, you begin with "HERO—from page 2." Some editors like to use cute or funny quotes to begin the jump pages, but they can confuse the reader if they aren't immediately recognized as coming from the same article. Again, the primary goal is clarity and making it easy for the reader.

Cutlines. Many editors underestimate the importance of cutlines (photo captions) as visual cues. Most readers scan through a magazine reading only the titles, cutlines, and **pull quotes** before deciding whether to read more. A carefully worded cutline can hook the reader into the article. To capture readers, cutlines should reveal more than a person's name. Just like good article titles and cover lines, cutlines should have a verb. For example, instead of labeling a photo with "Roger Smith, president of Widgets, Inc.," draw the reader in with a cutline like "Roger Smith turned red ink into black ink in less than one year as president of Widgets, Inc."

Dingbats. The cute signs and symbols that magazines use to conclude each article are called dingbats. They help readers navigate the pages, so they know when the article is done, and when to keep looking for more. Every magazine should carefully choose a dingbat that reflects its character, personality, or logo.

Clarity is Essential

Editor in Chief: A Management Guide for Magazine Editors describes three types of design flaws: the cryptic, the obscure, and the inside-out. Cryptic design elements have hidden meanings that the reader can't figure out by looking at or even studying them. The meaning may be known only to the designer. Obscure design elements do not illustrate the main theme of the article. They illustrate some part of the piece, often an obscure part such as an anecdote or quote buried deep in the article. The inside-out design element doesn't make sense until the reader has read the entire article.[8]

The positive side of these flaws means that every design element—whether it's a photo, illustration, or title and subtitle—must communicate the main message of the article in a manner that's immediately clear to readers.

That brings us back to where we started with this chapter. Bad magazine design distracts the reader, clutters up a page, confuses the reader, or makes reading more difficult. Good design makes reading a magazine easier. Bad design makes it harder. The secret to effective design is that simple.

Questions for Further Thought

1   What's the best-designed magazine you can think of? What design characteristics about it stand out?

2   What's the worst-designed magazine you can think of? What design flaws stand out?

3   What are your "pet peeves" about magazine design?

Shop Talk

Body text: The text within the body of the article—excluding its title, subtitle, pull quotes, and cutlines.

Cutline: An identifying description appearing below a photograph, which should offer interesting information not given in the article. Newspapers call them "captions."

Dingbat: A small design device used to designate the end of each article. Dingbats alert the reader to "stop" and not look for a continuation.

Display text: The text used in titles, subtitles, cutlines, ads, mastheads, and other visual elements of a magazine.

Folio: Information published at the top or bottom of every page that may include the page number, the date or month of the issue, and the title of the magazine.

Justified type: The type design in which all lines of text end evenly at the right side of the page. An uneven space between letters and words is what permits an even alignment at the end of each line.

Pull quote: Words pulled from the article that attract the reader's attention and break up large blocks of text. These enlarged quotes should be carefully chosen to highlight the article's main ideas.

Ragged-right type: The type design in which the space between letters is evenly distributed, resulting in a varying line length.

Subhead: A short phrase inserted between paragraphs of an article that give it an organizational structure and alert the reader to what's ahead.

Subtitle: Words appearing after a title and before the article that give additional information to the reader about its contents. Effective subtitles help "hook" and keep the reader reading.

Title: The identifying description of an article appearing above its text and in the table of contents. Like a good cover line, a title should have a verb.

Magazine Covers

Where Art Meets Commerce

When you walk down the aisle of any large supermarket or department store, you pass hundreds of products vying for your attention, time, and money. Take, for example, the cereal aisle. Cereal boxes come in all shapes, sizes, designs, and colors. Some boxes include a celebrity photo, while others have photos of children or of the product itself. The most common words on cereal boxes are those like *new, improved, free, healthy, fat-free.*

Walking down the cereal aisle is like looking at magazine covers. Each cereal product—like a cover—vies for your attention and asks you to stop and look at it. The teasers on the cereal box are like the **cover lines** from a magazine. If you like the cereal, you pick it up and put it in your cart. If you like the magazine, you pick it up and read it.

"Working on covers is one of the most exhilarating parts of my job. But it's also one of the most terrifying. The success of the magazine and your own personal reputation depends so often on newsstand vitality," Kate White, editor of *Cosmopolitan*, told a magazine publishing conference. *Cosmopolitan* sells 2 million copies on the newsstand every month—more than any other magazine in the world. White went on to say that she spends up to 80 percent of her time working on covers—more than she spends on any other part of the magazine.[1]

Consumer magazines are a discretionary purchase. Unlike food or medicine, you don't *have* to have them. You *choose* to buy them. Magazines are also an impulse buy. Some 60 percent of the readers who buy magazines on the newsstands have no plans to purchase a magazine when they come into a store, according to research by *Redbook*. Therefore, a magazine's cover has to work fast to capture the attention and dollars of any potential reader. Consequently, publishers spend huge amounts of time, money, and research trying to decide what to put on their covers. The dirty little secret of the magazine industry is that more than half of all magazines sent to newsstands end up in landfills. That's because the **sell-through rate**—the percentage of copies sold at retail outlets—averages 40 percent or less. A successful "sell through" means anything more than 50 percent for most publishers.

Top-selling magazines like *Cosmopolitan* are not the only ones that spend a lot of time on their covers. The editor of *Network Computing* said, "We use our cover not only to hook you in but also to make a statement about who we are. It's a fleeting chance to make a first impression, a glance from across the bar—a provocative headline, an interesting image or, hell, practically the entire table of contents."[2]

A good cover has certain design elements that are essential: title and logo, taglines, date, price, universal product code, web address (recommended), graphical images, and cover lines.

Essential (or Highly Desirable) Cover Elements

Title and Logo

The **title** is the name of the magazine, while the **logo** is the particular design for the title displayed on the cover. The title of your magazine—displayed proudly on the cover in the form of a logo—is a reader's first clue to your identity. The publication's title is perhaps the most important element on the cover. At first glance, it's all that differentiates your publication from another. The choice of title is a publication's first attempt to communicate with its readers.

When it comes to choosing a title for a new magazine, the promotional needs of marketers often clash with the prudent judgment of trademark lawyers. Marketers want descriptive names (which clearly convey the magazine's contents), while trademark attorneys want fanciful names (which are unique and easier to protect). Under trademark law, there are four types of marks:

- **Fanciful or arbitrary**: A secondary meaning need not be established. These are often made-up names (for example, Kodak, Exxon).

Sometimes they are arbitrary names (*Egg* magazine).

- **Suggestive**: A secondary meaning need not be established. These names suggest what the magazine is about, but do not actually describe it (*Playboy*).
- **Descriptive**: Must show a secondary meaning. These names have taken on additional meaning as being associated with the publication (*Parents*).
- **Generic**: Worthless. These names cannot be protected due to their generic meaning (*Consumer Electronics*). Sometimes a combination of two generic words can afford a degree of protection.

When Shirrel Rhoades owned *Opportunity Magazine*, his trademark was on the combination of the two words, with a disclaimer that he had no rights to either word by itself. That allowed for such competitors as *Small Business Opportunities* and *Income Opportunities* to thrive in a then-hot marketplace. But no one else could publish under the name *Opportunity Magazine*, a mainstay in that market niche since 1923.

Most marketers know that magazines with self-descriptive titles are easier to sell. You don't have to waste a great deal of promotional effort explaining the magazine's editorial position. For example: Is there any question what you'll find inside a magazine named *Fly Fisherman?* Do you have to think twice to know who should be reading a magazine titled *Elegant Bride?*

Other self-explanatory magazine titles include those like:

- *Soldier of Fortune*
- *Popular Mechanics*
- *Model Railroading*

Unfortunately, under trademark law, such descriptive names are more difficult to protect than fanciful ones.

Fuzzy and fanciful include such titles as:

- *Allure*
- *Saveur*
- *Vibe*

So you have a choice of extremes: titles that are self-explanatory or titles that conjure up images. Or the safest of all categories under trademark law—made-up names.

Which magazine would you be more likely to buy even if both cover the same topics? *Artichoke* magazine or *Entertainment Weekly?* The difference in circulation between the small, iconoclastic *Artichoke* and *Entertainment Weekly*, with its circulation of 1.8 million, tells the tale.

Not everyone knows that *Dr. Dobb's Journal* is a publication for computer buffs. But *Mac User* clearly identifies itself as a magazine designed for users of Apple's Macintosh computers. Some publications have overcome name obstacles with time. Practically everyone knows to expect intellectual opinions from *Harper's*—without stopping to think about the printers for whom it was named. But it has been around for over 150 years establishing the brand identity.

Magazine titles based on people's names can be risky. What value would you place on the financial advice found in a magazine called *Sylvia Porter's Personal Finance*, now that the syndicated columnist is deceased? Despite this risk, publishers know that titles based on celebrities—such as *Martha Stewart Living*—quickly communicate what the publication is about. Such titles accomplish this by trading on identifiable qualities or personalities associated with the celebrity—that's why Nike pays big bucks to Michael Jordan. This technique is known as **information transfer**.

But putting a celebrity's name in the title remains risky. Look what happened when Rosie O'Donnell and media giant Grunar + Jahr Publishing had a falling out: *Sic gloria transit* (good-bye!) to *Rosie*. And when a magazine's qualities are not so clear, the results can be expensive—as the late Francis Lear found when she vainly decided to name a publication after herself. Aimed at a new market for older women, *Lear's* was forced to rely on a tagline—"For the woman who wasn't born yesterday"—in order to get its positioning message across.

Some magazines are gutsy enough to use an abbreviated name:

- *GQ* was *Gentlemen's Quarterly*—a necessary change when the quarterly magazine went monthly.
- *CJR* stands for *Columbia Journalism Review*—shorthand for a publication that appreciates brevity.
- *W* comes from the publisher of *Women's Wear Daily*—a trendy title for a trendy magazine covering the fashion scene.

However, here's a word of warning about this approach: "Alphabet soup" may please your literati friends, but it doesn't necessarily help your newsstand sales. Not everyone will recognize your publication's "name" or guess its subject matter.

Another use of an alphabet title is to reposition a magazine's image. *Young Miss* became *YM*, which now—according to its tagline—stands for "Young & Modern."

One more warning about titles on covers: Uncle Sam has some strict (and somewhat arcane) rules about magazine covers. For example, no other type on the cover can be larger than the magazine's title. Best to check with the U.S. Post Office before mailing out your first issue.

Taglines

Taglines are your *second* chance—after the magazine's logo—to communicate your magazine's editorial purpose. Often positioned near the logo, they are like a subheading, whispering an additional word or three to further identify a magazine's editorial purpose. Some magazines can't rely on their name (that is, the logo) to explain to a new reader what content to expect inside. So the magazine uses a tagline in conjunction with its logo to supplement the publication's editorial identity or strengthen its positioning.

Some publishers try to play it safe with a belt-and-suspenders approach by using a tagline along with a descriptive name:

- *Spa:* "Travel, well-being, and renewal"
- *Popular Science:* "The 'what's new' magazine"

Fanciful titles always require further explanation:

- *Heart and Soul:* "Health and fitness for African American women"

What's in a tagline? Taglines can be very general in nature:
- *Playboy*: "Entertainment for men"
- *Penthouse*: "The international magazine for men"
- *Esquire*: "The magazine for men"

Or they can be specific to a given market:

- *Success*: "The magazine for today's entrepreneuring mind"
- *Income Opportunity*: "The original small business/home office magazine"

Or to position a publication by association with its ownership:
- *Smart Money*: "The Wall Street Journal magazine of personal business"
- *Your Money*: "A Consumer's Digest publication"

A tagline also can be descriptive:
- *Inc.:* "The magazine for growing businesses"
- *Nation's Business:* "The small business advisor"

Universal Product Code

Boring but essential, a universal product code **(UPC)** is used by wholesalers and retailers to track sales at checkout. Designers hate these bar codes, but woe to your sales if you omit them!

Web Address

More and more magazines display their web addresses on their covers. The magazine's web address is an increasingly important component of its business identity. It gives the casual newsstand browser an opportunity to delve into the magazine more and consider subscribing at a later time. "If your magazine doesn't have a web address on the cover, someone may wonder what's wrong," said Scott Moss, magazine marketing director for DRG Publishing.

Price

Price is a major factor in the purchase decision. Is the magazine a good value? Too expensive for the perceived value? Savvy publishers compare the pennies-per-page value of their publication with that of their competition. This is simple research: count the number of pages in a given issue and divide them into the cover price. Consumers don't consciously do this, but they're reacting to an innate sense of value when buying any product.

For example: A $4.95 magazine with 144 pages costs 3.4 cents per page. A competitor with a $3.95 cover price and 96 pages is charging 4.1 cents per page. Assuming equal quality, which is the better value?

Kobak said that putting a price on the cover is a "cardinal rule" of publishing. "Every magazine, even those that are circulated on a controlled basis, should have a price on the cover—the higher you can realistically make it, the better! Otherwise you are putting yourself in the same class as a catalog or any other throwaway," he said.[3]

Veteran newsstand marketers like to talk about the "two coin" theory—the idea that consumers tend to make impulse purchases when they don't have to fish for extra change. So handing a clerk a five-dollar bill for a $4.95 magazine gets less resistance than searching pockets for a quarter to go with three one-dollar bills for a less-expensive $3.25 cover price.

Date

Which issue is this? January? March? Summer? Fall? Dating is required, but it also serves as a marketing tool. Since nobody wants to buy an old, out-of-date magazine, publishers tend to date them far in advance. This ensures good shelf life and a sense of "freshness." A typical consumer magazine goes on sale the month prior to its cover date, but some magazines date their covers up to two months ahead of the on-sale date.

Graphical Images

They include either photographs or illustrations, whether single or multiple images. Generally, a strong graphic focal point (rather than a confusing muddle) makes the cover an eye-catcher.

The conventional wisdom about cover images, reflected through professional literature as well as the authors' magazine experience, includes five generally recognized principles. You will, of course, find exceptions to any of them.

1   Covers with people on them sell better than covers with objects or nature scenes. One study of every issue of *Life* magazine covers between 1936 and 2000 found that 74 percent had at least one person on the cover, while only 26 percent had none.[4]

2   Sex sells, and covers with women sell better than covers with men.

Even women's magazines put mostly women on their covers. Kate White said that *Cosmopolitan* covers must have "A certain type of celebrity, someone our reader would love to drive cross-country with; a certain expression on her face; killer hair, there has to be lots and lots of volume."[5]

3 Movie stars and entertainers sell better than politicians, business leaders, or sports celebrities. That's because they have the best name and face recognition in popular culture. However, this will vary with the market demographics. A magazine covering a special niche or market demographic can successfully use a cover "celebrity" in that field who is unknown to the general public.

4 Good news sells better than bad news, and positive sells better than negative. The editor of *Indianapolis Monthly* once said that her worst-selling issue ever used a handgun on the cover to illustrate a cover story about crime in the city.

5 The future sells better than the past, and solutions sell better than problems.

Richard Stolley, the founding editor of *People* magazine, once famously offered this prescription for magazine covers: "Young is better than old. Pretty is better than ugly. Rich is better than poor. TV is better than music. Music is better than movies. Movies are better than sports. Anything is better than politics. And nothing is better than the celebrity dead."[6] To these can be added such truisms as light covers sell better than dark, photographs sell better than illustrations, and blondes work better than brunettes. But for every rule we can show you exceptions—covers that sold well despite breaking the rules. Editors and marketers develop a sense of what "works" for their magazine. As Jerry Ward, one-time circulation director for Meredith, once said about cover images that worked on *Better Homes and Gardens*, "We've never had a bad pie."

Cover Lines

These "teaser lines" are brief article descriptions that magazines publish on their covers. When magazines are stacked together on newsstands, you usually don't see more than four or five inches of the left side of the cover. That's why most cover lines appear on the left side of the cover.

Magazines have four generally recognized types of cover design:

1 Single image, single cover line.
2 Single image, multiple cover lines.
3 Multiple image, multiple cover lines.
4 All typographic or all illustration

The second type—single image, multiple cover lines—is the most popular today and the one used by *Cosmopolitan* and most women's magazines. It has a couple of advantages. A single image has a single focal point and most likely attracts the casual browser's eye. Multiple cover lines, however, attract a wider variety of interests among potential readers who may not find the cover story the most interesting. You see the first type—single image and single cover line—in the weekly newsmagazines. You see the third type—multiple image and multiple cover lines—mostly among the supermarket tabloids. The fourth type—the all-typographic or all-image—is rare. The *New Yorker* is one of the few magazines that uses a single illustration on its cover without any cover lines.

Claudia Cohl, formerly an editorial director at *Scholastic*, likes to compare a magazine's cover to a tray of cookies. Someone may not like peanut butter cookies, but might adore oatmeal cookies. That's why you offer a variety of cookies to your guests to make sure there's something to please everyone. It's the same with cover lines.

Proven attention-getting words on magazine covers include: *free, now, exclusive, you, secret,* and *surprise.* Here are some more tips from Susan Ungaro, former editor of *Family Circle:*

- Use the power of the personal. Be sure readers know what's in it for them. Use personal pronouns and action verbs.
- Make believable and attainable promises. Don't use "bait and switch" lines that are inconsistent with the real content of the articles.
- Leave cleverness for the inside of the magazine. Cover lines should be clear and not coy, says Ungaro.[7]

New York designer J. C. Suares has redesigned numerous magazines, including *Shape, Fast Company, Discover, Runner's World, Prevention, Publisher's Weekly,* and *L.A. Weekly.* He said that covers with personal benefits packed in cover lines attract more readers. He calls it the "apple tree axiom" and uses this example:

Least effective: "Ode to an apple tree."
More effective: "Apple harvest time."
More effective: "From apple tree to apple tree."
More effective: "Is an apple a day effective?"
More effective: "How apples help you stay healthy."
Most effective: "How an apple a day *saved my life.*"

Suares believes that cover lines must contain an action verb. Verbless cover lines are motionless and boring. "There's no such thing as a cover line without a verb. If it doesn't have a verb then it's not a cover line. It's a title. I also hate gerunds [words ending in -*ing*]. You've got to come up with a sentence with a verb in it. I talk myself blue in the face [to editors] about having a verb in the cover line or headline," said Suares.[8]

To increase sales, Suares believes in aiming the cover at the "wannabes." Readers of magazines like *Runner's World* or *Writer's Digest,* for example, are mostly "wannabe" runners or writers, respectively. They sell more magazines to aspiring runners and writers than to the dedicated core of actual runners and writers. "The range of 'wannabes' changes from one magazine to another. Take for example health and fitness magazines; my studies indicate that the 'wannabes'—people who 'wannabe' fit—outnumber the core readers by ten to one," he said.

> When I went to help redesign *Shape*, I looked at four years of sales and figured out what it was that sold the magazine best in terms of image and language. I found out that for some reason, sexy women sold better. And in terms of language, everything had to be easy. If it said, "Six months to better abs," it wouldn't work. Everything had to be a quick fix. I lowered the flag, and I put the wannabe line above the flag. And we put a weight loss line on every issue, and the rest of the magazine was a combination of ways to stay healthy with the easiest possible process. That's what you find out from the history of the magazine.

Yet Suares stressed that the best type of cover will vary with a magazine's content and readership. "You have to come up with a compelling story and image. Compelling images depend on what's compelling to the reader of that magazine. For *Business Week*, it might be a stack of money. For any health and fitness magazine, it's the best-looking person you can find for that age."

Suares concluded by saying, "The job of the cover is to appeal to two different people: one is the core, and two is the wannabes, because that's how [magazines] increase sales."

Numbers

Readers like numbers on a cover. It makes them feel like they are getting lots for their money. Peruse your local newsstand and you will note such stand-out cover lines as:

- *80 Free Recipe Cards Inside*
- *10 Ways to Keep Your Man*
- *54 Cookie Recipes for the Holidays*
- *Midseason TV Preview: The Scoop on 25 New Shows*

Why do you see so many numbers when you do your newsstand survey? Because they work!

Photo Insets

Some TV sets allow you to watch a football game in a small inset in the corner while your wife watches her favorite soap opera on the rest of the screen. Magazines sometimes do the same thing—but both images are designed to attract the same viewer: a potential purchaser.

In addition to the main cover image, there may be a photo inset showing another image from inside the issue: a celebrity, a new cake, a game fish—depending on the magazine's editorial niche. These extra images catch the eye, promise bonuses inside, overcome the limits of the lazy readers who only glance at a cover.

When Myrna Blyth first took over as editor of *Ladies' Home Journal*, one of her first priorities was cover research. The results? She found that jazzed-up covers featuring photo insets, numbers, bars, and banners worked well—in addition to the traditional celebrity image.

Cover Style

A magazine's cover should reflect a recognizable personality for that publication. Just as you recognize the face of an old friend, you should be able to recognize the "face" of your favorite magazine. Even with the logo covered, a reader should be able to visually distinguish a particular publication from its competition. This is called style. One workable definition for *style* is "self-imitation."

Cover up the logos of *Playboy* and *Penthouse*. Most guys will be able to easily distinguish which is which, even with the name hidden. Why? Each publication has "a certain look."

Trade Dress

That combination of physical elements that gives your magazine's cover its unique look—the logo design, the typefaces, the use of colors, and so on—is called the trade dress. *Example:* The red border outlining the cover of *Time* is part of its distinctive trade dress. The red box housing the magazine's name on the cover of the *Economist* is part of its trade dress.

Trade dress can also help identify brand extensions. The familiar yellow box that surrounds a *National Geographic* cover is also used on *National Geographic Travel* and *National Geographic Adventure*. A little yellow box symbol is even used to identify the *National Geographic* cable channel.

Real Estate

The most important "real estate" on a magazine's cover is that vertical area on the left-hand side (the menu) and the space at the very top over the logo (the skyline). This is because of the way magazines are displayed at newsstands.

- On a mainline rack, magazines are fanned along a shelf with only the left-hand side showing.
- On other newsstand fixtures, magazines are stacked vertically with only their logo peeking over the top of the magazine below.

Thus, what your designer puts on this highly visible real estate can make or break a sale, because it might be the only part of the magazine exposed to a potential buyer's eyes.

Cover testing sometimes uses a simulated newsstand with two different covers of your magazine mixed with the competition. A target customer is first asked to point to your magazine. Of the two covers, the one selected most wins on visibility. Then, holding the covers in their hands, test subjects are asked which they would most likely purchase. The one selected most often scores on readability.

Visibility is more heavily weighted than readability, because if you don't see it you can't buy it! Most buyers first see a magazine on a newsstand rack from twenty or thirty feet away. Tiny images and small type may be a blur, not able to do their selling job.

Publishing veteran Adolph Auerbacher liked to use the "foot test." He drops the magazine on the floor at his feet. Looking down, are the cover lines legible? Is the graphic easy to understand? If the answers are affirmative, then the issue has a decent chance of success of the newsstand.

Scott Moss, magazine marketing director for Dynamic Resources Group, Inc., prefers to use the "squint test." Magazines on the newsstand are scanned from a distance. By squinting at the cover from a distance you get a better idea of how it will look to a casual shopper.

Protecting Your Magazine's Name

Trademark laws are designed to protect your "mark" used in trade. It's what identifies a product as being uniquely yours. The concept goes back to olden times, when silversmiths put an identifying mark on their handiwork to distinguish it from merchandise made by competitors. Today's intellectual property laws come to us from English tradition. This is a highly specialized legal field.

Trademark law differs from copyright law. Trademarks protect the identity of a product or service; copyright law protects the expression of an idea. The purpose of a trademark is to avoid a consumer's confusion between products.

Your magazine title should be trademarked. The first step is to affix a small "™" notice near the logo, announcing your claim to the mark. Once a trademark application has been approved and the mark is officially registered, an "®" can be affixed to signify ownership. Using the "®" prior to registration is forbidden and can result in the loss of the trademark rights.

■ ■ ■

Kate White, *Cosmopolitan* editor, offers this advice about a magazine's cover: "It should be juicy and have a really intense color and jaw-dropping cover lines."[9] J. C. Suares sums up his advice this way: "It should have a killer image and a compelling cover line."

Questions for Further Thought

1 What's the most memorable magazine cover you can think of? Analyze it in terms of the principles and ideas discussed in this chapter.

2 Do you think *Cosmopolitan's* cover designs help create its high single-copy sales rate? What is your opinion of *Cosmopolitan's* covers?

3 Spend at least half an hour studying magazine covers on any sales stand and discuss the colors, images, and types of cover lines you see most frequently.

4 What types of magazine covers do you find most distasteful or unattractive?

Shop Talk

Cover lines: The brief article descriptions that magazines publish on their covers.

Information transfer: Using identifiable qualities or attractions associated with a celebrity to help advertise or promote a product.

Logo: The particular design for the title of a magazine displayed on its cover.

Sell-through rate: The percentage of magazine copies delivered to retail outlets that are sold.

Tagline: A subheading positioned near the magazine's logo that further identifies a magazine's editorial purpose.

Trade dress: The combination of physical elements that gives a magazine's cover its unique look: the logo design, the typefaces, the use of colors, and so on.

Universal product code: The bar code used by wholesalers and retailers to track sales. Magazines sold at retail outlets must have them on their covers.

Why Advertisers Love Magazines

First, the bad news: Selling advertising is difficult—especially for a new magazine. "You had better face the fact early on that there will be no great rejoicing in the advertising world that you are starting a new magazine," writes James Kobak in *How to Start a Magazine and Publish It Profitably.* He said that advertisers and agencies may simply feel that they will have to deal with yet another set of salespeople. "The best you can hope for at the beginning is benign tolerance. They will probably put up with your visits— but please, not too many of them—out of the goodness of their hearts," he writes.[1]

It's tricky for aspiring magazine publishers because advertisers don't want to put their money into new magazine startups facing an uncertain future. They prefer to stick with established magazines, which have audiences with guaranteed size and quality. Aspiring publishers must find enough funds to get them through the first couple of years without depending on any guaranteed ad revenue. Most new magazines take at least three or four years before they turn a profit. Magazine publishers, therefore, face the formidable and tricky task of simultaneously building two sets of customers: the readers and the advertisers.

"Magazines are a unique business," said Samir Husni, author of *Launch Your Own Magazine.* "They must be sold not once, but twice: first to the readers and then to the advertisers."[2] While the editors are planning the content for upcoming issues, the advertising staff is out selling ads. The most successful magazines create a connection between a particular mix of products and a demographic group of readers willing to buy those products.

"You have to sell to both audiences, not only in the beginning, but every day," said Stewart Ramser, who launched *Texas Music* magazine in 2000. Advertisers often wait until they see that you have a good product. "We've had advertisers say, 'We've watched you for five years and have enjoyed the magazine and want to be involved now.' Two of our biggest clients came in after several years of contact," said Ramser in a telephone interview.[3]

The editorial content has to create the magic link that connects a group of readers with a group of advertisers. For example, *Crappie World* connects those readers who love fishing for this variety of fish with a group of advertisers who manufacture products to help them do so successfully.

The editor must make sure the advertising and circulation departments sell the same product he or she creates. The advertising sales staff must have a clear understanding of the editorial content and its readers in order to sell to those advertisers who want to reach them. The successful editor will work with the advertising and circulation departments in developing their promotional materials.

The "quality" of the audience is important to advertisers. A combination of factors helps determine the quality of a magazine's readership in the eyes of advertisers. All else equal, advertisers prefer affluent readers, young readers, and loyal readers who pay attention to both the articles and the ads in their favorite magazines.

Income level is an obvious indicator of reader quality. The more disposable income an individual earns, the more likely he or she will be able to purchase discretionary or recreational items advertised in the magazine.

Young readers—especially eighteen- to twenty-five-year-olds—are the most sought-after demographic group by advertisers. The reasoning among advertisers is that young readers haven't yet created permanent consumer habits. "Young readers are developing homes, lifestyles, and are still making up their minds which products to buy," said Dick Stolley, founding editor of *People* and former managing editor of *Life*. "The theory is that once you get to a certain age you buy the same kind of car, the same kind of toothpaste, same deodorant, etc.," he said.[4] Older readers are less likely to try out a new brand or product.

Demographics, however, aren't the only factor behind reader quality. *Loyalty* means that readers spend more time with and pay more attention to the content of one magazine than competing magazines and other media outlets. Renewal rates for subscribers is probably the best measure of reader loyalty. Greater loyalty means that these same readers also pay more attention to the magazine's ads and are more likely to purchase those products that appear in their favorite magazines.

Think about it for a moment. Are you more likely to pay attention to an ad in a favorite magazine for which you have purchased a subscription than an ad that flashes across the television screen? "The dirty little secret is that nobody watches TV ads any more," said Nina Link, president of the Magazine Publishers of America. "They're skipping them with Tivo or going to the kitchen for a snack."[5]

Another factor that goes into the quality of a magazine's readership is level and extent of public influence. This is a sophisticated way of talking about the potential for "word of mouth" advertising. In general, the higher the education level of a reader, the more likely he or she will be to influence a wide range of people. Everyone loves to tell their friends about good experiences with new products (as well as bad experiences). Advertisers know this and look for readers with wide social and professional networks.

Influence level is a key component of the economics behind business-to-business magazines. They offer free subscriptions to key executives with major buying influence in targeted fields. In order to "qualify" for a free subscription, the magazine requests certain information about the person's position and role in making purchasing decisions for his or her company. Advertisers of products for particular industries want so much to reach key executives that they will pay for ads with higher costs than those in traditional consumer magazines.

Some consumer magazines, such as in-flight magazines, depend only on controlled circulation. Others supplement their paid circulation with limited controlled circulation by distributing free copies in physicians' waiting rooms, hotel rooms, or airplanes. In every case, the readership has key demographic characteristics that are highly attractive to advertisers.

Selling magazine advertising is difficult because you are not selling a tangible product with measurable results. You must sell the intangible expectation that the space in your magazine will bring more sales for the advertiser's product. Today's advertisers increasingly look for a tangible **return on investment (ROI)**. Internet advertising can provide a specific ROI by measuring clicks, page views, and even viewing time—something print advertising can't achieve.

"ROI is critical," said Scott Crystal, publisher of *TV Guide*, in an interview. "The [advertising] industry is starting to look at engagement as a defining characteristic of our alliance. At the end of the day, our advertisers need to say, 'I know that it worked.' Not just that it worked because a lot of people saw it and it increased awareness, but it worked because it generated more sales," said Crystal.[6]

Magazines possess several advantages over other mass media that have always made them an attractive buy for advertisers. "When consumers buy a magazine, they consciously buy it with the understanding that there are ads inside," noted Steve Greenberger, a senior vice president at Zenith Media. "A large percentage probably buy the magazine predominately for the ads."[7]

Table 2: Consumer Rating of Media Choices

	Magazines	Network TV	Cable TV	Internet
The medium they trust and believe	43%	32%	15%	10%
The medium they enjoy ads appearing in	37%	36%	21%	6%
The medium they often make purchases as a direct result of seeing ads in	44%	34%	16%	6%

Source: Erdos & Morgan Media Choices Study (2005). Information provided courtesy of Time Inc.

Studies show that consumers trust advertising in magazines more than ads on television or the Internet. Since the advertising is related to the subject matter, readers are more likely to look at it and view it as an adjunct to the editorial content. A recent study found that consumers preferred magazines over network TV, cable TV, and the Internet as trustworthy sources of advertising.

In the same vein, another study found that magazines were among the venues consumers least wanted to eliminate as a source of marketing and advertising. When asked, "Where would you be in support of eliminating marketing and advertising?" 601 participants ranked magazines seventeenth, behind: (1) e-mail, (2) public schools, (3) mail, (4) faxes, (5) cable television shows, (6) before previews in movie theaters, (7) websites, (8) public television, (9) network television shows, (10) concerts, (11) radio, (12) sporting events, (13) billboards, (14) buses, (15) T-shirts, and (16) taxies. Ranking lower than magazines in the survey were bus stops, coffee mugs, blimps, and newspapers.[8]

The ability to provide detailed information to specific groups of readers has always been the strength of magazines in their competition for advertising dollars. "Magazines are a good place to run advertising that allows readers to consider products in a more leisurely way," said John Squires, publisher of *Sports Illustrated*, in an interview. "The auto companies have recognized that for years. When they want to do sight, sound, and motion, they put the ad on television and show the car driving down the Pacific Coast Highway. But when they want you to get a fuller understand of the benefits of an auto and its performance quality, magazines are a better place to do that than on television," he said.[9]

Ten Advantages of Magazine Advertising over Other Media

1. Targeted audience. Each magazine covers a specific field of interest, which attracts a precise market or group of people with specific demographics and intellectual characteristics. With a range of titles that appeal to a wide variety of demographics, lifestyles, and interests, advertisers can hone in on targets that fit their needs.

2. Self-selected audience. People buy a magazine because they want to read about the subject it covers. Therefore, they are likely to pay attention to all of the material in the magazine, including the advertisements. Multiple studies show that consumers are more likely to find magazine advertising enjoyable than advertising in other media. Other studies confirm that some people purchase some magazines primarily to read the advertisements.

3. Engaged audience. Reading is an active, participatory activity. The reader must actively comprehend the material and not sit back and wait to be entertained. Since the advertising is related to the subject matter, readers are more likely to look at it and view it as an adjunct to the editorial content.

4. Influential audience. Numerous studies indicate that heavy magazine readers possess higher levels of educational achievement than users of other media. Magazines are the medium of choice for "influential Americans"—the one in ten consumers who controls the levers of change and makes purchase decisions and recommendations.

5. Affluent audience. These same studies indicate that heavy magazine readers possess higher levels of occupational achievement and more discretionary income than users of other media. Across almost every demographic, the top twenty-five magazines out-deliver the top twenty-five TV shows. In addition, heavy magazine readers are likely to be among the largest spenders across most product categories.

6. Known audience. Most magazines conduct detailed studies on their readers' demographics, buying habits, and lifestyles and readily offer this information to advertisers.

7. Portability. Magazines can be picked up and reread many times in any location. Readers can keep and refer to them for years to come. The average magazine accumulates approximately 60 percent of its audience within a month's time. In addition, consumers refer to magazines multiple times, even saving them, giving advertisers the opportunity for added exposure.

8. Attractiveness. Graphic reproduction qualities in magazines can produce colorful ads with detailed, true-to-life illustrations.

9. Spaciousness. Magazine pages have more room for detailed explanations of products than most other media. They can also provide photos, sidebars, and illustrations of product details.

10. Interactivity. Magazine advertising offers many opportunities to encourage reader interaction: the ads can provide phone numbers, addresses, web addresses, inserts, order forms, coupons, and other interactive features. Magazine advertising moves the reader to action. Half of readers took action on magazine ads or had a more favorable opinion about the advertiser after viewing the ad, according to studies done by Affinity Research.

Sources: Starcom; Northwestern University Magazine Reader Experience Study, Affinity Research, How Media Measures Up, Documenting the Role of Magazines in the Mix, ROI for DTC, ROI for Kraft, Measuring the Mix, What Drives Automotive Sales, Dynamic Logic, Initiative, MRI Fall 2004, Roper, Neopets Youth Study, Media Choices.

The general-interest magazines of the 1960s, such as *Saturday Evening Post*, *Life*, and *Look*, learned that they could never match the size of TV audiences. So instead of trying to reach the largest possible audience, magazines adapted and recognized that they could do something better than television, radio, or newspapers. They could reach a specific group of readers who had a strong interest in specialized topics. Or they could reach an audience of predominantly men, African Americans, car enthusiasts, or Presbyterians. And they could deliver access to producers of products for those readers in a more economical fashion than any other media.

Contextual relevance is one advantage that magazines possess over other media, according to Crystal, of *TV Guide*. Contextual relevance means that the content of the articles is similar to the content of the advertising. "If you're a travel magazine, then travel advertising—that's your contextual relevance. If I am reading a travel magazine, then I am obviously motivated and interested by the destinations that are promoted in the advertisements.

"Clearly you have inquisitive readers in special-interest magazines. They're reading something actively, they're interested, they're enthusiastic and seeking more information. That's a terrific mindset for any advertiser

Table 3: America's Most Profitable Magazines (2004 data)

Rank	Magazine	Total Revenue (000)	Ad Revenue (000)	Circ. Revenue (000)
1	People	$ 1,271,057	$ 768,986	$ 502,071
2	Sports Illustrated	$ 1,031,824	$ 726,352	$ 305,472
3	Time	$ 1,018,100	$ 700,069	$ 318,031
4	TV Guide	$ 917,598	$ 377,571	$ 540,027
5	Better Homes and Gardens	$ 887,960	$ 715,335	$ 172,625
6	Newsweek	$ 662,386	$ 510,956	$ 151,430
7	Parade*	$ 616,087	$ 616,087	*
8	Reader's Digest	$ 556,291	$ 270,174	$ 286,117
9	Good Housekeeping	$ 543,611	$ 434,581	$ 109,030
10	Cosmopolitan	$ 472,819	$ 347,404	$ 125,415
11	Woman's Day	$ 449,756	$ 350,406	$ 99,350
12	BusinessWeek	$ 430,038	$ 365,562	$ 64,476
13	InStyle	$ 421,053	$ 357,519	$ 63,534
14	USA Weekend*	$ 416,271	$ 416,271	*
15	Family Circle	$ 395,517	$ 298,432	$ 97,085

*Sunday newspaper supplement

Source: Advertising Age Data Center.

to want to tap," said Crystal.[10]

Advertisers don't buy space on a magazine's pages—they purchase *access* to a magazine's readers. Anyone wanting to go into any aspect of magazine publishing should never forget that maxim: *advertisers don't buy space on a magazine's pages—they purchase access to a magazine's readers.*

"Advertisers are very skeptical people. They won't buy you until you've really got the readers," said John Squires, president of *Sports Illustrated*. "Do everything you can to figure out how to serve your reader and make your reader happy. Ultimately if you're concentrating on the reader, the rest of the business will work."[11]

Table 3 illustrates that only two of America's fifteen most profitable magazines (*TV Guide* and *Reader's Digest*) receive more revenue from circulation than from advertising.

Circulation is the best predictor of a magazine's advertising rates and what it can charge. The higher the circulation, the greater the magazine can charge for space on its pages. But circulation isn't the only factor. Advertisers will generally pay a premium for younger readers or those with higher-than-average incomes. One research study found that magazines with gender homogeneity (mostly men or mostly women) are more attractive to advertisers than those with mixed readerships.

The Price of Advertising

How much can you charge for advertisements? The largest consumer magazines charge $200,000 and up for one full-page color ad. A small magazine with only a few thousand readers may be lucky to attract $1,000 for a full-page ad.

Once a magazine determines its rates, it publishes them in a rate card, which includes a complex breakdown of rates according to the following variables:

- Full-color versus black-and-white ads.
- Premium rates for inside front and back cover and front-of-the-book pages.
- Half-, third-, quarter-, and eighth-of-page rates, and classified section rates.
- Discounted rates for advertising in multiple issues.

Yet, today magazine rate cards are like sticker prices on automobiles and furniture. Few advertisers expect to pay the full rate, and publishers give frequent discounts off the card rate. Magazine publishers should determine the rates based on what they need to make a profit, but expect advertisers to negotiate for discounts.

How do advertisers decide whether to pay $1,000 for an ad in a small-circulation ad or $100,000 for the same ad in a high-circulation magazine?

Magazines use a mathematical formula known as **cost per thousand (CPM)** to determine the cost of their ads. You can figure the CPM by dividing the cost of a full-page ad by how many thousands of readers the magazine has. Let's say a national magazine has 5.4 million readers and charges $185,000 for a full-page color ad. Its CPM is $185,000 divided by 5,400,000 divided by 1,000, which equals $34.26. That means an advertiser pays $34.26 in order to reach 1,000 of its readers.

Suppose a local city magazine has a circulation of 60,000 readers and charges $2,500 for one of its full-page color ads. Its CPM is $2,500 divided by 60,000 divided by 1,000, which equals $41.67. Even though the high-profile national magazine charges seventy-four times as much as the city magazine for a full-page ad, it reaches ninety times as many readers. That means its CPM—the cost of reaching 1,000 readers—is less.

Advertisers and advertising agencies use the CPM to compare the cost of advertising across different media, since it enables them to measure the

Table 4: Reader Demographics and Cost of Advertising for Fifteen Highest-Circulation Magazines (2005 data)

Circ Rank	Magazine	Total Paid Circ.	4-Color Full Page Ad	Cost per 1000 (CPM)	Median Age	Median HH Income
1	AARP: The Magazine	22,559,956	$417,000	$18.48	62.9	$ 49,057
2	Reader's Digest	10,081,577	$221,600	$21.98	50.6	$ 52,473
3	TV Guide	9,073,543	$177,700	$19.58	43.9	$ 48,465
4	Better Homes and Gardens	7,634,170	$339,700	$44.50	47.1	$ 58,540
5	National Geographic	5,431,117	$185,480	$34.15	45.8	$ 60,570
6	Good Housekeeping	4,639,941	$286,525	$61.75	49.4	$ 55,976
7	Woman's Day	4,209,130	$220,120	$52.30	49.2	$ 51,965
8	Family Circle	4,147,657	$216,400	$52.17	49.8	$ 53,073
9	Ladies' Home Journal	4,132,910	$213,000	$51.54	51.1	$ 56,328
10	Time	4,034,061	$234,000	$58.01	45.7	$ 66,176
11	People Weekly	3,652,022	$216,200	$59.20	41.2	$ 62,888
12	Sports Illustrated	3,339,229	$279,450	$83.69	39.0	$ 63,830
13	Newsweek	3,125,971	$210,000	$67.18	46.6	$ 67,842
14	Cosmopolitan	2,982,508	$184,700	$61.91	32.2	$ 55,636
15	O: The Oprah Magazine	2,622,718	$139,975	$53.37	43.1	$ 66,327

Source: MediaMark Research, Inc.

cost of newspaper versus magazine versus television ads. Most magazines have CPMs in the range of $30 to $60. Strong demand for advertising space in magazines has caused ad rates to increase more rapidly than the subscription and single-copy prices. One academic study determined that average advertising rates in the top eighty consumer magazines increased by more than 150 percent in inflation-adjusted dollars between 1980 and 2000. At the same time, the price of an average subscription declined in inflation-adjusted dollars.[12]

Readers per Copy

It gets even more complicated. Magazine circulation is looked at in two ways: primary audience (that is, the actual circulation of that publication) and total audience (the total number people reading the magazine based on its pass-along readership). The theory is simple: You buy a magazine, but yours may not be the only eyeballs to scan its pages. Your friend may thumb through it. A neighbor may borrow it. And some copies of the magazine (say, those in a doctor's waiting room) get perused by many more sets of eyes.

Syndicated research companies such as MediaMark Research, Inc. (MRI), measure this pass-along factor for each magazine (readers per copy, or RPC) and report it to advertising media buyers. Thus a magazine with a primary audience of 200,000 with 3 RPC has a total audience of 600,000—giving it an advantage over a competitor with a larger circulation of 250,000 but a lower RPC of 2, giving it a total audience of only 500,000.

Media Buyers

Advertising agencies help their clients make "media buys." For example, if an account manager has a client that manufactures gasoline engine-powered garden equipment, the manager will help the company decide whether its return on investment (ROI) is most likely to come from television, newspaper, radio, or magazine advertising. While television ads reach the most people the quickest, TV ads are expensive. While newspaper ads are cheaper, the account manager determines that the majority of newspaper readers are not likely purchasers of this type of equipment. A little more research by the account manager may reveal that males with household incomes of more than $60,000 account for the majority of purchases of gasoline-powered lawnmowers, edgers, trimmers, and tillers. Therefore, the account manager advises the company that it will get the best return on its investment in a magazine with a specialized niche audience—such as *House and Garden.*

Ad agencies typically get 15 percent of the cost of ads from their clients. So if the full-page *House and Garden* ad for new lawn tractors cost $100,000, the agency bills the manufacturing company for $100,000. But it keeps $15,000 and sends the remaining $85,000 to the magazine.

The Advertising Sales Staff

The size of the ad sales staff varies from one person at the smallest magazine to dozens of people at large magazines. All magazines, however, have a similar range of advertising duties to fulfill, regardless of the titles given to persons handling them. Larger magazines may break out the sales staff into specialized categories: the automotive manager, the person who handles HABA (health and beauty aids) accounts, the person who manages travel sales, and so on.

Sales Director or Manager

The head of the advertising department trains and supervises the sales staff, but also has other duties. First, the ad sales director must create revenue estimates for the next one to five years. The revenue estimate is crucial to the magazine's operation because it influences the level of spending throughout the magazine's departments. Second, the advertising director must develop the long-range sales strategy. That includes determining which types of markets and customers to target in the magazine's sales efforts. It may also include working with the editors to create editorial calendars with monthly themes. Themes help editors plan their content in advance, but they also help sell advertising to companies that sell products with related themes. For example, a September "back to school" theme in a parenting magazine enables the ad sales director to develop a strategy targeting department store chains, clothing, and school supply companies.

Regional Manager

Most large magazines have branch managers in major cities who are responsible for finding and servicing advertising accounts located in that assigned geographic area.

Advertising Sales Representative

The day-to-day sales staff is always looking for new customers, as well as handling existing accounts. They develop word-of-mouth contacts and scan for potential advertisers in yellow pages, newspapers, and competing publications. They create and arrange presentations to prospective clients and advertising agencies.

Some magazines supplement their advertising sales efforts by using an outside rep firm, an independent sales organization that may cover a region the magazines' salespeople can efficiently reach or bring in specialized contacts such as a rep based in Detroit who specializes in automotive accounts. Generally they work on commissions or draw against commissions.

The Promotions Staff

The promotions staff fulfills a different function than the ad sales staff and has a separate department at large magazines. Unlike direct selling, magazine promotion concerns itself with the long-range development of the magazine's image and reputation. The promotions department does everything from sending press releases to getting the magazine publicized elsewhere to attending conventions, conferences, and trade shows.

Many advertising directors are creative, bundling ad pages with co-branded **paid promotions.** This might range from special appearances to giveaways, product endorsements to free magazine distribution.

A master at this art is David McKillips, associate publisher of *MAD* magazine and ad director for DC Comics. "It's deal-making at its finest," he said. "And savvy marketers love it."

His promotions for *MAD* have included putting the *MAD* logo on a NASCAR, offering free White Castle hamburgers to readers of the magazine, and handing out copies of the What-Me-Worry humor magazine at comedy clubs.

Adopting a cradle-to-the-grave publishing strategy, McKillips has spun off a *MAD Kids* for younger readers and *MAD Classics* for the older diehard fans. And these increase his promotional opportunities.

Yet, promotions and ad sales cannot be separated that simply. An effective long-range promotional strategy will make selling advertising easier. An advertiser will more likely purchase an ad from a magazine that he has read about in a newspaper or heard about on a television news report. Some of the specific department positions and their duties follow.

- The sales promotion director creates promotional programs and material to support advertising sales, which includes arranging promotional presentations for potential advertisers.
- The research director plans and executes research projects to analyze existing and potential customers, markets, and ad rates.
- The copy writer is responsible for creating ideas for promotional material and working with other staff members to create material that improves the magazine's public image and reputation.
- The marketing art director is responsible for the visual component of advertising and promotional material for the magazine.

The Media Kit

Magazines develop media kits as sales tools used to promote the magazine to its prospective advertisers. Media kits should contain as much of the following information as possible to help sell the magazine to its advertisers:

- An explanation of the magazine's editorial purpose and content.

- A description of how the magazine differs from its closest competitors.
- Recent articles from the magazine or copies of the magazine itself.
- Circulation figures and demographic information about the magazine's readers.
- A rate card with full- and partial-page advertising rates.
- Testimonial letters from satisfied advertisers and readers.
- Articles about the magazine from newspapers and other publications.
- A list of awards and notable accomplishments of the magazine or its staff members.
- An editorial calendar highlighting themes and special issues.
- Deadlines and closing dates for future issues.

For example, in the following paragraphs, we have used *Vanity Fair's* online media kit to illustrate these types of content.

Editorial purpose. *Vanity Fair* summarizes its content with a quote from its editor: "The biography of our age—one month at a time." It continues, "With a unique mix of image and intellect, *Vanity Fair* captures the people, places and ideas that are defining modern culture. From the arts and entertainment, to sports and media, to politics and world affairs, *Vanity Fair* is what the world is talking about now."

Detailed demographics. *Vanity Fair* has a total average paid circulation of 1,136,824, which consists of 21 percent men and 79 percent women with a median age of 40.4 years. Sixty-eight percent of its readers come from subscription sales, while 32 percent come from newsstand sales. The median household income is $68,889. Forty-one percent of its readers graduated from college, while 31 percent hold professional and managerial positions. *Vanity Fair's* media kit also gives a more detailed breakdown of its readership by age and income categories.

Many magazines have a guaranteed rate base, which is 1,075,000 for *Vanity Fair*. That means it guarantees a minimum of 1,075,000 readers for the length of the advertising contract. If the circulation falls below 1,075,000 during the life of the contract, the magazine must offer a lower rate to its advertisers.

Rate card. The rate card displays the rates for full- and partial-page ads. The cost for a one-time, full-color, full-page ad in *Vanity Fair* is $114,860 (2006 rates). The card offers a gradually decreasing cost for full-page ads if purchased for more than one issue. If an advertiser commits to twelve months of ads, the cost decreases to $102,225; the cost is $93,037 for a forty-eight-month commitment.

A half-page ad is $71,795, which gradually decreases to $63,898 for a six-month commitment. A full-color, one-third-page ad is $51,685, which gradually decreases to $47,550 for a twelve-month commitment. The cost of two-color ads is approximately 20 percent less than full-color ads, and the cost of black-and-white ads is approximately 35 percent less than full-color ads.

Magazine information. *Vanity Fair* is published by the Condé Nast Media Group. Its media kit points out that the magazine twice won the highest honor in magazine publishing—the National Magazine Award for General Excellence for magazines with a circulation of more than 1 million. Advertising Age recognized *Vanity Fair* as one of the five best magazines of 1998. Its editor, Graydon Carter, was named Advertising Age's Editor of the Year in 1996 and Adweek magazine's Editor of the Year in both 1997 and 2003.

Editorial themes. *Vanity Fair's* media kit listed six months of upcoming theme issues for 2006: "Hollywood Issue" (March), "Forever Sexy Issue" (April), "Television Issue" (May), "International Best-Dressed List" (September), "New Establishment Issue" (October), and "Music Issue" (November). Other themes were not announced at the time this information was published.

Closing dates. For *Vanity Fair,* the closing date for any monthly issue is generally two months prior to the date of that issue. For example, the closing date for the December 2006 issue was October 2, 2006, while the on-sale date for the December issue was November 7.

The Church-State Conflict

Advertisers who spend large amounts of money in magazines sometimes expect—and unfortunately get—favorable product mentions in editorial content and even articles written about their companies. This **"church-state conflict"** is one of the oldest and most persistent ethical issues in magazine publishing. Its frequency and prevalence can't be proven in any study because no editor will admit to publishing favorable articles about an advertiser to obtain future contracts or support. But everyone in the business knows that it occurs. It's sometimes obvious, when favorable articles or product mentions occur in magazines close to full-page ads from those same companies, but usually it's more subtle.

A 2005 report from a media consulting firm revealed that product placement was influencing every segment of media, including periodicals and newspapers, video games, the Internet, books, and even radio and recorded music. The same report said that product placement in magazines was expected to grow 17 percent, to $161 million, in 2005.[13] With increased pressure for product placement in magazine articles, the American Society of Magazine Editors announced revised guidelines in October 2005 to ensure a clear line of demarcation between advertisers and editorial content. ASME's

American Society of Magazine Editors Guidelines for Editors and Publishers (Adopted October 2005)

DESIGN: Advertisements should look different enough from editorial pages that readers can tell the difference. To avoid confusion, any ad that looks enough like an editorial story or feature that it could be mistaken for one should be slugged "Advertisement" or "Promotion" at the top of each page in type as prominent as the magazine's normal body type.

COVERS: The front cover and spine are editorial space. Companies and products should appear on covers only in an editorial context and not in a way that suggests advertisement. (This includes use of cover "stickers.")

ADJACENCIES: Advertisements should not be placed or sold for placement immediately before or after editorial pages that discuss, show or promote the advertised products.

LOGOS: Advertiser logos should not appear on editorial pages except in a journalistic context. A magazine's logo should appear on advertising pages only in connection with advertisements for the magazine and its promotions or when an advertised product is touting editorial awards that it has won.

SPONSORSHIP: Sponsorship language (i.e., "sponsored by," "presented by," etc.) should not appear in connection with regularly occurring editorial features. Such language may be used in connection with editorial extras (special issues, inserts, onserts and contests) as long as the editorial content does not endorse the sponsor's products and any page announcing the sponsorship is clearly an ad or is labeled "Advertisement" or "Promotion" in a type size as prominent as the magazine's normal body type. Single-advertiser issues that don't include sponsorship language do not have to be labeled, but should include an editor's or publisher's note disclosing the special arrangement to readers.

ADVERTISING SECTIONS: Editorial-looking sections or pages that are not produced by a magazine's editors are not editorial content. They should be labeled "Advertisement," "Special Advertising Section" or "Promotion" at the top of every page in type as prominent as the magazine's normal body type.

PRODUCT PLACEMENT/INTEGRATION: Advertisers should not pay to place their products in editorial pages nor should they demand placement in return for advertising. Editorial pages may display and credit products and tell readers where to buy them, as long as those pages are solely under editorial control.

EDITORIAL STAFFING AND TITLES: A magazine's editorial staff members should not be involved in producing advertising in that magazine. Advertising and marketing staff should not use titles that imply editorial involvement (e.g., merchandising editor).

EDITORIAL REVIEW: In order for a publication's chief editor to be able to monitor compliance with these guidelines, every effort must be made to show all advertising pages, sections and their placement to the editor far enough in advance to allow for necessary changes.

ADVERTISING REVIEW: While editors or publishers at their discretion may share the general topic matter of upcoming editorial content with advertisers, specific stories, layouts or tables of contents should not be submitted for advertiser review.

newly revised "ten commandments" include statements such as "Advertisements should look different enough from editorial pages that readers can tell the difference," and "Advertisers should not pay to place their products in editorial pages nor should they demand placement in return for advertising."

"Nothing could be more damaging to our position as the medium consumers trust most, both in editorial and advertising, than blurring the readers' ability to know the difference between an editorial and commercial message," Magazine Publishers of America chairman Jack Kliger told the *American Magazine* conference in 2005.

Rejecting Ads

Magazines sometimes reject ads they believe might offend segments of their readership or are inconsistent with their editorial standards. Many magazines will not accept cigarette or alcohol advertising, for example. While sometimes framed as a "freedom of the press" or "censorship" issue by rejected advertisers, courts have always upheld the rights of publishers to control their own editorial and advertising content.

John Squires, president of *Sports Illustrated*, said that SI rejects ads about "a dozen times a year." He said the magazine rejects ads "largely on matters of taste" when they believe an ad "will offend our readers." He said it also rejects advertisements that make health claims or other kinds of claims, such as those made by companites selling performance-enhancing supplements, that can't be substantiated. Finally, he said, "We reject certain ads that promote behavior that we feel is unacceptable and will not accept ads that promote online gambling."

The Targeted Nature of Magazines

In a recent issue of *Folio*, executives from several major companies commented about the strengths and weaknesses of magazine advertising. Steve Sturm, vice president of marketing for Toyota Motor Corporation, said, "We have a large product line where each product appeals to a distinct demographic, and print is good at delivering a very targeted message for different demographics. . . . Print is more sophisticated—you can get into more details about product benefits and features."[14]

Michael Hines, global marketing chief with the Prudential Insurance Company, said that the strength of magazines is that "People have a real relationship with magazines. They're very targeted. Readers have an unspoken dialogue with a publication over time. That builds trust, and that trust translates, to some degree, to the publication's advertisers. Magazines are very good when you target the right message in the right publication."[15]

Questions for Further Thought

1   Do you think you pay any more attention to advertisements in magazines than those in newspapers or on television? Why?

2   Have you ever noticed a possible "church-state violation" when a magazine wrote a favorable article about or made a favorable mention of one of its prominent advertisers?

3   Is a magazine's rejection of an ad that editors feel might offend their readers a form of censorship? Do advertisers have the same right of free speech as journalists?

4   Can you name a magazine whose ads you find particularly enjoyable and interesting?

Shop Talk

Church-state conflict: Pressure that magazine advertisers place on editors to publish articles that are favorable to or that mention their products. Advertisers also pressure editors to place their advertisements close to favorable or non-controversial content.

Contextual relevance: The similarity between the content of the advertising and the content of the editorial material in special-interest magazines. Contextual relevance increases the appeal of the magazine to advertisers in that field of interest. Media kit: The purpose of a media kit is to "sell" the magazine to prospective advertisers by promoting the quality of its content and its audience. Media kits include advertising rate cards, demographic information, circulation details, and other literature such as awards or newspaper clippings the magazine can use to promote itself.

Return on investments: Precise and quantitative measurements of the effectiveness of advertising in a particular media outlet.

Recommended Websites

Advertising Age: www.adage.com

Audit Bureau of Circulations: www.accessabc.com

MediaMark Research, Inc.: www.mriplus.com

Standard Rate and Data Service: www.srds.com

Finding and
Keeping Readers

The circulation director has a difficult job that never ends. Just to maintain a ten-thousand-subscriber rate base, the circulation director has to find up to five thousand new subscribers every year. Most magazines average around a 40 percent conversion rate and a 60 to 70 percent renewal rate. **Conversions** describes those subscribers who renew their subscriptions after the first year. **Renewals** refers to those who have converted and renewed their subscription again for the second or third year. Suppose a magazine starts out with ten thousand subscribers. With typical attrition rates and no new subscribers, its circulation will look like this:

Year 1: 10,000 subscribers
Year 2: 4,000 subscribers (40 percent renewal)
Year 3: 2,400 subscribers (60 percent renewal)
Year 4: 1,560 subscribers (65 percent renewal)
Year 5: 1,092 subscribers (70 percent renewal)

And these are typical industry figures. That means the circulation director is always having to work hard to find new subscribers. But keep in mind that each source of subscriptions renews differently. Direct mail might convert at 40 percent, but direct-mail agents might only come in at 20 percent. Insert cards might convert at 45 percent or better, but school plan subscriptions may be 15 percent. Therefore, the source mix will affect the overall conversion and renewal rates.

Circulation means the number of people who receive an issue of a particular magazine.

Magazine publishers set advertising rates based on circulation and are usually expected to provide audited proof of their circulation to advertisers. There are two approaches to delivering circulation: paid and controlled.

Most consumer magazines use **paid circulation**, which includes copies sold through subscription and single-copy sales. Many business-to-business magazines go after **controlled circulation**, which means offering free subscriptions to a highly selective and targeted audience, such as airline travelers or key decision-makers in targeted industries.

Consumer Marketing

A consumer marketing director, as the name implies, has the job of marketing the magazine to consumers. Another common term for this function is circulation director. Circulation directors must possess three very different qualities:[1]

1 Creativity in developing new ways of reaching and attracting readers. Circulation directors must be able to write creative marketing letters and design compelling ads for the magazine—or hire people who can. They must continually look for new venues and outlets in which to market the magazine. They must know the demographics of their magazine readership exceedingly well and purchase the right mailing lists from brokers to reach that market with the most economy and efficiency.

2 An understanding of statistics. Circulation directors must use spreadsheets to calculate copies delivered, sell-through rates, returns, cancellations, bad debts, and renewals and determine how those variables affect their profit and loss. For example, the circulation director must be able to use statistics to determine the "point of diminishing returns" in direct-mail promotion. The additional revenue obtained from five thousand new subscribers may not equal the cost of sending out the 150,000 direct-mail circulars it may take to obtain those subscribers.

3 The ability to deal with infinite details. Circulation directors may deal with thousands of pieces of incoming and outgoing mail every week, low-paid clerks, computer problems, and things that just don't go right. They must have the patience and attention to detail necessary to solve these problems every day. A publisher who doesn't possess these skills (and most journalists don't) must hire skilled people who do.

Possessed with these qualities, a circulation director has three main responsibilities:

1   Managing the rate base. He or she must deliver a guaranteed circulation to advertisers.
2   Finding the proper audience. The readership the director builds must be attractive to advertisers, and they must renew their subscriptions every year.
3   Delivering a profit for the magazine.

Unfortunately, these goals tend to work in direct conflict with each other. First, pressure to increase a rate base means going deeper into the magazine's readership universe. This costly process of finding new subscribers works against bottom-line profits on a circulation basis. It may also dilute the quality of the audience demographics.

Second, reaching a specific audience segment involves greater (and more costly) targeting. It narrows the universe and puts increased pressure on achieving the rate base.

Third, going for profit involves less concern for volume or for targeting a narrow audience.

To accomplish this juggling act, the circulation director must find the proper balance, based on the magazine's numbers and its publishing goals.

Every magazine, whether consumer or business, has a "natural" level of circulation. According to most experts, the highest possible circulation for any potential magazine is 10 percent of the number of people who practice, follow, or enjoy the subject matter of that potential magazine. For example, if there are 20 million left-handed Americans, a magazine for left-handers could expect a circulation of up to 2 million subscribers. If there are 1 million people who enjoy widgets, then such a magazine could anticipate a circulation no greater than 100,000. That is its "natural" level.

Every publisher is tempted to push circulation to its highest possible level in order to get a higher ad rate. But the additional subscribers beyond the "natural" level of circulation are expensive to reach and slow to renew. They can actually decrease the profitability of a magazine.

The Building Blocks

The circulation marketer has three major building blocks with which to create a circulation rate base. Each block is comprised of various, but somewhat similar, sources.

Direct-to-Publisher

Direct-to-publisher sales include all methods of selling subscriptions whose revenues come directly to the magazine publisher. On average, 85 percent of all magazines sold come from subscriptions, and only 15 percent from single-copy or newsstand sales. Subscriptions result from direct-mail campaigns, insert cards, and space ads in other publications. According to Anne Finne, vice president of consumer marketing for the Magazine Publishers of America, direct-to-publisher sources are "the dominant subscription source used by magazines."

Advantages. The publisher controls the volume, the timing, and the creative design. And the publisher keeps all the money.

Disadvantages. The publisher has to pay up front for the mailing, which includes creative costs, printing, postage, and billing.

Agency-Sold

These subscriptions are sold by third parties whom the publisher authorizes as sales agents. Subscription agencies do the work and pay the expense of subscription acquisition, and keep a high commission on all subscription deliveries. Examples of subscription agencies include school plans, catalog agents, and direct-mail agents such as Publishers Clearing House.

Advantages. The agent does all the work, and it doesn't cost the magazine publisher any time or money to sell these subscriptions.

Disadvantages. The agent keeps most of the money, too—usually around 90 percent of the subscription price. Although publishers lose money on these subscriptions, its helps them maintain their rate base. They also hope these new subscribers eventually become profitable renewals.

Newsstand Sales

Single-copy sales at newsstands and other retail outlets have declined dramatically over time. They now account for about 15 percent of all magazine sales—down from about 40 percent in the 1960s. The reasons for the decline are multiple—too many magazines, too many media choices for consumers, self-checkouts at grocery stores—and the inefficient magazine distribution system. Single-copy sales are generally handled through a **national distributor** (acting as banker and facilitator), who deals with the four major **wholesalers** who send their trucks out to place copies in over 150,000 retail outlets. These include supermarkets, convenience stores, drugstores, department stores, terminal accounts, and sometimes actual newsstands. Some special-interest publications distribute directly to **affinity outlets**, which are stores that sells products similar in nature to the content of the magazines (example: *Rolling Stone* to record and music stores).

Advantages. Single-copy sales in department stores, newsstands, or retail chains are the best way to catch the attention of new readers. Newsstand is a great sampling device. It allows people to try an issue of a particular publication before making the larger financial commitment of subscribing.

"One of the reasons why we are on the newsstand is to make our audience younger," said John Mack Carter, who is the former editor-in-chief of *Good Housekeeping.* "It brings young people to the marketplace. It introduces our magazine to people who don't know about it through subscriptions."

Disadvantages. Generally the sell-through rate for single-copy sales is less than 50 percent, and the publisher earns about 50 percent of the cover price of those copies that actually sell. That means that if a publisher sends out ten thousand copies of magazine with a $5 cover price, the publisher's actual dollar return will average about $12,500.

Subscription renewals are a fourth area. Although technically a direct-to-publisher activity, renewals extend the life of subscriptions obtained by both direct-to-publisher and agent-sold methods. Therefore, we'll examine renewals separately.

Table 5: Demographic Profiles: Percent of Buyers by Source of Subscription

	Direct Mail	Insert Card	Agency Sold	Other Sources
SEX				
Male	46	47	43	44
Female	54	53	67	56
INCOME				
$35,000 or More	44	55	46	49
$15,000-$34,999	44	35	41	35
Less than $15,000	12	10	13	16
EDUCATION				
Some college or more	58	53	56	54
Completed high school	25	32	28	28
Some high school	17	15	16	18
AGE				
18-34	30	38	39	37
35-54	33	31	36	33
55+	37	31	25	30

Source: Audits and Surveys, Inc.

Sources

Each method of selling subscriptions is called a **circulation source**. Many different sources make up the categories above. Each source is like a separate business, with different sales techniques, different cost structures, different payups, different renewal rates, and thus different profitability levels.

Age is the only demographic that seems to make a difference in sales success. Direct mail seems to attract fewer eighteen- to thirty-four-year-olds and more fifty-five-plus subscribers, while households reached by direct-mail agencies tend to be younger—75 percent under the age of fifty-five.

Direct-to-Publisher Sources

Direct Mail

Direct mail is the best-known example of direct-to-publisher subscription solicitations.

A typical **promotional package** consists of a six-by-nine-inch outer envelope, four-page letter, brochure, order card, and business reply envelope. A common variation is including a lift letter ("I can't understand why you wouldn't want to take advantage of this offer . . .").

However, DM packages come in many sizes and shapes: jumbo packages, self-mailers, polybags, double postcards, and sweepstakes formats are among the more common.

Advantages. Direct mail is the most common and effective means for magazines to obtain new subscribers. A publisher can buy mailing lists of people whose interests are highly similar to the content offered by the magazine.

Disadvantages. Direct mail is expensive. The typical promotional package costs about fifty cents to create and mail, and the typical paid-up return rate for new subscriptions is about 2 percent. That means, in effect, that a publisher will spend $1 million on a mailing to 500,000 prospective subscribers to acquire only 10,000 paid subscriptions. That's the main reason that starting a new magazine is so expensive and requires huge amounts of capital investment.

"Few publishers can deliver a meaningful rate base without a healthy reliance on direct mail," said David Ball, vice president of circulation for Meredith Corporation, the second-largest media company next to Time Warner.[2]

Direct-mail promotions have two kinds of basic offers. The first—a

hard offer—asks for a check or credit card number with the order. Hard offers are seldom used in new magazine promotions. The second—a **soft offer**—is a "send no money now" promotion that promises to send a bill after the first issue of the magazine is delivered. The customer is told to "simply write 'cancel' on the bill if you aren't completely satisfied with the magazine." While soft offers bring higher return rates, their actual pay-up rates average less than 50 percent. The average overall rate of return for soft offers is 3 to 4 percent, but only half of those usually pay the bill after they receive it. According to Brian Beckwith, president of a magazine publishing company, a good pay-up rate is 50 percent, and a good overall net response to a direct mailing is 1 to 2.5 percent.[3]

Like we've said before, selling magazines is a tricky business.

Some magazines offer a **premium** with their subscription offer. A premium is a free gift offered as an incentive to prospective subscribers. Common premium items include videos and DVDs, calendars, or books with some relationship to the content of the magazine. While premiums can increase the return rate, experienced publishers warn that if a premium is more valuable than the magazine itself, those renewal rates are low. They attract only those subscribers who want the free gift—not the magazine itself.

Forbes, a magazine that has largely stayed away from premium offers, used to run ads showing a Rolls-Royce, with a jibe against its competitors, *Fortune* and *BusinessWeek*, saying, "I Wonder What They Will Offer Next?"

Nevertheless, as we learned from Cracker Jacks, "a prize in every box" is a workable sales technique.

The Internet

The Internet now accounts for an estimated 8 to 10 percent of new consumer magazine subscribers.[4] Direct-mail campaigns can cost millions of dollars for each mass mailing. But subscribers attracted through the magazine's website are inexpensive to obtain. "When you can attract subscribers for free through your own website, it's the most valuable kind of subscriber. You get someone who has sought out your brand, and we're not paying for that," said Chris Haines, the managing editor for the *U.S. News and World Report* website.

More and more magazines are finding that that their websites are an important source for new subscriptions. About 89 percent of all magazines sell print subscriptions on their sites.

Attracting new readers to their print magazines is, in fact, the primary objective of the Time Inc., websites, according to Ned Desmond, president of Time Inc., Interactive. The company uses what he calls the "curtain strategy" for the online editions of its print magazines. That means that most of the online content is free, but if you want to read all of it, you have to order a print subscription at a modest cost. "What we discovered was that renewal rates on those orders was extremely high. So it became a very rich source of subscriptions," he said in an interview.[5]

Insert Cards

Insert cards are either bound inside a magazine or blown in. While they annoy everybody, insert cards are a good, inexpensive way to get subscriptions. They are easy to use, get passed along to other readers, and enjoy the long shelf life of most magazines. The blow-in cards pull slightly better, despite the annoyance factor. Cards in newsstand copies average a 2 percent response rate, while subscription copy cards average about 1 percent. That's not surprising when you consider that a newsstand buyer is often a new reader and subscribers are already getting the magazine.

Exchange Ads

Exchange ads involve a free exchange of space with other magazines. The space of running the other magazine's ad in your magazine is your only cost. And this is often remnant (unsold) space. Sometimes a bind-in card is included. These exchanges can be based on: (a) circulation size for circulation size, (b) dollar value for dollar value, or (c) one ad for one ad. In other words, the negotiation is up to you. "It's a pain to work out the deal and response is low," said Susan Allyn of *TV Guide*. "But the cost is low."[6]

Remnant Television Time

RTV relies on remnant television time to sell subscriptions. Men's titles usually do best on late-night TV, women's titles in daytime. The TV spots perform best at two-minute segments, but time available usually requires them to be one minute or thirty seconds. An 800 number is displayed on the screen for much of the time, giving viewers ample opportunity to grab a pencil and take down the number.

Gift Promotions

Gift promotions involve a donor and a donee. Some magazines get as many as 25 percent of their subscriptions from gifts. The majority of gift subscriptions are made as Christmas presents. "This is usually your most profitable circulation source other than white mail," noted Bob Cohn, a consultant with an extensive magazine publishing background. "The average donor orders one and a half gift subscriptions, and the pay-up rate is high. After all, who wants to look like a deadbeat by not paying for a Christmas present?" he said.[7]

White Mail

White mail results from unsolicited subscriptions that come in over the transom. They're called "white mail" because people write in on plain paper asking for a subscription and enclosing a check. Since there's no promotional expense, these cash-with-order subscriptions are a magazine's most profitable source.

Agent Sources

Direct-Mail Agents

These agents sell subscriptions via direct-mail packages that include a stamp sheet featuring multiple magazines. The best known of these agents is Publishers Clearing House. The late Jack Shurman, a longtime PCH executive, once described these promotions as a "newsstand in the mail." Just as newsstand buyers peruse a rack of magazines trying to decide which ones to buy, the PCH customer looks over a stamp sheet of magazine titles to pick his or her selections.

Catalog Agents

These agents sell to schools and libraries. Libraries don't want the bother of dealing with three hundred different publishers when selecting magazines for their periodical departments, so they do one-stop shopping through a catalog agent—picking out magazines, as the name implies, from a catalog. "There's hardly any point in sending out renewals to this category," explained circulation consultant Vince Dema. "Libraries prefer to renew through the agent who handled the order in the first place."[8]

School Plan Agents

These agents use school kids or scouting organizations to sell magazine subscriptions as a fundraiser. The young salespeople rarely venture farther than next door and sell mainly to family members. The best known of this type of agent is QSP (short for Quality School Plan), owned by *Reader's Digest*. "Our strongest sales period is in the fall when schools are raising money to buy computers or basketball uniforms by selling magazine subscriptions," said Lawrence Freeman, of QSP.[9]

Paid-during-Service Agents

PDS agents often sell by telephone, usually multiple magazine packages with the money collected during the service of the subscription. These are often long-term subscriptions of three to five years, a handy subscription base for mass-circulation magazines to reduce turnover of the file.

Cash Field Agents

Cash field agents are more sophisticated these days, but their roots go back to door-to-door magazine selling ("I'm working my way through college . . ."). Sales teams were recruited and sent out into the field to sell subscriptions.

Partnership Marketing

These sales come from negotiated arrangements with department stores, banks, catalog companies, or any other businesses that serve a field of interest similar to that of the magazine. For example, publishers who want to sell subscriptions to their fishing magazine will look for a sporting goods chain that will place their brochure in customer mailings or shopping bags. Publishers who want to promote a personal finance magazine will look for a bank that will distribute a promotional brochure to their customers.

"When it comes to generating strong renewal rates and a high volume of subscribers in the right demographics with low customer attainment costs, partnerships have more potential than anything else I know of right now," said Chip Block, Ziff Davis Media's publishing strategist.[10]

Partnership-sold subscriptions have come under fire recently by the Audit Bureau of Circulations and they are rewriting the rules. This impacts the rate bases of magazines such as *BusinessWeek*, which have relied on partnership subscriptions to take up the slack left by the shrinkage of direct-mail agent subscription production.

Renewals

Many advertising-driven magazines choose to lose money on acquiring new subscribers, knowing they can make it back over time through **renewals**. New subscriptions cost magazines up to $30 each to acquire—more than the cost of the first year's subscription. Renewals, however, are the real profit center because they might cost the magazine only $3 each. Renewals are created by "reselling" a subscription by sending out a series of renewal reminders. Each letter in the series is called an *effort*. A typical renewal series is composed of six or seven efforts in all. The series may be supplemented by substituting telephone calls or magazine wrap-arounds for efforts.

Consider this: Selling a new subscription is like talking to a stranger, while a renewal is like talking to an old friend. After all, these people have already indicated their interest in your publication by subscribing to it the first time around. Therefore, it's not surprising that renewals are much more cost effective than new acquisitions.

"The rule of thumb," said direct marketing consultant Junius R. (Sandy) Clark III, "is that you can keep mailing renewals until the cost starts approaching that of acquiring a new sub."[11]

Renewals give great financial leverage to a new magazine. Try this calculation: When launching a new title with a proposed circulation of 200,000 subscriptions, that total number must be acquired from scratch the first time around. It will probably cost $30 a subscription, which means an acquisition cost of $6 million in year one. If 40 percent of the 200,000 new subs become conversions, that's 80,000 second-year subscribers at a total cost of $240,000. In order to deliver the 200,000 rate base, you need another 120,000 replacement subs at $30 each, which will cost you $3.6 million. That plus the $240,000 renewal cost means you spend $3.84 million in year two versus the $6 million in year one to maintain your 200,000 subscribers.

In year three, 40 percent of the 120,000 new subs will convert at a cost of $3 each, or $144,000 for 48,000 subs. And a greater percentage of the previous conversions will renew, because you have now qualified them as being really interested in your magazine. If you can renew 60 percent, that's 48,000 at $3 each, or another $144,000. Without getting lost in the figures, the point of this is to say that maintaining the rate base in year three will cost $3.4 million compared with the $6 million it cost in year one to maintain that many subscribers.

That's why editorial content is so important to economic success. Strong editorial brings high conversion and renewal rates, which means less money spent on acquiring new subscribers.

Some naive first-time publishers think that if they publish a great magazine, readers will automatically flock to renew. But as Steve Aster, president of Primedia's Consumer Marketing, likes to point out, "I've seen magazine screw-ups prove beyond a doubt that if you don't send out renewal efforts, your renewal percentages will definitely go down."[12]

Single-Copy Sales

The newsstand industry has an unwieldy, archaic distribution system for selling magazines one copy at a time. Although called "newsstand," only a small percentage of single-copy sales are sold at traditional newsstands. Today, supermarkets comprise the largest category of retail outlets.

Some specialty magazine publishers rely almost totally on newsstand sales for their bread and butter. These tend to be "opportunistic" publishers who are quick at catching a new trend and throwing a magazine about that subject onto the newsstand to "see if it sticks." (Such companies include Harris Publications and Starlog Group.)

With little advertising revenue and fewer subscriptions, these are clearly circulation-driven publications. The publisher must manage them based on newsstand sales efficiency. Each issue's profitability depends on exceeding a certain newsstand break-even percentage. There are about 150,000 retail

Table 6: Single-Copy Magazine Sales Location

Place	Percentage of Sales
Supermarkets	38.3
Mass merchandisers	16.6
Bookstores	11.4
Drugstores	10.3
Terminals	6.0
Convenience stores	7.4
Newsstand and misc.	10.0

Source: Magazine Publishers of America.

outlets selling magazines in the United States. Since 1994, the largest increases in sales have come from mass merchants and bookstores. Some 4,700 titles are sold at retail outlets. The average supermarket carries 700 titles, with 300 or 400 on sale at any given time. The top 100 titles represent 51 percent of the business, the top 500 represent 80 percent, and the bottom 1,800 titles represent less than 1 percent.

Hudson, News Group, Levy, and Anderson are the major wholesalers today. Thirty years ago there were more than four hundred, but consolidation has ruled the day—and destroyed regional efficiencies. With heavy debt loads and a broken financial model, wholesalers are looking for ways to cut delivery costs, eliminate inefficient titles, and reduce draws. "I remember back when Anderson was about selling one more copy; now, it's about handling one less," commented veteran newsstand marketer Jim Sokolowski, who has worked on both sides of the desk.[13]

Table 7: Typical Price Shares for a Magazine with a $4 Cover Price

Source	Percent	Amount
Magazine publisher	45	$1.80
National distributor	5	$.20
Retail display allowance, shipping, etc.	10	$.40
Regional wholesaler	20	$.80
Retail store	20	$.80
TOTAL	100	$4.00

The number of copies a publisher puts on the newsstand (or other single-copy venue) is known as the draw. The actual number sold is known as the sale. The sell-through rate is expressed as a percentage. With a draw of 100,000 copies and a sale of 30,000, you would have a 30 percent sell-through rate. The industry average has declined steadily over the past few decades, averaging less than 30 percent today.

Supermarkets and mass merchants sell magazines at the checkout line as well as on a mainline rack elsewhere in the store. Checkouts are perfect for the impulse purchase of magazines, but the publisher is competing for that space not only with each other, but with tobacco, film, and chewing gum. Therefore, you must buy the right to be at the checkout by paying an extra per-pocket fee—the **retail display allowance (RDA)**. This is an expensive game, best afforded by large advertising-driven titles, mass-selling women's magazines, and weeklies. Others must be satisfied with shelf space on the mainline. Other retailer chains offer special displays in exchange for a promotion fee paid by the publisher. Bookstores (like Barnes and Noble and Borders) frequently put together promotional programs by category (children's titles, crafts, and so on).

Leonard Mogel, author of *The Magazine: Everything You Need to Know to Make It in the Magazine Business,* offers five pieces of advice to the new publisher to develop single-copy sales:

1. Pay a visit to a magazine wholesaler and learn firsthand the problems of distribution.
2. See one of the major national distributors. Ask questions about percentages of advances, promotional efforts, size of field staff, and so on. Call on one of their major magazine accounts for their opinions.
3. Visit the regional office of a major supermarket chain. Ask about the company's attitudes on magazine sales in general, and find out how it promotes new titles and what its display policy is.
4. Study the placement of magazines and the display formats for as many retail outlets as possible. This can also help you evaluate which cover techniques are most effective.
5. Examine the story of a new magazine that has been successful on the newsstand. Find out what kinds of promotional techniques its publisher used.[14]

Fulfillment—Keeping the Subscriber Happy

How many magazines are published in Red Oak, Iowa—a town of six thousand? None, to be exact. But millions of dollars of magazine subscription and renewal checks go through its post office every year. That's because it's the location for a branch of Communications Data Services. CDS is an international data management company that provides customized fulfillment services to publishers and direct marketers of all sizes. A subsidiary of the Hearst Corporation, it manages 150 million names of active subscribers for nearly four hundred magazine and direct-mail clients. In 2004, for example, CDS sent 499 million pieces of mail and received 182 million pieces of mail for its customers. Serving the magazine industry are four major fulfillment companies—CDS, Palm Coast Data, Kable, and SFG—along with many smaller ones.

As John Meneough, president of Palm Coast Data, said, "As complicated as magazine fulfillment can be, it's a wonder everything goes so smoothly."[15] But it does, mainly because most publishers rely on an outside fulfillment service—a company specializing in maintaining subscriber records and producing labels for mailing out copies to those subscribers.

Magazine **fulfillment** is the process of fulfilling magazine subscriptions to consumers. Fulfillment means processing new orders, renewals, changes of address, cancellations, and expirations, and printing mail labels. It's a complicated job that requires special expertise, large computers, and complex software for companies with hundreds of thousands of subscribers. Therefore, most publishers find it more economical to hire an outside company than do their own fulfillment. According to one expert, "Rarely, if ever, does an in-house fulfillment operation save hard dollar (out-of-pocket cash) compared to the use of an outside service."[16]

Fulfillment consists of the following activities:

1 Producing labels.
    a Doing the main file run for each issue
    b Producing supplements (usually biweekly updates).
    c Doing postal code pre-sorts.
    d Producing postal forms.
    e Transmitting labels (physically or electronically) to printer.
2 Completing customer transactions.
    a Opening mail, removing and validating subscription orders.
    b Agency clearing (tape transfer) and validating customer payments.
    c Endorsing and making bank deposits.
    d Producing cash reports.
    e Entering orders.
    f Maintaining batch controls.
3 Maintaining subscriber file.
    a Keeping subscriber addresses current.
    b Suspending non-paying subscriptions.
    c Filing change-of-address requests.
    d Notifying expired subscriptions.
    e Identifying and correcting address errors.
4 Billing customers.
    a Preparing subscription invoices.
    b Managing account receivables.

    c   Updating credit suspensions.

    d   Preparing and mailing renewal notices.

    e   Billing new and renewal subscription requests.

5   Handling customer Service.

    a   Sending missing issues to subscribers.

    b   Handling cancellations.

    c   Handling renewals.

    d   Dealing with customer complaints.

6   Miscellaneous.

    a   Filing circulation verification documents.

    b   Creating offsite backup files.

How do you choose a fulfillment company? The company should demonstrate an understanding of the economics of the magazine business and how it works. A fulfillment company also needs to understand the importance of keeping subscribers happy with prompt and timely answers to their questions. It should understand the publisher's need for sound and timely statistics about new subscriptions, renewals, pricing, and other data used in computer planning models.

Subscribers versus Single-Copy Buyers

While some magazines are sold mainly by subscription and others mainly by single copy, subscription sales outnumber single-copy sales by four or five to one. However, if you examine the figures on a *people* basis—rather than on an *issues-purchased* basis—you discover a more even split in buying patterns. About 60 percent of all adults subscribe to magazines during the course of a year and about 60 percent also buy magazines at newsstand.

Although there's a significant overlap of people who buy by subscription versus single copy, there are also strong segments of people who buy *only* by subscription or *only* by single copy. According to one survey, 24 percent of all people purchase magazines by subscription only, while 17 percent purchase single copies only. Fifty-nine percent of all readers purchase both subscriptions and single copies.

Demographic Profiles

Single-copy buyers tend to be younger females, while subscribers tend to be older females and males. This perhaps explains why *Cosmopolitan* sells 70 percent of all of its magazines through single copies—the highest of any magazine. Condé Nast—a publisher specializing in women's titles such as *Glamour, Self, Allure, Mademoiselle,* and *Vogue*—has a stronger single-copy base than subscriptions. These facts also reflect the important role of supermarkets as a key retail distribution point for single-copy sales.

Psychographic Profiles

As you might expect, subscription buyers tend to have higher socioeconomic profiles than single-copy buyers. They are more likely to have a checking account and credit card and to have traveled, stayed at a hotel, or attended a concert than single-copy buyers. Single-copy buyers are more likely than subscription buyers to have attended movies, bought records or paperback books, or made camping or biking trips.

Pricing

In 2004, the average single-copy price paid for a magazine was $4.40. This is a healthy increase over the $2.81 of ten years ago. The average one-year subscription price in 2004 was twelve issues for $25.93. This is lower than the $28.51 average of ten years prior.

This trend toward higher single-copy pricing and heavy subscription discounting have shifted the circulation bottom line. From 1999 to 2003, the bottom-line contribution from subscriptions has increased by a percentage point, while that for single copy has declined by one point.

Paid circulation requires readers to purchase their magazines within Audit Bureau of Circulations (ABC) or Business Publications Audit, Inc. (BPA) guidelines. Publishers establish a *basic price*, the regular retail price at which anybody can buy the magazine at any time. Then marketers tend to discount—within the strict ABC or BPA rules—subscription offers against the basic price.

The cover price on the front of the magazine is considered its *basic single-copy price*. The one-year price listed in the fine print of the publisher's statement inside the magazine will be the basic subscription price. Lower

Table 8: Percentage of Subscribers versus Single-Copy Buyers		
	Mostly Subscriptions	Mostly Single Copies
Stayed at a hotel/motel	57	45
Went to a play/concert	44	31
Took an airplane trip	34	27
Went to movies	65	76
Bought paperback books	56	62
Bought records	47	57
Went camping/biking	42	52
Have a checking account	86	67
Have a credit card	72	48
Ordered by mail in the past year	42	33

Source: Lieberman Research, Inc.

price offers—discounts against those basic prices—may be found elsewhere in the magazine on insert cards or space ads.

Positioning

Positioning is the technique of establishing your product's market "position" in the mind of a potential consumer. The classic example is the Avis ads that proclaimed, "We're Number Two—But We Try Harder!" That catchy phrase effectively positioned the smaller rental car company against its more successful competitor, turning Hertz's number one market position to Avis's advantage.

There are two types of positioning: *target positioning* and *product positioning.*

Target positioning is designed to emotionally impact how you feel about a product. Those telephone ads that show a son in a far-away city calling Mom on Mother's Day, putting a smile on her face and a tear in her eye, are designed for maximum emotional effect. Product positioning pits your product in a positive light against a competitor. One famous example is the Coke versus Pepsi taste test.

The price of a magazine can be used for positioning purposes. When launching *Cricket*, a literary magazine for children, in the mid-1970s, it was priced higher than other children's magazines to emphasize its "top of the line" positioning.

"In direct marketing, we have four great motivators," said Shirrel Rhoades, who oversaw the magazine's launch, "exclusivity, greed, pride, and guilt. *Cricket*'s strategy was based on guilt. Rhoades explained, "Parents feel vaguely guilty that they don't spend enough time with their kids, and an upscale literary magazine that might help their kids grow up smarter and go to college helps relieve that sense of guilt."[17] And *Cricket* squarely hit its target audience—affluent, college-educated families—with its higher pricing positioning.

Circulation: Where's It Headed?

The term *circulation* has evolved into *audience development* in many companies, noted Barry Green, director of circulation for Hearst Business Media. "We are the keepers of the database that feeds so much of what is being offered to our advertising audience and our readers and web registrants."[18]

"Two mega trends portend what the practice of circulation will be like in twenty years," Susan Allyn, circulation director at *TV Guide*, told *Circulation Management* in its twentieth-anniversary survey. "The first trend involves the Internet and its pervasive effect on all media. The other is the growing influence of media agencies in defining circulation quality."[19]

John Mack Carter, former president of Hearst Magazine Enterprises, once said years ago that newsstand sales were the "acid test" for any new magazine. When asked if he still believed that, he replied, "I still believe it, and the difference between now and then is the acid bath is a lot more bitter and vitriolic than it was then. It does not take as long to succumb to the acid as it used to take. But it is still the test."[20]

Questions for Further Thought

Circulation experts say that long direct-mail letters of three to four pages always bring a higher return rate than shorter letters. Why do you think this is true?

2   Single-copy magazine prices now average about $4.50. What kind of content does a magazine have to have for you to spend this much?

3   Study the demographic profiles of single-copy versus subscription magazine purchasers and make some generalizations about their differences.

4   Are you less likely to subscribe to a magazine whose content is available free on the Internet? What qualities of the magazine will motivate you to purchase a subscription?

Shop Talk

ABC: Audit Bureau of Circulations, Inc. An independent, nonprofit organization based in Schaumburg, Illinois, that measures and verifies the circulation of its member magazines. Magazine publishers pay to belong to ABC so that their circulation rates will have credibility with advertisers.

Affinity outlet: A retail store that sells consumer products similar in nature to the content of the magazines sold at the store.

Arrears: Continuing a subscription to the reader after its official expiration date. Some publishers continue subscriptions in arrears hoping that the reader will eventually renew.

Insert cards: The little bind-in or blow-in cards cards inserted in magazines that offer a valuable and inexpensive source of new subscribers for most magazines.

BPA: Business Publications Audit, Inc. Another auditing organization—similar to the Audit Bureau of Circulations—that measures and verifies the circulation of business-to-business magazines for their advertisers.

Circulation sources: The different methods publishers use to find new subscribers—direct mail, agents, insert cards, package stuffers, white mail, and so on.

Controlled circulation: Free subscriptions offered to a highly selective and targeted audience, such as airline travelers or key decision makers in targeted industries.

Conversion rate: The percentage of first-year subscribers who continue their subscriptions for the second year. Conversion rates average around 50 percent for most magazines.

Direct mail: The subscription promotion package sent by magazines to prospective subscribers. Most magazines have found direct mail to be the most effective means of obtaining new subscribers even though the paid-up return rate averages around 2 percent.

Draw: The number of magazines delivered to wholesalers or retail outlets.

Fulfillment company: Most magazines contract with fulfillment companies to manage their subscription list and process new subscriptions, delete expired subscribers, and make address changes and updates. The fulfillment company also sends out renewal notices and processes new orders.

Hard offer: A subscription offer that requires the recipient to pay by check or credit card before receiving the first issue of the magazine.

National distributor: A national company that contracts with publishers to deliver their magazines to wholesalers, who in turn deliver them to retail outlets. National distributors contract with shipping companies and usually don't physically handle the magazines.

Premium: A free product offered as an incentive to prospective subscribers. Common premium items include videos and DVDs, calendars, and books.

Regional wholesaler: The intermediary company that receives magazines through the national distributor and delivers them to the stores and retail outlets. The wholesaler usually receives about 20 percent of the cover price of each magazine.

Renewal rate: Usually refers to the percentage of subscribers who continue their subscriptions after the second year. The first-year renewal is called a conversion. Renewal rates average 60 to 70 percent for most magazines.

Retail display allowance: A fee paid by the magazine publisher to place the magazine at the checkout stand or in another prominent place in a store.

Sell-through rate: The percentage of magazines delivered to retail outlets that are actually sold.

Soft offer: A "send no money now" offer that asks for a subscription order; a bill is sent after the first issue of the magazine is delivered. Pay-up rates for soft offers average less than 50 percent.

Subscription liability: The number of magazines that a publisher "owes" each subscriber after the subscription is paid for. Subscription liability is an important component of the transaction price when magazines are bought and sold by publishing companies.

White mail: Unsolicited subscriptions that come in over the transom. They're called "white mail" because people write in on plain paper asking for a subscription and enclosing a check.

Launching a Magazine, Step by Step

Amy Love had a dream. She wanted to change women's sports and especially the image of women's sports in the media. That's why she started her own women's sports magazine, *Real Sports*, in 1998. In just a few years, its circulation soared to 150,000 readers.

Her dream began as a nine-year-old soccer player in Danville, California, where she was selected for the all-star soccer team in the 1970s. However, after the roster was turned in, the state organization "disallowed" her participation because the team was reserved "for boys only." When her parents tried to explain why she couldn't be on the team, she asked them, "What does the fact that I'm a girl have to do with my ability to play soccer?" That led to a class-action lawsuit, initiated by her parents, seeking the right for any girl to have access to elite teams. This landmark case was settled in federal court, allowing her and all girls the right to play on team sports.

She went on to earn business degrees from Texas Tech and Harvard. After working a few years for Procter and Gamble and Haagen-Däzs, she started thinking about starting a women's sports magazine. She first shared her dream with friends in a Christmas card letter in 1995. Three years later, she launched *Real Sports*, dedicated to "the real representation of today's women and girl athletes in all sports." The magazine's mission is "to remain cutting edge, with a bit of an attitude, to challenge convention and take media coverage of girls' and women's sports to an unprecedented level."

Twenty percent of *Real Sports* readers are men. "It's not about gender; it never has been about gender. It's about great stories. We want to publish a magazine that a father can sit down with and talk about with his daughter. We're proud that our readers are calling *Real Sports* 'the authority in women's sports coverage,'" she said in a speech at Ball State University.

Magazine launches start with an idea. "Hey, I've got an idea for a magazine about widgets," you say one day to your friends. They will likely give you a polite smile, knowing that you are either daydreaming or have taken complete leave of your senses.

Next try out the idea on some publishing professional you come across. The old pro will explain to you that only one third of new magazines survive, and that it's an expensive and risky proposition. In short, he or she will try to talk you out of it. If you remain undeterred, you have a faint chance of success, for only the insanely determined should proceed beyond this point.

At this point, you will probably start dreaming up articles and exciting editorial features. That's important. But it might pay to do some other homework before you get diverted with the fun stuff.

Draw up a list of competitive magazines—those publications most similar to your concept. If there are no competitive titles, then you have a problem. A mistake made by many aspiring publishers is thinking they have an original concept because no one has ever published a magazine serving that field before. Advertisers are pack animals; they don't like being first in a market. They are wary enough about new magazines as it is—they read the failure statistics too. And you have to ask yourself the hard question: If this is such a good idea, how come nobody else is doing it? If there are no magazines serving your field, then it's probably because others have tried and failed or there's simply no market demand for a magazine in that field.

Second, how is your magazine different from its competitors? Yes, all of them may be magazines about widgets, but each has a unique personality and slightly different positioning. You should avoid trying to publish a me-too. The idea that you can beat established competitors at their own game reflects dangerous conceit. Put some thought into how your magazine will be distinguished from its competition, and why the market needs yet another magazine about widgets.

Next, make a list of advertisers appearing in the competitive magazines. Will these advertisers be interested in your take on the market? This exercise will give you a target list for your future advertising sales. It will also help you decide on a reasonable number of ad pages to project in your marketing plan.

How many pages do your competitors average per issue? What's the ad/edit ratio? What do they charge per page—both the out-of-pocket expense and cost-per-thousand circulation (CPM)? Get a copy of your competitors' statements from the Audit Bureau of Circulations, which will show you their circulation and how they achieved it. This report will give you a gauge of what circulation level you need to achieve in order to compete. Magazines with bigger circulation can charge bigger ad rates. Bigger circulation gives the illusion of bigger success. Just how expensive will it be for you to "keep up with the Joneses"?

How much of your competitors' circulation is subscription versus single copy? This will give you a good notion of what to expect on the newsstand.

Does it appear that they do a lot of direct mail? Do they rely heavily on subscription agents? What is the basic subscription rate and cover price? How heavily do they discount subscriptions? Is there any geographic bias to their circulation? You will get a good hint where widget aficionados live—the Midwest, Northeast, or the Deep South, for example. Are they located in urban counties or rural counties?

You will find all this and more on an Audit Bureau pink sheet or the Business Publications Audit, Inc. equivalent. These are great resources of information.

At this point you may want to talk with a **national distributor** (such as Curtis or Kable or WPS) to get an estimate for what quantity of single-copy distribution they can provide. Just because a competitor sells 100,000 copies on the "newsstand" each month doesn't mean you will. Your competitor has likely had the time to build sales in this channel, gather the required authorizations, perhaps invest money in promotions. You cannot expect to achieve this straight out of the gate, at least not without ample spending.

In 2004, 86 percent of total magazine circulation came from subscriptions, while single-copy sales accounted for the remaining 14 percent. To assess the subscription potential, you may want to talk with list brokers to find out what lists they think might work for your magazine and how many names are available for rent. These companies see lots of mail results, and while they can't share proprietary information that belongs to another client, their judgments *are* informed.

You (or an experienced publishing consultant) can take all this information and create a circulation plan for your new magazine. This will tell you "how big, how fast, at what cost." The circulation numbers will be the skeleton around which you flesh out your publishing plan.

You now have enough information to make certain assumptions about your magazine launch: How many copies you need to print for the newsstand draw (a combination of estimated sales and returns). How many subscription copies you need to print (paid copies plus bad pay copies). How many copies you need for office use (promotional and advertising) and complimentary subscriptions (for ad agencies, vendors, your aunt Mary). This will give you the print order.

Based on your research of the competition, you should have a good idea how many ad pages you expect to sell. You have an idea of the ad/edit ratio you need, which will help you determine the average "book size." You can decide what paper weight and cover stock you want for your new publication. A printer will give you a quote on printing your desired number of copies of a magazine with your desired "specs."

Before setting out to create a budget for your marketing plan, you should peruse the Magazine Publisher's Association Financial Survey. This will show you the publishing economics of magazines similar to yours. The survey breaks out participants by circulation size and by advertising revenue, so you can get a good fix on where your magazine would fit. Since the actual numbers are proprietary, the survey looks at expenses as a percentage of revenue. This will show you how much you *should* be spending on each department based on your expected revenue. Compare your estimates against these percentages and see how you fare. If there are large discrepancies, be prepared to explain them. Any smart investor *will* ask about them.

You will want to make a five-year plan. Investors want to see how their funding will pay off. The rule of thumb is that most consumer magazines take three to five years to break even. This is due to the cost of building circulation and ad sales over time.

The timing and expenses are dependent on your launch strategy. There are generally two approaches. One is sometimes called the "Hearst Method." The other is often referred to as the "Time Inc., Method."

Hearst will frequently test a new magazine concept by trying it as a one-shot on the newsstand. If it shows promise, the publisher might increase its frequency to quarterly or bimonthly—a step-by-step process as they verify the reader acceptance. This is easier for Hearst to do than you or me: the large publishing empire owns its own distribution company (ICD), and it has muscle with the wholesalers who carry other Hearst bestsellers such as *Good Housekeeping* and *Cosmopolitan*.

Time Inc., is more likely to test a new magazine concept via direct mail. The response and pay-up analyzed over a wide spectrum of mailing lists will give them a reliable barometer of a new magazine's reader appeal. You can do the same if you put up the money for a direct-mail test.

Can you afford this? Or more likely the question is, Do you think you can raise this much money?

Most likely you will raise some seed money from friends and family (see chapter 9) to do the direct-mail test. Then, armed with good test results and your marketing plan, you will set out to raise the launch money or find a well-heeled publishing partner.

Five Criteria for Choosing a Successful Niche

Some people choose a magazine niche because of a personal interest. "I love widgets and think there ought to be a magazine for widget aficionados," they say.

Others start magazines because of greed—and we mean that in the nicest sense of the word. "Do you know how many people buy widgets? It's a huge market!"

It's good to love your subject matter, but always remember that you are not publishing to please yourself. You must please your readers. Narcissism will not succeed in the economics of publishing. This is not to say you don't have to become an expert on your market—you must! But the readers' interests come first.

The French say, "Cherchez la femme."

Watergate's Deep Throat said, "Follow the money."

We say, "Follow the market."

Concept That Meets a Need in the Magazine Marketplace

First of all, the concept must meet a need in the magazine marketplace. "A magazine exists because people have an interest. If that interest is strong enough—and a magazine satisfies it—the magazine will be profitable," said magazine expert James B. Kobak.[1]

For example, can you think of a magazine aimed at helping the newly divorced with the difficulties they face after going through a divorce? When millions of Americans experience divorce every year, you would think a magazine would be needed to serve this population. Although many magazines do publish articles about divorce, there really are none devoted solely to this topic.

It's not hard to understand why. Practical problems resulting from divorce may last less than a year. Therefore, a publisher has little chance to acquire thousands of long-term subscribers. Nobody wants to read about divorce for the rest of her life. Most people read magazines for pleasure. Divorce is a painful and unpleasant topic. People want to get through it and get on with their lives. They don't want to read articles reminding them month after month that their marriage has failed.

A major error in creating new magazines is creating a title of strong interest to the would-be publisher, but with little appeal to a wider audience. College students developing prototypes and business plans for new magazine concepts often focus on entertainment, music, or travel magazines aimed at students. Yet magazines aimed solely at college students also have difficulty succeeding. Can you think of any? College students are a transient audience with a constantly changing composition. Not only do students frequently change their places of residence, their interests change quickly once they graduate and face new challenges. Therefore, it's difficult for a publisher to find and acquire the high percentage of long-term subscribers that are necessary for any magazine to succeed.

Ruby Gottlieb, a senior vice president for Horizon Media, said she's seen lots of magazine ideas that don't really have an audience. For example, she cited *Smart TV,* a failed magazine geared toward the "educated, intellectual television viewer." She told *Folio,* "That's like an oxymoron: How many people are there out there who really could be classified as 'smart' TV viewers?"[2]

Simple and Easily Understood Concept

Second, the concept for the magazine must be succinct and simple. You must be able to state what your magazine is all about in a few words. Successful publishers call it the "lighted match test." If you can't explain your concept in the time it takes for a match to burn and go out, then you don't have a clear concept.

One of the most successful launches of the last twenty-five years was Rodale's *Men's Health,* which has a simple concept and clear target audience. Ted Spiker, former senior editor, explains its success: "I think it talks to real men—it gives them good, useful, surprising advice and insights into their world. And it does it with a tone and a voice that you trust, that you laugh at, and that's not afraid to kick you around if you need it. A big brother, in a way, that knows what you need to know."[3]

Why is this simplicity so essential? The answer is marketing—to customers, to advertisers, and to investors. New magazine entrepreneurs have to sell their concept to all three sets of customers. If you don't immediately grab their attention with an innovative concept, or if it requires a complex explanation, then you're likely to lose them before you ever get their money.

Sustainable Content

Third, the field of interest served by the magazine must generate constantly evolving news, developments, and innovations. In other words, it must create a constant source of material for news and feature articles. If the potential editorial material is new—but not constantly evolving—then perhaps a book is a better idea than a magazine.

Clearly Defined Audience with Mutual Interests

Fourth, the magazine entrepreneur must clearly identify the group of people who are interested in the magazine's particular content. Not only must the publisher identify it, he must be able to prove to advertisers and investors that the size and demographic characteristics of this group are desirable to them. It's not enough to say that "people are interested in such-and-such." The response from direct-mail tests and other market research must yield statistical evidence of the precise size and characteristics of this audience.

The entrepreneur must also prove that his or her audience has mutual interests and values that the magazine will reflect. This requirement is why there are so few magazines aimed at residents of particular states. While every state has a clearly defined population, people in most states have such diverse interests and values that no magazine can successfully serve all of them. The best-known exception is *Texas Monthly*, which has achieved notable success as a statewide magazine, perhaps because of the state's unique cultural identity. Citywide magazines have better success because they serve large urban populations with common interests in dining, entertainment, and lifestyle opportunities.

Advertisers with Products Aimed at Those Interests

Finally, common interests and values in an audience create a need for products and services to meet their needs. Some generic consumer products do serve a wide range of interests—automobiles, household products, health and beauty products, and so on. A new magazine, however, has little hope of attracting advertising from producers of these products—such as General Motors, Procter and Gamble, or Johnson and Johnson. Those companies either advertise on television or work closely with a small group of established national magazines.

The best hope for a new publisher is finding a small market niche that advertisers interested in that niche have difficulty reaching through existing media outlets. For example, widget manufacturers can always advertise on television or in local newspapers. But in doing so, they will pay a lot of money to reach a lot of people who have no interest in widgets. They can reach thousands of widget enthusiasts for a much lower cost by advertising in a magazine devoted to these devices.

What Makes a Magazine Fail?

Lack of capital and poor management are often named as two of the greatest culprits in why a magazine fails.

As Kobak said, "Too often we hear the complaint that the project would have succeeded but 'we were undercapitalized.' Sure you were, but whose fault is that? Two possibilities: either you didn't plan right, or you didn't raise the amount you knew you needed."

Miscalculation

Take *WigWag*, for instance. The publishing plan called for $6 million back in the late 1980s, but Lex Kaplen's team raised only $3 million. Not to worry, they told themselves. They would publish such a great magazine that when they needed the second $3 million, investors would line up for the privilege of providing it. And, just as promised, they produced a great magazine: great editorial, great visual style, great readership. But when they went back for the second round of financing, the magazine industry was in a slump and investors did not step up. The magazine had no choice but to cease publication after fifteen great issues—despite its rave reviews.

Misreading a Fad

Advertisers loved science magazines in the 1980s because they delivered a strong male audience. But the plethora of magazines like *Science 89*, *Science Digest*, and *Discover* had a short lifespan. Only *Discover* remains, as a struggling survivor. In late 2005, Disney Publishing Worldwide announced that it had signed an agreement to sell the twenty-five-year-old science magazine to Bob Guccioni, Jr.'s freshly formed Discover Media, LLC.

Misreading the Audience

Mature Outlook, *Golden Years*, *Prime Time*, *Lear's*, *McCall's Silver*, *New Choices*—where are these senior magazines today? Deceased, unfortunately. As Kobak points out, "They failed because old people don't want to read magazines for old people." The exception is *Modern Maturity*. It has the largest circulation of all magazines, but probably not because of its popularity with readers as much as the many additional benefits that come with belonging to a large lobbying association for seniors—AARP.

Poor Execution

Early in 1983, Time Inc., set out to take on well-established *TV Guide* with a new magazine called *TV-Cable Week*. The new publication promised to provide state-of-the-art programming information to cable owners across the country. Six months later, the magazine folded, having chalked up a staggering $47 million loss. Christopher Byron describes the failed launch in a book called *The Fanciest Dive: What Happened When the Media Empire of Time/Life Leaped without Looking into the Age of High-Tech* (the title coming from a Shel Silverstein poem about a guy executing a high dive into an empty swimming pool). Despite Time Inc.'s unrivaled success in developing new magazines, this debacle proves that "it ain't as easy as it looks."

Conflicting Goals

When former *Harper's* exec Bob Schneirson was recruited by the World Wide Church of God to launch a positive-outlook magazine called *Quest*, he negotiated with them to give him editorial freedom. In the end, his mainstream execution did not satisfy the mission of the magazine's church backers.

Divided Audience

Alan Bennett took over management of *California* magazine thinking he could replicate the success of *Texas Monthly* and other regional publications. But, true to the title, he tried to make it serve all of California—not understanding that while L.A. and San Francisco may be located in the same state, their residents' mindsets are worlds apart.

Wrong Targeting

Savvy was conceived as a magazine for up-and-coming female executives— a business magazine for the fairer sex. But, as Diane Brady, the magazine's original circulation director, pointed out, "Women execs wanted to read the same magazines as their male counterparts—*Forbes*, *Fortune*, and *BusinessWeek*."[4] Despite all efforts, the magazine wound up appealing to secretaries who aspired to be female executives.

Wrong Reasons

When the late Malcolm Forbes was turned away from a downtown club in New York City, he decided to launch a hip club magazine that would ensure his entry into that world. Hence, a new title called *Egg*. All the money in the world was behind it, but the success was marred by a company confused by the boss's nonstrategic side venture.

■■■

James Kobak offers these six pieces of advice to prospective magazine publishers:

1   Test carefully before committing. Conduct focus groups and in-depth research with potential readers to determine interest. Conduct real-time testing of the sale of subscriptions or single copies; find lists and send out direct mail for testing purposes. Test whether advertising can be sold.
2   Develop realistic projections. And don't forget to do some downside forecasts as well as the optimistic ones you want to believe. You probably won't get more than a 2 percent paid-up return on direct mail, and don't plan for more than a 50 percent renewal rate on subscriptions.
3   Make sure that you understand how the business works. That doesn't just mean an understanding of each component—edit, advertising, circulation, and production—but involves the ability to put them all together intelligently.
4   Don't reinvent the business. Go through the steps and processes that have worked for years, or you will be sorry.
5   Don't launch if you know you're undercapitalized. As with any small business, the number-one killer is insufficient capital to see

the enterprise through its first years when cash flow usually doesn't cover expenses.

6   It's harder to turn a profit on general-interest magazines than those for special interests. It's the niche, stupid.[5]

Questions for Further Thought

1   Create some concepts for new magazines and discuss their likelihood of success based on the five criteria discussed in this chapter: (1) concept that meets a need in the magazine marketplace, (2) simple and easily understood concept, (3) sustainable content, (4) clearly defined audience with mutual interests, (5) advertisers with products aimed at those interests.

2   Why do you think science magazines have difficulty creating long-term success?

3   Why are celebrity magazines so popular today? Which companies advertise in these magazines and which audience are they trying to reach?

4   Why do you think *Real Simple* has been one of the most successful magazine launches of the last few years? Who are its advertisers?

Shop Talk

Direct mail: The typical solicitation package for new magazine subscriptions, which includes a pitch letter, descriptive brochures, return order card and envelope.

National distributor: A company that contracts with magazine publishers to ship their magazines to regional wholesalers, who in turn deliver the magazines to retail outlets.

Writing
a Business Plan
and Attracting
Investors

Texas native Stewart Ramser saw how popular Texas music was around the world after seeing Texas groups perform in Sweden, Germany, and France. So he had a hunch that there was a worldwide market for a magazine focusing on Texas music and musicians. "I wrote a business plan for *Texas Music* during my final quarter of M.B.A. school in 1998," he said. "That was when all my friends and business-school classmates were getting 'real' jobs and I thought, 'Well, this would be an opportunity for me, just coming out of business school, to maybe spend a year and try to develop this idea and see if I could make it fly."

Seeking advice and help from others every step of the way, Ramser tapped Austin City Limits and the Texas Music Office. He planned the magazine for a year and a half before launching the first issue. He did a lot of research on potential advertisers, studied the demographics, wrote a business plan, started a subscription drive. "I did all of my homework, and everything I did was grounded in the numbers," said Ramser, in an interview. "You don't need an M.B.A. to launch a magazine, but you do need to have a sense about spreadsheets, accounting, cash-flow, and profit and loss statements."[1]

He launched *Texas Music* in December 1999. The first issue, featuring Lyle Lovett on the cover, was available in just two stores in Texas. Today, *Texas Music* reaches fans in forty-eight states and twelve countries. It's also available on newsstands in forty-three states, and in more than 2,500 stores across the country.

You may be saying, "I have this great idea for a new magazine but I don't know what to do next."

You need a business plan. The business plan is a crucial document outlining the principles, concept, scope of the market, table of organization, cash projections, and the financial assumptions upon which these projections are based.

While a business plan will help guide you through the launch process, the main purpose of a business plan is to attract investors. Potential investors need tangible, concrete evidence that your magazine concept is economically viable. They won't rely on your enthusiasm or throw money at a bad idea. A strong, detailed business plan will prove to skeptical investors that you have an idea that will bring them profits.

What does a business plan need to contain? Publishing executive John Klingel provides this "Table of Contents" for a new magazine's business plan:

1   Executive summary. A one- or two-page summary of the entire plan, budget outline, and timeline for expected profitability.

2   The market.

    a   Market demand—explain why there's a need for this magazine. What public information need isn't met by existing magazines?

    b   Readers—explain demographics and interests of targeted readers and prove that a sizeable readership potential exists.

    c   Advertisers—identify key advertisers who need to reach this readership market with its products. Explain advertisers' affinity with editorial product.

    d   Competition—explain titles, content, and circulation of similar magazines. If none seems to exist, prove that there's a need for this kind of magazine.

3   The editorial product.

    a   The editorial niche—how will your content differ from similar magazine titles? What editorial need will your magazine fulfill that others don't?

    b   The content—explain the editorial formula, its editorial mission, some article ideas, and provide a sample six-issue editorial theme calendar.

4   Marketing strategy.

    a   Circulation—explain the market strategy for acquiring subscriptions and getting single copies to retail outlets. Include pricing strategy.

    b   Advertising—explain where you will find advertisers and how you will reach them with your sales staff and their promotional efforts.

    c   Other sources of revenue—identify any other key funding sources.

5   The people. Identify qualifications of key people involved in the launch. Convince investors you have the right people to launch a successful magazine.

6   Five-year financial projections.

   a   Summary of timeline for expected profit and loss.

   b   Detailed breakdown of expected expenses and revenues over five years.

   c   Major assumptions—explain the projected circulation, price, printing costs, and so forth on which you based your budget outline.

   d   Potential investment return—tell your investors how much they will make and when.

"Investors will rarely read your plan all the way through, so keep it succinct and to the point," suggested Paul Hale, an investment banker specializing in magazines.[2] He advises that the business plan be no more than twenty pages in length. You should think of the business plan as a summary. But make sure you have the backup material handy in case a potential investor decides to ask questions.

How Far Should You Project Your Magazine's Financials?

Projecting a budget through four or five years of a new publication is next to impossible. Far too many variables make these figures unpredictable. Yet investors expect these projections, so they must be calculated.

Writing the Business Plan

Publisher Carl Pugh devised a simple checklist to help. He said, "Follow these steps one at a time and you will discover you have a business plan for your new magazine right in your very own hands."

The Concept

Write your mission statement, your guiding light, in no more than three sentences. In fact, if you can boil it down to one sentence, you're better off. Make it clear and concise, and then memorize it like it's your own name.

The Contents

Break your magazine's contents down into departments, columns, and features (don't forget the table of contents page and the letter form the edi-

Table 9: Sample Five-Year Budget for Magazine Launch

	Pre-launch	Year 1	Year 2	Year 3	Year 4	Year 5
BASIC ASSUMPTIONS						
Subscription sales						
Single-copy sales						
Total paid circulation						
Cost per full-page color ad						
Cost per full-page B&W ad						
Color CPM						
B&W CPM						
Subscription price						
Single-copy cover price						
Editorial/advertising page ratio						
Total pages per issue						
Issues per year						
Conversion and renewal rates						
Paid-up direct-mail response rates						
EDITORIAL AND ADMINISTRATION COSTS						
Staff salaries						
Staff benefits @ 25% salary						
Freelance writers and photographers						
Office administration, rental, supplies, etc.						
CIRCULATION AND ADVERTISING						
Direct-mail marketing						
Fulfillment company fees						
Other promotion/advertising						
Advertising sales expenses						
PRODUCTION COSTS						
Paper, printing, and binding						
Periodical-rate postage						
TOTAL EXPENSES						
CIRCULATION REVENUE						
Single-copy sales (net)						
Subscription sales (net)						
AD REVENUE						
Color ad sales (net)						
B&W ad sales (net)						
OTHER REVENUE SOURCES						
TOTAL REVENUE						
NEEDED INVESTMENT CAPITAL						
(expenses minus revenue)						

tor). For the business plan, you'll need to drape six issues' worth of specific contents over this skeleton. This gives any potential investor some ideas and stories so he'll have a better idea about what you're up to.

Letter from the Editor

It may seem premature, but go ahead and write the letter from the editor for the premiere issue. Remember to explain your motives to the readers, and make them feel like the magazine belongs to them.

Audience Analysis

Once you've done research on your audience, boil it down to demographics and psychographics. Lay it all out here for you potential investors and advertisers to chew on.

Competition Analysis

Scan the newsstand, check the reference books, and list your competition. Dedicate one page per major competitor, providing their circulation, ad rate, concept, and, above all, the weaknesses upon which you will capitalize. Then list your minor competitors, minus the individual weaknesses and without dedicating an entire page to each one. At the end of the list give a summary of the entire minor lot.

Once you've got all competitors enumerated and analyzed, write a two- or three-paragraph executive summary detailing what you've found. This page should lead off this section.

Advertising Analysis

This is what we call the "wish list." Thumb through your competitors' publications and make a list of all the advertisers you'd like to steal from them. Then, add to the list all those advertisers they don't have but you want.

Circulation Analysis

Remember that acquiring readers costs money. That's why this section is so crucial. In this part of your business plan, outline your strategy for moving your magazine from the press to the people. It's more complex than it seems and therefore can become expensive. Determine what percentage will go to single-copy sales, to direct mail, and to promotional freebies.

The direct mail solicitation effort is often the biggest single expense for any magazine launch. Remember that the typical direct-mail package costs fifty to sixty cents each, and that you can't expect more than a 2 to 3 percent paid-up response rate—on good days! That means you have to send out 1 million pieces of mail (which will cost you $500,000) in order to obtain 20,000 paid subscribers. If those 20,000 subscribers send you $25 each, you will break even. That's why most magazine publishers only break even or lose money on first-year subscribers. Their profits don't come until subscribers renew regularly and they don't have to spend so much money on subscriber acquisition.

Staff

Determine whom you will need and what you will pay them. The key staff positions to fill are editor (finding editorial content), design director (doing layout and design), advertising director (acquiring the advertisers), and circulation director (acquiring readers). Employees can get expensive, but your magazine (and your marriage) will suffer if you have an under-staffed launch. One person can't do two jobs—much less all of them.

The Budget

This is the most time-consuming and complex element in your business plan. You've got to lay out all of your expenses and revenues for the next five years. Your investor may turn to this section first, so take your time and do it right. Make the bottom line clear for each fiscal period and, most impor-tant, be honest. You can't publish a magazine from prison.

The Contingency Plan

It's the home stretch. Take all of the above elements and boil them down to a single page. Your potential investors don't want to have to read the entire business plan on first sight. Instead, give them the highlights from each section so they can get an idea of what you're doing in five min-utes or less.

Putting It Together

Once you've assembled each section of your business plan, once you've thought it all through, analyzed it, planned ahead, and prepared for the worst, put it all together in a well-organized folder or notebook.

Don't believe the old saying that you can't judge a book by its cover. If your business plan looks like it came from an amateur, your investor will think it's a waste of time and won't give you a dime. Give it a little design. You could even borrow the services of your soon-to-be graphic designer to give it a lit-tle pizzazz.

Grand Finale

Now is the time to put your words into action. Magazine ideas come by the dozens and aren't worth a dime. It is the proper execution of the idea that will make a great magazine. So, without further delay, get out of your seat and launch the best new magazine ever published.

Economics of Magazine Publishing

To get an idea of what it costs to publish a magazine, let's look at the results of a 2003 survey of 151 consumer magazines by the Magazine Publishers of America. According to their results, the typical large consumer magazine has more than 1 million subscribers and sixty-four employees. It sells 86 percent of its magazines by subscription and 14 percent by single-copy sales. About 52 percent of its revenue comes from advertising sales and 48 percent comes from circulation revenues. About a third of its expenses pay for paper, printing, postage, and delivery expenses. About 11 percent goes toward the cost of selling advertising, while 27 percent pays for the cost of selling subscriptions and single copies. Only 12 percent pays the salaries of editors and writers. After all the bills are paid, this typical magazine earns about a 15 percent profit. Tables 10 and 11 give more details of the results of this survey.

Keep in mind that this breakdown of expenses and revenues will not be "typical" for a new magazine launch. For new magazines, expect a much lower percentage of advertising revenues and a considerably higher percentage of direct-mail costs for selling new subscriptions.

Here are some "basic assumptions" that may help you to develop your own launch budget. Based on industry averages, these figures are a little optimistic but let's assume you're going to publish a great magazine!

- Third-class periodical postage: 30 cents per issue per paid subscriber, depending on total weight of magazines, percentage of ads, and other variables.
- Printing: 50 to 75 cents per issue for up to 50,000 copies—depending on paper weight, coating, amount of color, and quantity printed (please talk to a printer and get your own quotes). Printing and paper costs average 25 percent of all expenses for most magazines.
- Fulfillment cost: $1.25 per year per subscriber for labels, address changes, renewal notices, and so on.
- Direct mail to prospective subscribers: 45 to 60 cents each (includes postage).
- Paid-up response rate to direct mail: 2 to 3 percent. A 4 percent response to a "soft offer" is good, but pay-up rates on soft offers average around 50 percent.
- Sell-through rate for single copies: 30 percent of total distribution to retail outlets.
- Net income from single-copy sales: 50 percent of cover price. Keep in mind that you collect this income on copies sold only—not copies distributed.
- Advertising CPM (cost per thousand readers): $40. You can use this figure to determine per-page ad rates based on total projected circulation.

- Conversion rate (first-year renewals): 40 percent of total first-year subscribers.
- Renewal rate (second-year and thereafter): 50 to 70 percent.
- Advertising sales expense: 20 percent of total ad revenue.

Based on these assumptions, you can use table 9 as a worksheet for developing your own circulation, budget, and revenue projections.

Finding Investors for Your Magazine

"It is vital for the new publisher to have adequate financing to sustain the venture through the first three years. It's often difficult to obtain additional monies from investors," said Leonard Mogel, former publisher of *National Lampoon* and other magazines.[3]

Getting investors is a quixotic quest facing many windmills. Where do you get the money to launch your brilliant magazine idea?

Friendly Neighborhood Banks? Not Likely!

Nope, banks do not finance new magazine startups. It's too risky. Besides, these conservative lending institutions always look for collateral. Want to put up your house? If so, they can be a good source for financing for the acquisition of an established magazine. Banks like to see a performance history, cash flow, a customer list—in short, some assets.

Find a Big Brother? Look Out!

Large publishing companies sometimes make good partners, especially if you're partway there or have encouraging test results—and the magazine is a good strategic fit for their stable of publications. Years ago, many large publishers felt they didn't need any help, thank you very much. But many

---

Table 10: Circulation and Staffing Breakdown for the 150 Largest Consumer Magazines

Monthly subscription sales	1,160,139	86%
Monthly single-copy sales	195,694	14%
Total monthly circulation	1,355,833	100%
Editorial dept. employees	28	44%
Advertising dept. employees	19	40%
Other dept. employees	17	26%
Total employees	64	100%

Source: Magazine Publishers of America.

Table 11: Average Expense and Revenue Breakdown for the 150 Largest Consumer Magazines

TOTAL REVENUE		
Net advertising revenues	$ 26,465,757	52.0%
Subscription sales revenues	$ 17,201,184	33.0%
List rental revenues	$ 308,993	.6%
Single-copy sales revenues	$ 6,959,224	13.7%
Total magazine revenue	$ 50,935,158	100%
TOTAL EXPENSES		
Advertising		
Selling costs	$ 3,253,072	
Research and promotion costs	$ 1,506,000	
Total advertising expenses	$ 4,759,072	11.0%
Subscriptions		
Commissions to agencies	$ 5,780,375	
Subscription promotion costs	$ 3,850,691	
First-class postage costs	$ 338,625	
Third-class postage costs	$ 692,836	
Fulfillment costs	$ 935,132	
Total subscription expenses	$ 11,597,658	26.9%
Single Copy		
Commissions on single-copy sales	$ 3,424,849	
Other single-copy promotion costs	$ 611,237	
Total single-copy expenses	$ 4,036,086	9.4%
Editorial		
Manuscripts and art	$ 2,628,349	
Staff salaries and other expenses	$ 2,705,553	
Total editorial expenses	$ 5,333,901	12.4%
Production		
Paper costs	$ 5,504,382	
Printing and bindery costs	$ 4,589,625	
Total production expenses	$ 10,094,007	23.4%
Distribution		
Subscription postage costs	$ 3,783,579	
Single-copy distribution costs	$ 317,316	
Total distribution expenses	$ 4,100,895	9.5%
Other Administrative Costs	$ 3,201,855	
Total expenses	$ 43,123,474	
Total revenue	$ 50,935,158	
Net profit	$ 7,811,684	15.3%

Source: Magazine Publishers of America.

companies have come to appreciate the nimble determination of entrepreneurs, realizing that new launches can be diverting and a successful launch often requires blinders to failure and a champion to lead the charge.

But there's always a catch. The large publisher often requires a buyout option, the guarantee that if the launch is successful the company can buy you out. In other words, it's like being a surrogate mother: if it's a healthy birth you agree to give up the baby.

Find a VC?

Venture capitalists (sometimes simply referred to as VCs) are investors and investment groups willing to take higher risks—like launching a magazine. However, great risk requires great rewards. As John Veronis, a principal at the Veronis Suhler Stevenson investment-banking group, has observed, "It used to be you got to keep ninety percent and give away ten percent. But today that's likely to be reverse."

Hit up Investment Bankers?
Be Prepared to Strike Out!

Veronis Suhler Stevenson is an investment-banking group that specializes in private equity investing and magazine financing. Since 1987, VSS has managed four private equity buyout funds with commitments exceeding $2 billion and has invested in thirty-seven portfolio companies including over 180 add-on acquisitions in the media, communications, and information industries. No, investment banking groups do not fund new business launches; they concentrate instead on helping their clients buy and sell existing properties.

Most entrepreneurs are forced to raise the money to launch a new magazine the hard way: on their own.

Here are a few examples of how it has been done.

Use Other People's Money

When Shirrel Rhoades decided to launch a regional travel magazine, he went to the chief investment officer of the Trust Corporation of the Bahamas, a repository for "offshore money." Fortunately, he was armed with a letter from Time Inc., saying it sounded like a good idea (even though the media behemoth had declined to invest). With that "endorsement," he had the money for *Directions* the very next day!

Mortgage the House

Roy Reiman took a mortgage on his house and used the money to print sample copies of *Taste of Home*, which he mailed to prospective subscribers with a promotional wrapper. Circulation topped 2 million in two years. Now at 4 million, it's larger than all the other food magazines combined. By putting his money where his mouth was, Reiman founded a publishing empire that was later sold to *Reader's Digest* for $760 million.

Sell Your Car

John Lawrence used his Volvo to start *Harrowsmith*, a Canadian magazine for country dwellers. The charter issue was financed by a $3,500 bank loan putting up his car as collateral and a Chargex card with a $2,000 limit.

Find 150 Friends

When Lex Kaplan left the *New Yorker*, he dreamed of creating his own publication, "one that would defy the laws of advertising, ignore celebrities, and make room for high-level culture writing and smart illustration." That was *WigWag*, a magazine publishing memorable literary journalism and fiction. Described by a colleague as a "moneyed odd bird," Kaplan raised $3 million through family and supportive friends.

Look for Friends in High Places

Owen Lipstein had an idea for a health magazine. He took the proposal to a foundation with money to invest and launched *American Health*. It didn't hurt that his father was on the foundation's board. He later sold the publication to *Reader's Digest*.

Pay for It Yourself

When Lew Miller, a former medical economics executive, wanted to launch his own magazine, a decision-making publication called *Life Options*, he put up his own dime. Despite an array of savvy publishing consultants, the direct-mail test didn't show enough life in *Life Options* and he shelved the project, to his own financial loss.

Marry It

When Helen Benham married Dick Robinson (the chairman of Scholastic), she had an idea for a magazine for the day-care market. Guess what? Scholastic launched what's now known as *Early Childhood Today* with Helen as the founding publisher!

Divorce It

Lear's was a feminist magazine "for the woman who wasn't born yesterday." To launch her namesake magazine, the late Francis Lear used part of her $120 million divorce settlement from TV producer Norman Lear (*All in the Family, Sanford and Son*).

Spend Your Inheritance in Advance

When Theodore Marston launched *Plants Alive*, it was financed with family money. The magazine was highly successful for a period of time, and then the market faded. This luckless venture was essentially spending his inheritance in advance.

Charge It

Robin Wolaner writes in her book *Naked in the Boardroom*, "In 1986 I had my own idea for a start-up and raised $5-million from Time Inc. for a joint venture that launched *Parenting* magazine, one of the most successful new magazines in the past twenty years." But the truth was, it wasn't quite that simple. She used her personal credit cards to finance a direct-mail test that produced a terrific response, convincing the media giant to buy into her dream. Stewart Ramser used his credit cards for most of the startup expenses for *Texas Music*, but only after he had exhausted all other sources for finding investors.

■■■

"Bootstrapping it" is difficult. Even the most enthusiastic staff member turns surly when the payroll check bounces. The friendliest of printers will keep the presses rolling only so long without steady payments. And the post office does not deliver magazines on credit.

The point: Shepard your funds wisely. A common mistake for an inexperienced entrepreneur is to spend in the wrong places.

For example, don't put all your money into fancy offices. Those lavish magazine offices you see in the movies exist only at large companies like Time Warner or Condé Nast. The majority of small magazines are published in Spartan surroundings. A ritzy address or expensive carpeting is a signal to your investors that you're not putting their money where they want it to be: in the product.

But while it may be exciting to see your ideas come alive by creating a prototype, don't let it turn into an ego trip that uses up valuable funds. Sometimes there's not enough money left to get the enterprise off the ground.

When Otto Fuerbringer, a former managing editor of *Time*, tried launching a national parks magazine, the seed money was spent on a beautiful prototype—but investors didn't step forward. The magazine didn't have enough money left to get off the drawing board.

That said, a prototype *can* be useful in perfecting an idea, providing something tangible for a focus group to examine, and explaining your concept to both potential investors and advertisers. At Scholastic, the staff decided that a prototype was necessary for its 1983 launch of *Family Computing*, since the large educational publishing company was not known for its ability to publish consumer magazines. A prototype allowed it to demonstrate to advertisers that the publication would not have a textbook flavor.

Ramser, founding publisher of *Texas Music*, offered the following three pieces of advice for aspiring magazine entrepreneurs.

1   Learn the business side of publishing. "Learn about cash flow, income balances, spreadsheets; everything shows up in the numbers. Spend a lot of time developing the plan," he said.

2   Spend whatever time it takes to plan before you launch your first issue. "A lot of planning pays off. I spent a year and a half working on my plan before I launched my first issue."

3   Put out the best possible product you can. "You never get a second chance to make a first impression on readers and advertisers. Use high-quality color and paper. If you put out a good product, then the readers and the advertisers will follow."[4]

Questions for Further Thought

1   Experts say that individual entrepreneurs have a successful launch rate that is at least as high as that of established publishers. Why do you think this is the case when major publishers have enormous financial advantages?

2   Why is a new magazine concept that has no obvious competitors with similar titles not likely to succeed?

3   Besides finding the funds, what do you perceive as the major obstacle to launching a new magazine?

How Magazines Embraced the Internet

On August 6, 1991, Tim Berners-Lee, who invented the software that led to the World Wide Web, announced the invention from his research lab in Geneva, Switzerland. In a message to a newsgroup, he wrote, "The WWW project merges the techniques of information retrieval and hypertext to make an easy but powerful global information system. . . . To follow a link, a reader clicks with a mouse. To search and index, a reader gives keywords or other search criteria. These are the only operations necessary to access the entire world of data."[1] He made quite an understatement.

Fifteen years later, most experts agree that no other technological advancement has affected the magazine industry more than the **Internet**. It has provided new revenue platforms, a more effective means of marketing and subscription management, as well as the digitization of content to reduce the expense and time of shipping materials and repurposing content. The **World Wide Web**, one component of the Internet, has enabled publishers to make their content and photos easily accessible to an international audience.

Victor Navasky, publisher of the *Nation*, sees advantages and disadvantages to the Internet. "It has speeded up the news cycle in a way that will be beneficial in the short run but possibly destructive in the long run," he said in an interview. "The impulse to beat the opposition to the story can lead to a kind of sensationalism that used to be the province only of the tabloids. That has spilled over into more mainstream journalism. An ocean of non-fact-checked information is ultimately degrading to the profession," he said.[2]

On the other hand, Navasky said, it makes a lot of things possible. "It enables you to consult a lot of sources that you didn't used to be able to consult in very short amounts of time. There is a benefit to interconnectivity and interactivity that we've only begun to glimpse. There is a new possibility for fact-checking," he said.

Has the Internet helped or hurt the magazine industry? The answer is "both." While some statistics indicate that some magazine circulation and readership has declined, most evidence indicates that most magazines are making a profit on their websites, which are also attracting new subscribers for their print editions.

"The result for magazine publishers and media companies is that the traditional business model is being forever altered," said Bert Langford in a *Folio* article titled "Six Ways Technology Is Changing Publishing."[3]

"The biggest challenge for all media companies today . . . is how they move in the online world; the companies that can't make the transition, in five to 10 years, may be obsolete," Reed Phillips, of media investment bank DeSilva and Phillips, told *USA Today*.[4]

In August 2002, John Motavalli, a technology journalist and media critic, published *Bamboozled at the Revolution: How Big Media Lost Billions in the Battle for the Internet*. Motavalli examined how many media companies, especially Time Warner, lost hundreds of millions of dollars in failed efforts to capture an Internet audience.

Yet Motavelli's obituary for magazines proved premature. After the fall of so many Internet content sites in the few years after 2000, a powerful cultural attachment to magazines endures. Magazines provide their readers a unique tactile, visual experience. Readers can flip through the pages, pausing to admire a beautiful photo or laugh at a cartoon. Web content has not replaced magazines as once predicted; instead, it has evolved to extend the presence and depth of a magazine's content. It has extended the availability of magazine information to new audiences and given publishers a more efficient means of subscription management.

The chief executive officer of Meredith Corporation—America's second-largest publishing company—said, "The Internet is your friend. Once viewed as a threat, the Internet is a medium that magazines are using as a growth catalyst on many fronts." William Kerr continues, "For our editors, it allows us a more frequent dialogue with readers. For our marketers, it provides another source of potential revenue generation. For our circulation professionals, it provides a low-cost alternative for generating magazine subscriptions. And it is growing at a phenomenal rate."[5]

If anything is being cannibalized by rich-content magazine websites, it's public libraries. Michael Rogers, general manager of Newsweek Interactive, told *Folio* magazine, "Being able to read a magazine without paying for it is not new, and being able to read a magazine's archives without paying for them is not new," he said. "Both have always been possible . . . in your local library."[6]

Effects of the Internet

In its 2005 *Communications Industry Forecast*, Veronis Suhler Stevenson reports that the average number of hours (per year) adults spent reading consumer magazines declined from 134 in 1999 to 124 in 2004. Newspapers and broadcast television also lost ground. At the same time, consumer Internet usage increased from 65 hours per adult in 1999 to 176 hours in 2004. The average number of magazines read by each American adult per month declined from 1.80 in 1999 to 1.65 in 2004.[7] A summary of the results is presented in table 12.

Yet magazine industry leaders argue that "time spent" is not an effective measure of media consumption, especially of magazines. "Time spent is not a valid criterion of measurement for media today," said Nina Link, president of the Magazine Publishers of America, in an interview. "So many people are multitasking and using media as 'wallpaper' while they're doing other things," she said. People will often play the television or radio or surf the Internet while they're talking on the telephone or doing other things. When they read magazines, they're more likely to be focused solely on the magazine and less likely to be doing anything else, she explained.

She's right. While the average person spends 241 minutes a day watching television, about 69 of those minutes are spent using some other medium—using e-mail or the Internet, talking on the telephone, or listening to music—at the same time. They are most likely to be using the Internet, e-mail, or tele-

Table 12: Hours per Person per Year Spent Using Consumer Media

	Broadcast TV	Cable and Satellite TV	Newspapers	Consumer Internet	Consumer Magazines
1999	797	630	205	65	134
2000	793	674	201	104	135
2001	744	744	197	131	127
2002	719	800	194	147	125
2003	696	847	192	164	121
2004	678	868	188	176	124

Source: Communications Industry Forecast, 2005-2009, 19th ed. (New York: Veronis Suhler Stevenson, 2005), p. 421.

phone while they watch TV and less likely to be reading a magazine.

Those are the results of a ground-breaking 2005 study, *Concurrent Media Exposure,* by Ball State University scholars.[8] Their study defined *concurrent media exposure* as "exposure to content from multiple media simultaneously available through shared or shifting attention." They observed 394 media users and compared their multiple exposure to television, radio, e-mail, the Internet, telephone, music, newspaper, magazine, books, videos, DVDs, and game consoles.

Consumers are "more involved" with magazines than the Internet, television, or radio, according to a survey commissioned by the Magazine Publishers of America. When asked how much attention they paid to each

Table 13: Demographics of Internet Users ["Use the Internet, at least occasionally"*]

Total adults	**68%**
Women	67%
Men	69%
Age	
18-29	84%
30-49	80%
50-64	67%
65+	26%
Race/Ethnicity	
White, non-Hispanic	70%
Black, non-Hispanic	57%
English-speaking Hispanic	70%
Community Type	
Urban	72%
Suburban	70%
Rural	59%
Annual Household Income	
Less than $30,000	49%
$30,000-$50,000	73%
$50,000-$75,000	87%
More than $75,000	93%
Educational Attainment	
Less than High School	29%
High School	61%
Some College	79%
College +	89%

*Source: Pew Internet & American Life Project, May-June 2005 Tracking Survey. N=2,001 adults, 18 and older. The current two-part question reads, "Do you use the internet, at least occasionally?" and "Do you send or receive email, at least occasionally?"

media while consuming it, the seven thousand respondents said that magazines received "all of my attention" 28 percent of the time. The Internet was close behind, with 27 percent, while television received 10 percent and radio 4 percent. As the medium in which people pay the most attention to advertising, magazines ranked first, with 48 percent; television second, with 32 percent; radio third, with 6 percent; and the Internet last, with 4 percent.

The Pew Internet and American Life project, funded by the Pew Charitable Foundation, tracks Internet adoption rates and usage. The project's 2005 findings determined that 68 percent of all American adults and 84 percent of all adults under thirty use the Internet at least occasionally. Income and education are the greatest predictors of Internet usage, according to the Pew study. It found that 84 percent of all college graduates and 93 percent of all households with an annual income of more than $75,000 regularly use the Internet. The results of the Pew study appear in table 13.

It's difficult to pinpoint cause-and-effect relationships between the Internet and magazines with circulations at more than eighteen thousand magazines. If the Internet is stealing any readers from print publications, however, it's hurt-

Table 14: Combined Circulation per Issue of Audit Bureau of Circulations–Audited Magazines, 1970–2004

Year	Subscription	Single Copy	Total
1970	174,504,070	70,231,003	244,735,073
1975	166,048,037	83,935,424	249,983,461
1980	189,846,505	90,895,454	280,741,959
1985	242,810,339	81,076,776	323,887,115
1990	292,444,099	73,667,773	366,111,872
1991	292,852,615	71,894,865	364,747,479
1992	291,613,749	70,694,310	362,308,059
1993	294,905,373	69,418,673	364,324,046
1994	295,648,763	67,917,148	363,565,911
1995	299,050,282	65,846,048	364,896,329
1996	299,532,710	65,984,883	365,517,593
1997	301,244,640	66,133,817	367,378,457
1998	303,348,603	63,724,643	367,073,246
1999	310,074,081	62,041,749	372,115,830
2000	318,678,718	60,240,260	378,918,978
2001	305,259,583	56,096,430	361,356,013
2002	305,438,345	52,932,601	358,370,946
2003	301,800,237	50,800,854	352,601,091
2004	311,818,667	51,317,183	363,135,850

Sources: Magazine Publishers of America (www.magazine.org). Averages calculated by the MPA from ABC statements each year.

ing the most popular, high-circulation general-interest magazines. The total circulation of about four hundred of the largest magazines (those whose circulations are verified by the Audit Bureau of Circulations) declined about 4 percent, from a peak of 378 million in 2000 to 363 million in 2004.

Special-interest niche magazines continue to succeed, which reflects a trend that occurred with television's growth between 1950 and 1970. What kinds of magazines are succeeding in the cluttered media environment of the early 2000s? *Magazine Dimensions 2005* reports, "The answer is publications that serve newer, more sharply focused interests (*Men's Health, Cooking Light, Maxim, Family Fun* and *O, The Oprah Magazine*), as well as those catering to our insatiable interest in entertainment and celebrities."[9] These "lifestyle" magazines registered a 10 percent gain in circulation between 2000 and 2004, while "men's magazines" climbed by 9 percent during the same period. Magazines targeting young Latino women soared in popularity, with *Latina* gaining 36 percent and *Cosmopolitan en Español* climbing 80 percent.[10]

Link doesn't view the Internet as a threat, but as an opportunity for the magazine industry. "New media benefit magazines. I think we're bringing in people who are not necessarily the subscribers who are forming new relationships with magazine brands," she said.[11]

A lot of evidence supports her claims. *Routes to Success for Consumer Magazine Websites* contains the results of a survey of magazines made by the Federation of the International Periodical Press (FIPP) in 2005. This international survey had three main objectives: (1) to examine practices of successful online magazines, (2) to learn about the ways in which these publishers had achieved online success, and (3) to share some of the lessons they learned.[12]

Results came from 71 magazines in more than a dozen countries. These magazines had an average (median) 115,000 site visitors each month. About a fourth (26 percent) received less than 50,000 visitors per month, while a fifth (18 percent) received more than 1 million.

More than half (54 percent) reported that their online editions were profitable, 18 percent said they were breaking even, and only 17 percent said they were losing money. These encouraging results represented healthy progress since 2003, when in a similar survey only 26 percent of successful websites reported profitability and 38 percent said they were losing money.

The FIPP survey results included five parts. Its questions focused on (1) major website objectives, (2) website content, (3) readership, (4) advertisers, and (5) profitability.

Major Website Objectives

Most magazines (84 percent) responding to the survey said they hoped to use their websites to expand their audience beyond the print audience base

Table 15: Objectives for Web Editions of Print Magazines

Rank	Objective	%
1	Expand the audience beyond the print base by creating an online audience.	84
2	Use website to attract new readers for the printed product.	81
3	Create new revenue streams/profits in long term.	76
4	Build a community around the magazine's brand.	67
5	Communicate with the target audience on a more frequent basis.	57
6	Allow audience access to content at times and places convenient to them.	42
7	Create new revenue streams and profits in the short term.	40
8	Increase your product lines (e.g., news flashes, archive retrieval, etc.).	33
9	Provide website ads as added value for print advertisers.	27
10	Form online partnerships with others to develop more powerful services.	22

Source: *Routes to Success for Consumer Magazine Websites* (London: Federation of the International Periodical Press, May 2005).

by creating a new online audience. Almost as many (81 percent) said they hoped to attract new readers for the print magazines. The third-ranked objective (76 percent) was to create new long-term revenue streams and profits. Table 15 contains details about these magazines' reported objectives.

Attracting new readers to their print magazines is, in fact, the primary objective of the Time Inc., websites, according to Ned Desmond, president of Time Inc., Interactive. The company uses what he calls the "curtain strategy" for the online editions of its print magazines. That means that most of the online content is free, but if you want to read all of it, you have to order a print subscription at a modest cost.

"The best example is at *Fortune* magazine," he said in an interview.

A couple of years ago *Fortune* had some tough situations on its circulation front. What they did was a combination of things. They put several years of articles online and you could find them easily. You could begin reading the article, but when you tried to continue, you had to subscribe. But the subscription was a very small amount, maybe $2.99 or $3.99 for three or four issues. But you had to pay with a credit card. That *Fortune* audience who was eager to get that business information was more than willing to put credit card down and pay that small amount.

What we discovered was that renewal rates on those orders was extremely high. So it became a very rich source of subscriptions. Over the past couple of years, *Fortune* really turned around its circulation economics.[13]

Direct-mail campaigns for new subscribers are expensive and can cost millions of dollars for each mass mailing. But subscribers attracted through the magazine's website are inexpensive to obtain. "When you can attract subscribers for free through your own website, it's the most valuable kind of subscriber. You get someone who has sought out your brand, and we're not paying for that," said Chris Haines, the managing editor for the *U.S. News and World Report* website.[14]

Jon Rosswurm, Internet marketing director for magazines owned by Indiana's Dynamic Resources Group, Inc., reports that nearly 20 percent of the company's new magazine subscriptions are coming from online marketing.

Website Content

"If you think about what the Internet is good for—it's not really great for reading a long article. It's not great for watching moving images. It's great for getting information quickly; things that require instant access to information and are not graphic-heavy and do not require a lot of time spent looking at the same thing work well on the Internet," said Chris Haines, of USNews.com. He described the website's purpose as: "To extend the brand, reach new audiences, bring in revenue, and present it in a way that works on the Web."[15]

Eighty-six percent of the magazines responding to the FIPP survey publish information on their websites that has not appeared in their print editions. The survey asked the magazines what type of content attracted new audiences. The four most common answers were (1) time-critical information, (2) interactive content, (3) searchable databases and archives, and (4) personalized content.

Time-Critical Information

This content includes frequently updated news on the subject area covered by the magazine. Most of the successful websites in the survey (72 percent) update their content daily with news not appearing in the print magazine. Some magazines update their site continuously throughout the day. Only 11 percent reported that they updated monthly. Online classified advertising was a pull for several sites. Several magazines mentioned the availability of free electronic newsletters as an attractive feature.

Other examples of time-critical information included a database of kitchen food for a cooking magazine, a "hot spot" finder, and city and country guides for travel magazines. A finance magazine mentioned website-only investing, personal finance, and real estate columns, and an investment portfolio Q&A. A car magazine stated that the site contained far greater depth of information on car models than could be published in the print edition.

For some websites, 80 to 90 percent of the content was written exclusively for the site.

Thirty percent of the surveyed magazines offered RSS, or **Really Simple Syndication**. RSS offers a website the facility to automatically supply registered users with continually updated headline information about specific topics the user requests. News content is the most common example of RSS—including news for specialized interests such as daily film or automotive news. One site offers not only news headlines but also a summary of all fresh content that appeared on the site that day. Other types of RSS content provided by at least one site include magazine content; branded blogs; all on-site articles; a variety of sections of the site such as foreign affairs, the economy, and politics; and weekly motivational messages to registrants of various clubs.

Eighty percent of the surveyed magazines give free access to the whole site to all visitors. About 19 percent of sites charge for access to parts of the site or allow only print subscribers to access certain areas. The proportion of the site that is paid-only or print subscriber–only varies between 5 and 90 percent.

The *New Republic* is one magazine that allows subscriber-only access to most of its online content. Only about 25 percent of its weekly content is accessible by nonsubscribers. Yet if a new customer subscribes online, he or she gets immediate access to the magazine and its archives. Lori Dorr, circulation director, told *Folio*, "Having the digital versions of the magazine available for new subscribers allows them to engage in the product instantly, rather than having to wait four weeks for the print copy to show up."[16]

Table 16: Types of Interactive Content Provided

Rank	Objective	%
1	Subscription request for print edition.	89
2	Chat room or message board discussion.	60
3	E-commerce-products and services for sale.	48
4	Offers and discounts exclusive to subscribers.	38
5	Freelance articles or blogs submitted for publication.	34
6	Other interactive facilities.	34
7	Hyperlinks to related external sites.	29
8	Classified ads from site visitors.	28
9	Online subscription to members-only area.	26
10	Fee-charged online articles, reports, and features.	18

Source: Routes to Success for Consumer Magazine Websites (London: Federation of the International Periodical Press, May 2005).

Interactive Content

The FIPP questionnaire asked for ways in which visitors to a website might interact directly with the site's publishers and/or other visitors. The most popular type of interactive content (89 percent) was a page for print subscription orders. Other types included chat rooms (60 percent), and e-commerce (48 percent). Respondents were asked what types of content they provided on their own sites; the results are summarized in table 16.

U.S. News and World Report is known for its annual ratings of colleges, universities, and hospitals. Besides these annual print directories of schools and hospitals, the magazine charges a fee for the same information on its website. But it has also expanded its free interactive content by adding free access to directories of thousands of hospitals, charitable organizations, auto reviews, and travel and retirement guides.

"Something that we have really taken and run with is data and directories, which are volumes and volumes of data about each institution that's not qualitative or ranked," said Haines. "We went into partnership with the American Hospital Association, which collects data on six thousand member hospitals. So they provided that data to us for free, and we turned it into a consumer product and gave them the tools to search it. That's definitely a direction we're going in."

The *U.S. News* website also offers the magazine's writers a chance to publish material that won't fit in the print edition. "More and more writers have come to us and volunteered. With the advertising crunch, our magazine is pretty thin. They can't do what they want to do, which is write. But we don't have any space constraints. So we tell them, 'If you want to write, we will publish your stuff every day.' We have people now who are volunteering to do more writing for us, and we're creating places for that to happen," he said.[17]

E-commerce

About 35 percent of online magazine sites conduct e-commerce, which includes selling branded goods, such as mugs, shirts, caps, and so on. Twenty-two percent sell types other branded goods. A few sites also sell unbranded goods such as toys, garden plants, and decorating and cooking accessories.

Readership

Most magazine websites in the FIPP study found that they attracted significant numbers of new readers who did not read the print products. The number of site visitors received each month varied enormously. Eighteen percent received more than one million site visits per month, while the median was about 115,000. More than half found that their sites attracted 20 percent more readers than their print products. Only 6 percent found that they had gained "no significant new audience" from their websites.

Advertisers

About 66 percent of the consumer magazine websites gained new advertisers on the web who did not advertise in the print products. Advertisers appreciate three characteristics of online advertising: First, the Internet is an excellent direct response medium. Site visitors who click through to an ad are show themselves to be "hot prospects" and ready to buy the advertiser's product. Second, the audience is measurable. Site owners can prove not only the number of visitors but also the click-through rates for advertisements. And third, the web audience tends to be younger than the print audience, which appeals to advertisers.

Profitability

More than half the surveyed sites (54 percent) were profitable, 18 percent were breaking even and only 17 percent were losing money. This represented a healthy increase in the two years since the 2003 survey, when only 26 percent of successful websites were profitable and 38 percent said they were losing money.

Conclusion

During the last five years, it appears that the Internet has had some negative effect on top-tier consumer magazine circulation. Veronis Suhler Stevenson's 2005 *Communications Industry Forecast* reports that magazine readership decreased from 134 hours per year per person in 1999 to 124 hours per year per person in 2004. Consumer Internet use increased from 65 to 174 hours per year per person. Total combined circulation of all ABC-audited magazines declined from a high of 378 million in 2000 to 363 million in 2004.

Yet any losses from declining print readership are equaled or surpassed by increased revenue from online ad sales and inexpensive new subscriptions obtained via the magazines' websites. Many smaller niche-oriented magazines continue to grow, and the number of new launches every year surpasses nine hundred. Some segments, such as Latino, men's, and celebrity magazines, are growing.

Most magazine editors and publishers believe that the Internet has offered them another ad revenue stream, an inexpensive means of obtaining new readers, managing fulfillment, expanding their brand exposure, and increasing reader loyalty.

Josh Macht, editor and general manager at Time.com, said, "The sky's the limit for the success of this thing. It's still very early. There are so many more people to reach, and the advertisers are clamoring to reach them."[18]

Questions for Further Thought

1   Compare the print content of your favorite magazine with its Web content. Does the website have more, less, or identical content? What other differences do you note?

2   Do you enjoy reading screen content as much as print content? Can you tell any difference in your reading speed or what types of content you're more likely to read online versus in print?

3   Teenagers and young adults have grown up with the Internet. How do you think their reading habits differ from those who are older than forty?

4   Do you think the Internet will significantly harm circulation of newspapers and magazines as wireless reading devices become smaller and less expensive?

Shop Talk

Internet: The international network of mainframe and personal computers that originated in the 1960s and allowed users to communicate with one another using e-mail, the world wide web, file transfer protocol and other software applications.

Really Simple Syndication. RSS offers a website the facility to automatically supply registered users with continually updated headline information about specific topics the user requests.

World Wide Web: A component of the Internet invented in the early 1990s that allows a user-friendly interface to create an interactive experience with text, photos, audio, and video.

A Brief History
of Magazines

Vanity Fair shocked the world when it became the first of any publication to reveal the identity of Watergate hero "Deep Throat" as Mark Silk, the ninety-one-year-old former associate director of the FBI. Silk was the famous anonymous source in Woodward and Bernstein's 1973–74 *Washington Post* investigation that led to President Richard Nixon's resignation. Silk remained anonymous for thirty years, until the *Vanity Fair* story. John D. O'Connor, the Silks' family attorney, wrote the article that appeared in the magazine's July 2005 issue. He had negotiated with the magazine for two years to publish the article. Joan Felt, the daughter of Mark Silk, said in an interview that the family had many reasons for revealing her father's role in Watergate, but didn't deny that "to make money was one of them."[1]

Magazines have always occupied a unique role in American history because they created a "middle ground" between books and newspapers. Magazines found their niche, first, because they could offer more in-depth information to more specialized audiences than newspapers. Second, magazines could publish more frequently with more up-to-date information than books.

Printing originated in China around 1045 with "block printing" techniques made from clay or wood. Characters were carved into a wooden block, inked, and then transferred to paper. Since each word, phrase, or picture was on a separate block, this reproduction method was expensive and time-consuming.

Magazines evolved from the pamphlets, booklets, posters, and almanacs— not to mention newspapers and books—made possible by Gutenberg's printing press in the fifteenth century. The first American magazines were published in 1741, about fifty years after the country's first newspapers.

European Origins

Johannes Gutenberg, a goldsmith from Mainz, Germany, invented movable type around 1440, which made mass production of printing possible. The Gutenberg press, with its wood and later metal movable type, brought down the price of print materials and made them affordable. By 1500, after only fifty years of printing, more than 9 million books had been published.[2]

Johann Rist, a German poet and theologian, published the first periodical in 1663. His *Erbauliche Monaths-Unterredungen* ("Edifying Monthly Discussions") was aimed at an elite intellectual audience. The first periodical to call itself a "magazine" was *The Gentleman's Magazine*, published by British printer Edward Cave in 1731. Taking the best content from other leading periodicals, "It was more like a *Reader's Digest* in its eclectic choice of content, which ran the gamut from the literary to the political, from the critical to the biographical," according to magazine historian Sammye Johnson.[3]

American Magazines

Two American printers competed to publish the first magazine in the United States. Benjamin Franklin, who achieved initial success as a printer, planned to publish the first American magazine. To his surprise, however, rival Philadelphia printer **Andrew Bradford** beat him by three days. Bradford published the first issue of his magazine, *American Magazine; or, A Monthly View of the Political State of the British Colonies*, on February 13, 1741. Three days later, the first issue of Franklin's magazine, *The General Magazine and Historical Chronicle for All the British Plantations*, was published. (Despite popular legend, Benjamin Franklin did not publish the first issue of *Saturday Evening Post*—although it was printed on the same presses he used.)

Bradford's magazine survived for only three months, while Franklin's survived for six. Both were heavily influenced by the British magazines, which Bradford acknowledged in his first issue: "The Success and Approbation which the MAGAZINES, published in Great-Britain, have met with for many Years past, among all Ranks and Degrees of People, Encouraged us to Attempt a Work of the Like Nature in America,"[4] he wrote.

By the end of the eighteenth century, about one hundred magazines had been launched in America. Among the more successful were the *Columbian Magazine* (1786–92) and the *American Museum* (1787–92) of Philadelphia, the *Massachusetts Magazine* (1789–96) of Boston, and the *New York Magazine* (1790–97) of New York.[5] The eminent magazine historian Frank Luther Mott calls these four magazines the "most important" and "longest-lived" of the eighteenth century.[6]

Both the number and circulation of magazines grew throughout the nineteenth century. Mott estimates that about 600 magazines were published in 1850, 700 in 1865, 1,200 in 1870, and 3,300 by 1885. These figures don't reflect the number of unsuccessful starts made in the period. Mott estimates that at least four thousand magazines with an average lifespan of two years each were launched between 1800 and 1875.[7]

During the seventeenth and eighteenth centuries, magazines faced three major problems that limited their successful expansion: transportation problems, low literacy rates, and high production costs.

First, because magazine distribution was possible only by stagecoach, horseback, or canal, circulation was limited primarily to large eastern cities. Second, most of the population was illiterate and, thus, couldn't read magazines. Third, the cost of magazines made them affordable only to affluent readers. Consequently, the majority of magazine readers up until the late nineteenth century were concentrated among the educated and affluent populations of Boston, New York, Philadelphia, Chicago, and Washington, D.C.

The opening of the Pacific railroad in 1869 made national distribution of magazines logistically possible. Ten years later, Congress stimulated the growth of magazines by providing low-cost mailing privileges followed by postal delivery to rural areas. The number of rural free delivery routes increased from 44 in 1897 to 25,000 in 1903. Rotary presses replaced the slow flatbed presses in the 1880s, increasing the production speed tenfold while decreasing production costs. These advances in transportation, technology, and postal delivery helped make possible the mass-circulation magazines of the twentieth century.

Oldest Monthly Magazines

The popular-science magazine *Scientific American* has been published monthly since August 28, 1845, making it the oldest continuously published magazine in the United States. Widely read, it has a monthly circulation of 100,000 in the United States and 100,000 internationally.

Harper's is a general-interest magazine covering literature, politics, culture, and the arts. It is the second-oldest continuously published monthly magazine in the United States. *Harper's* was launched in June 1850 by the New York City book-publishing firm Harper and Brothers. The initial press run of 7,500 copies sold out immediately, and within six months circulation had reached 50,000. Today, its circulation is slightly more than 200,000.

A New Business Model

Up until this time, magazines sold few ads, relying primarily on circulation revenue. This business model was part of the reason magazine subscription and cover prices were too high for most people to afford. During the 1890s, a few publishers realized that they could make more money by dropping the price of their magazines and making them affordable to working-class Americans. By selling their magazines for less than the cost of production, they could still make a profit because of the high volume of advertising that large circulations attracted.

Munsey's magazine was the highest-circulation magazine at the turn of the twentieth century. Although started in 1889, it was still losing money until **Frank Munsey** (1854–1925) dropped the price from a quarter to a dime in 1893. His move increased circulation from 60,000 to 700,000 in the next seven years. *Munsey's* became the first low-price, mass-circulation magazine. The magazine continued until 1929 and the onset of the Great Depression. Munsey died in 1925 after launching more than a dozen magazines.

Another leading magazine of the time that adopted the low-price, high-circulation model was *McClure's*. **Samuel S. McClure** (1857–1949) founded *McClure's* in 1893 as an inexpensive illustrated monthly. Each issue contained articles on exploration, science, trains, and personalities, as well as fiction. By 1900, *McClure's* boasted a circulation of 370,000, which was second only to *Munsey's*. In 1902, *McClure's* initiated the muckraking movement. It began with Ida M. Tarbell's exposé of monopolistic practices of the Standard Oil Company, which ran for two years.

The Growth of Advertising

The growth of advertising had three major effects on magazines between 1900 and 1920. First, the Audit Bureau of Circulations was created in 1914 to monitor and verify circulation figures for advertisers. In the scramble for high circulation that low-priced magazines enabled, some publishers padded their figures while others sought to maintain secrecy. Advertisers pressured magazine publishers to join and cooperate with the new bureau in providing accurate and reliable figures. Today, most leading magazines belong to the Audit Bureau of Circulations based in Schaumburg, Illinois, and it remains the leading industry source for accurate circulation figures.

Second, advertising stimulated the improvement of magazine design and layout. In 1896, Edward Bok, editor of *Ladies' Home Journal*, was the first to move advertising from its segregated section at the back of the magazine. Before long, most magazines were mixing advertisements and editorial matter throughout their pages.

Most companies hired agencies to design their advertisements. Their visually attractive advertisements stimulated editors to improve the graphic presentation of their editorial material. Since many advertisers preferred color advertisements, their display stimulated the use of color in the graphic design and presentation of articles.

The third effect of advertising on magazines was standardization in size. Since some advertisers place the same ads in several publications, magazines that were larger or smaller than the normal-sized magazines faced a competitive disadvantage. Most of the large general-interest magazines, such as *Collier's* and *Saturday Evening Post*, were a large 10-by-12-inch format until their demise or restructuring in the 1960s and '70s. Since then, 8.5-by-11-inch magazines have become the norm. Notable exceptions are *Reader's Digest* and *National Geographic*, with their digest formats. Because of their high circulations, advertisers were willing to prepare special ads for them.

Table 17: Highest-Circulation Magazines and Year Started

Circ. Rank	Name of Magazine	2005 Paid Circulation	Year Started
1	AARP: The Magazine	22,559,956	1958
2	Reader's Digest	10,128,943	1922
3	TV Guide	9,073,543	1953
4	Better Homes and Gardens	7,634,170	1922
5	National Geographic	5,431,117	1888
6	Good Housekeeping	4,606,800	1885
7	Family Circle	4,298,117	1932
8	Ladies' Home Journal	4,131,243	1883
9	Time	4,050,589	1923
10	Woman's Day	4,015,392	1937
11	People	3,779,640	1974
12	AAA Home and Away	3,675,663	1980
13	MediZine Healthy Living	3,505,353	1994
14	Sports Illustrated	3,339,229	1954
15	Prevention	3,331,686	1950

Source: Audit Bureau of Circulation, June 2005 figures.

Magazines That Made History

In 2004, two Italian journalists, Norberto Angeletti and Alberto Oliva, published the book *Magazines That Make History*.[8] They profiled eight magazines that they considered history's most innovative and influential. Five were American magazines: *National Geographic, Time, Reader's Digest, Life,* and *People*. The others were *La Guerre* (French), *Hola!* (Spanish), and *Der Spiegel* (German).

National Geographic

National Geographic was started in 1888 as a publication of the National Geographic Society. For its first fifteen years, it was a dull, print-heavy publication aimed at the society's members, who had an academic interest in geography. The editor who transformed the magazine—**Gilbert Hovey Grosvenor** (1875–1966)—was hired as assistant editor in 1899 when he was twenty-three years old. His vision for the magazine—a photo-oriented magazine that would popularize recent geographic findings and expeditions—clashed with the society's editorial committee, whose members wanted to keep the magazine's technical, academic orientation. Fortunately, Grosvenor won out. After becoming editor-in-chief in 1903, he led the *National Geographic* for the next fifty years as a pioneering photojournalism magazine. Over the years, it scored many photojournalism "firsts" and consistently ranked among the top five circulation leaders.

Reader's Digest

The affluence of the 1920s brought the birth of some the century's most successful magazines, including *Time* and *Reader's Digest*. Technological advances nearly doubled industrial production between 1921 and 1929. Employment was high, corporate earnings were soaring, and prices were stable. *Reader's Digest*, started in 1922, found its niche by providing practical and useful information at a time when most of its competitors were publishing fiction or erudite essays. Its editorial formula was simple: reprint the best articles from the country's leading periodicals after condensing them into a short, readable format. Today *Reader's Digest* is the world's largest independently published magazine. Its forty-eight international editions publish 23 million monthly copies, read by an estimated 100 million people in nineteen languages and sixty countries.[9]

DeWitt Wallace (1889–1981) and his fiancée, **Lila Bell Acheson** (1889–1984), started *Reader's Digest* in 1922 on a shoestring. The son of a college president and Presbyterian minister, Wallace worked in St. Paul, Minnesota, for a publisher of farm magazines and textbooks. Laid off from his job in 1921, he borrowed $5,000 from friends, and he and his fiancée rented an office in New York, clipped and condensed dozens of articles for their new magazine, and prepared a circular to solicit subscriptions. On their wedding day, October 15, 1921, they mailed thousands of promotional circulars. When they returned from their honeymoon, their mail included fifteen hundred charter subscriptions at $3 each.

The Wallaces created an editorial formula guided by three criteria: applicability, lasting interest, and constructiveness. "Applicability" meant that readers should feel that the subject concerned their lives. "Lasting interest" meant that an article should be worth reading a year later and not go out-of-date. "Constructiveness" meant that articles promoted optimism, good works, and constructive approaches to life's problems.

"The magazine has always been a family magazine. I think we're probably the only true family magazine out there, because everyone in the family can read it," said Jacqueline Leo, editor-in-chief, in a recent interview. "Young teenagers and all the way up to Grandma. It can tie a family together over an idea instead of over an argument or a problem. They wind up talking about a story in the magazine they can talk about at the dinner table."[10]

Time

Time magazine made its mark in 1923 by summarizing the world's news in one convenient, easy-to-read magazine. Using a model similar to that of *Reader's Digest*, its innovation came not in its content, but in the convenient way in which it packaged and delivered it. Whereas the *Digest* focused on service articles of practical interest, *Time* focused on news and current events.

Henry Robinson Luce (1898–1967) and **Briton Hadden** (1898–1929) were Yale classmates who decided while they were still in college that they wanted to start a newsmagazine. Luce grew up in China as the son of Presbyterian missionaries, while Hadden was the son of a Brooklyn stockbroker. After college, Luce became a reporter for the *Chicago Daily News* and Hadden worked for the *New York World*. By chance, they were both offered jobs on the *Baltimore News*. Reunited there, they resumed planning a weekly newsmagazine they tentatively called *Facts*.

In less than a year, these two twenty-four-year-old men quit their jobs and moved to New York with little money, plenty of ambition, and a typewritten dummy for their new magazine. They spent a year raising money and selling shares in their new venture, mostly to former classmates or Yale alumni. After raising $85,000—$15,000 short of their goal—they decided to proceed anyway. The first issue of *Time: The Weekly News-Magazine*, containing thirty-two pages and selling for fifteen cents, appeared on March 3, 1923. The partners had fulfilled their goal: reducing the world's news into twenty-two departments in a magazine that could be read in less than an hour. By January 1924, circulation had climbed to thirty thousand. By the end of the year, it had reached seventy thousand.

During the first six years, Hadden was editor-in-chief, while Luce was the publisher and business manager. Hadden, however, was stricken with a streptococcus infection in 1928 and died on February 27, 1929, at the age of thirty-one. Luce became editor and majority shareholder. Soon thereafter, he started planning for the first of three magazines his company was to create: *Fortune* (1930), *Life* (1936), and *Sports Illustrated* (1954). After his death in 1967, his successors at Time Inc., continued his creative legacies by starting *Money* (1972), *People Weekly* (1974), and many more magazines.

Life

The first cover of *Life* magazine, published November 23, 1936, showed a **Margaret Bourke-White** photo of the newly completed Ft. Peck Dam in Montana, built by Roosevelt's Works Progress Administration. The first inside photo displayed a surgical-masked doctor in a crowded delivery room. With the caption "Life begins," the full-page photo presented a baby boy in the doctor's gloved hand.

From its first issue, sales far exceeded even Luce's expectations. His business plan predicted that it would take two or three years to reach a "break-even circulation." Nevertheless, all 466,000 copies of the first issue sold out the first day. By the end of 1937, *Life's* circulation had reached 1.5 million. *Life* has the distinction of being the only magazine to ever lose money its first year because of its success. Because Luce had set first-year ad rates based on modest circulation expectations, those ad revenues could not cover the high printing costs resulting from unexpectedly high circulation figures.

Life published weekly issues from November 23, 1936 to December 29, 1972.

Life reached a circulation high in 1969—8.5 million subscribers. But *Life* could never attract sufficient advertising revenues to offset the cheap subscription rates it had to offer to attract that many readers. Relaunched as a monthly magazine in 1978, *Life* persisted for another twenty-two years, until the company stopped publication for the second time with the May 2000 issue. But its colorful legacy and wide name recognition were too valuable for the company to ignore. For the third time, Time Inc., launched the magazine, on October 1, 2004, in a different format. This time it emerged as a weekly magazine in Friday editions of seventy daily newspapers. The company called it a "newspaper-distributed magazine" and not a "supplement" like its competitors *Parade* and *USA Weekend*.

People Weekly

On March 4, 1974, *People* hit the market with a cover featuring Mia Farrow, who was starring in *The Great Gatsby*. Founding editor Richard B. Stolley wrote in its first issue, "*People* is a magazine whose title fits it perfectly. There is nothing abstract about the name. People is what we are all about."

People was an immediate hit. "Within eighteen months we were making money, which was very quick, and within two years we had paid back the initial investment, which I think was about $40 million," said Mr. Stolley in a telephone interview.[11]

Although it never ranked near the top in circulation, its popularity with advertisers made it the nation's most profitable magazine—a position it still retains. "I think *People*'s success comes from three places," said Joe Treen, a former executive editor.

> It offers much more than just celebrity gossip, fashion stories and 'eye candy' photos. You also get news, human interest, social issues, etc.—stories you do not get in the magazine's competition. No doubt newsstand buyers pick up the magazine because some celebrity is on the cover. But once they get inside, they very much relate to the whole range of stories, including those that do not involve celebrities at all.
>
> Second, the magazine is very well-reported. It simply has more information than its competitors. And the information is accurate. Nothing is made up or padded or piped. Third, *People* has surprisingly high integrity. The magazine is copiously fact checked. It operates under Time Inc.'s tough conflict of interest and code of ethics policies. In other words, a *People* story may seem frothy and gossipy but the reporting took place under the same kinds of rules you find at The *New York Times* or the *Washington Post*.[12]

In 2005, *People* was named *Advertising Age*'s Magazine of the Year "for handling the Katrina disaster more deftly than the government . . . [and] reaching the highest circulation in its 31 years, holding its position atop Time Inc.'s formidable magazine portfolio and confidently navigating the foamy, sometimes filthy, currents of celebrity weeklies."

Time Inc., expanded its media empire during the 1980s. It paid $14 billion for Warner Communications, Inc., in 1989, creating the world's largest entertainment and media concern. The first year, Time Warner created Time Warner Publishing to oversee all of the company's publishing activities and launched new magazines such as *Martha Stewart Living* and *Entertainment Weekly*. The second mega-merger came with Turner Broadcasting in 1996, a move that saw CNN founder Ted Turner join the group as deputy chairman. The third came in January 2000, when America Online acquired Time Warner for a $160 billion stock exchange. The merger, which was approved by the FCC a year later, was the largest corporate merger in U.S. history and resulted in a new company with an estimated value of $350 billion at the time.

In the next two years, however, the company's stock plummeted by 75 percent, and *Fortune* (a Time Inc., magazine) called the AOL–Time Warner deal "one of the great train wrecks in corporate history." In January 2003, the company reported a $98.7 billion loss for fiscal 2002, the largest in U.S. corporate history. Reflecting widespread discontent, the company's board of directors voted on September 18, 2003, to remove "AOL" from the company name. AOL chief executive officer Jonathan Miller had requested the name change and said that the AOL–Time Warner name had become "a symbol of failed mergers," which was hurting its public image.

By 2005, Time Inc.—the magazine publishing unit of Time Warner—had become the world's largest magazine publisher, with 170 titles. Luce's creative legacy is seen in the fact that three of the world's most historic magazines—*Time*, *Life*, and *People*—were started by him or his company.

Other Magazine Publishers

Meredith Corporation, best known for *Better Homes and Gardens* and *Midwest Living*, became the second-largest U.S. publisher in June 2005 with its $350 million purchase of *Family Circle*, *Parents*, *Fitness*, and *Child* magazines from Gruner + Jahr USA, a division of the German company Bertelsmann AG. Meredith's origins began as a wedding present. The grandfather of **E. T. Meredith** (1876–1928) gave him the controlling interest in his farm newspaper in Des Moines, Iowa, along with a note saying, "Sink or swim." After leading the paper to profitability, Meredith sold it and began publishing a service-oriented farm magazine called *Successful Farming* in 1902. It grew to more than half a million subscribers by 1914. In 1922, he started a magazine named *Fruit, Garden, and Home*. After changing its name to *Better Homes and Gardens* in 1924, the magazine's fortunes began to climb. It became the leading monthly magazine and held a circulation of 8 million for more than two decades.

Condé Nast (1873–1942) began his magazine empire when he purchased *Vogue* in 1909. Four years later, he purchased *House and Garden*, which trans-

Table 18: Magazine Growth in the United States, 1950–2000

Year	Single-Copy Copy Sales per Issue	Sub. Sales per Issue	Total Circ per Issue	US Pop.	Mag. Read per Person	# of HH	Mag. Read per HH	Avg HH Size
1950	62,804	84,160	146,975	151,232	0.97	43,554	3.37	3.5
1955	68,770	104,366	173,126	164,302	1.05	47,874	3.62	3.4
1960	61,770	127,503	189,172	180,671	1.05	52,799	3.58	3.4
1965	65,231	148,342	213,573	194,303	1.10	57,436	3.72	3.4
1970	70,231	174,504	244,735	205,052	1.19	63,401	3.86	3.2
1975	83,835	166,048	249,983	215,973	1.16	71,120	3.51	3
1980	90,895	189,846	280,742	227,726	1.23	80,776	3.48	2.8
1985	81,077	242,810	323,887	238,466	1.36	86,789	3.73	2.7
1990	73,668	292,444	366,112	249,948	1.46	93,347	3.92	2.7
1995	65,846	299,050	364,896	263,044	1.39	98,990	3.69	2.7
2000	60,240	318,678	378,919	281,422	1.35	105,480	3.59	2.6
Change	-4%	279%	158%	86%	39%	142%	6%	-26%

Source: Magazine Publishers of America, Audit Bureau of Circulations

formed into a leading interior design authority. In 1914, he introduced *Vanity Fair*, a magazine that quickly set publishing standards in arts, politics, sports, and society. In 1939, he launched *Glamour*, the last magazine he would personally develop before his death. By 2005, Condé Nast Publications holdings included about twenty magazines, including *Bon Appétit, Condé Nast Traveler, GQ, Lucky, Mademoiselle, Popular Mechanics*, the *New Yorker, Redbook, Self, Seventeen*, and *YM*.

Nast's enduring contribution to magazine publishing was creating the concept of "class" publications directed at particular groups of readers with common interests. He preferred to attract a select group of readers of a high social profile over a mass-circulation magazine. As he pointed out in a 1913 essay, "A 'class' publication is nothing more nor less than a publication that looks for its circulation only to those having in common a certain characteristic marked enough to group them into a class."[13]

Condé Nast Publications was purchased in 1979 by S. I. Newhouse and became a division of Newhouse's empire, which also included newspapers, book publishers, and cable television companies. Newhouse expanded its magazine titles by purchasing Street and Smith Publications, Inc., a publisher of sports magazines (1959); *Gentleman's Quarterly* (1979); *Tatler*, a British monthly (1983); *Gourmet* (1983); *Details* (1988); *Architectural Digest* (1993); and *Bon Appétit* (1993). The company revived the *Vanity Fair* title in 1983, which had been merged with *Vogue* since 1936, and launched *Condé Nast Traveler* in 1987 and *Allure* in 1991.

In 1945, **John H. Johnson** started *Ebony*, which was to become America's most successful magazine aimed at a predominantly African-American audience. "In a world of despair," he wrote, "we wanted to give hope. In a world that said Blacks could do few things, we wanted to say they could do everything. We believed in 1945 that Black Americans needed positive images to fulfill their potential."[14] Johnson also started *Jet*, "The Weekly Negro News Magazine," in 1950, which focused on current events and trends affecting African Americans. At the time of Johnson's death in 2005, both *Ebony* and *Jet* still ranked as circulation leaders among American magazines.

Television and Its Effect

The 1960s marked the beginning of the most profound adaptation that American magazines made in the twentieth century. As magazines realized that they could no longer compete with television for ad dollars for a broad audience, magazine content became increasingly specialized. New magazines identified audience niches with special interests and found advertisers who wanted to reach that audience. "These two trends of the 1960s, the precipitous decline of the large general-interest magazine, and the sudden rise of the leisure-active specialized magazine, were historical absolutes," writes magazine historian David Abrahamson.[15]

Between 1946 and 1956, the number of television stations multiplied from 6 to 422, while the number of homes with television sets increased from 8,000 to 34 million. During the same period, TV advertising revenue rose from virtually nothing to $1.2 billion in 1956. Although the magazine industry's share of total advertising revenue fell from 13 percent to 8 percent, its total income actually rose, from $426 million to $795 million in 1956.

The magazine industry suffered some high-profile casualties. *Woman's Home Companion, American Magazine, Collier's, Coronet, Saturday Evening Post, Look,* and *Life*—with combined circulations that once reached 37 million—all ceased publication between 1956 and 1973. *Life* and *Saturday Evening Post* later reemerged as monthlies and restructured shadows of their former selves. Aside from these highly visible casualties, however, television's effect on the economic health of the magazine industry is debatable.

What the failed magazines had in common was, for the most part, that they were all aimed at a "general" audience of all ages, races, and genders. Television also appealed to the same broad audience, so television and these particular magazines were competing against one another for the same advertising dollars. Few, if any, of these magazines had suffered dramatic circulation losses at the time of their demise. What they were suffering was the loss of advertisers of everyday household products who found they could better promote their wares on television. Television provided not only larger audiences, but also sound and pictures to describe the products.

As a result, we have seen a steady trend over the past fifty years from general-interest magazines to special-interest magazines. Titles published by Hachette Filipacchi Media tell the tale: *Flying, Car and Driver, Popular Photography, Metropolitan Home, Mobile Entertainment,* and *Cycle World.* Today, new launches fill specific niches; examples include titles such as *Budget Travel* and *Budget Living*—both brainchilds of entrepreneur publisher Don Welsh. Other successful concepts include *Cigar Aficionado* and *Wine Spectator,* both from M. Shanken Communications, Inc.

International Publishing

In 1910, Hearst became the first American company to publish overseas when it acquired Nash's *Pall Mall* in the United Kingdom. Condé Nast soon followed by launching a British edition of *Vogue* in 1916. *Reader's Digest* launched its magazine in the United Kingdom in 1938 and now publishes nineteen editions in forty-eight languages throughout the world.

"But it was not until Hearst began to license its brands and content during the early 1970s that international publishing by US groups began to take off," writes John T. Cabell, CEO of an international magazine consulting firm.[16] Today, most of the largest consumer magazines publish localized editions around the world. Most publishers enter these international markets by partnering with local publishers through licensing deals. *Magazine World* reported in 2005: "There have been more cross-border licensing deals established in the past ten years encompassing more world markets and more industry sectors than at any other time in publishing history."[17]

Magazines and "the New Journalism"

The 1960s saw the rise of a phenomenon known as "the New Journalism" in magazines, newspapers, and books. In later years, "literary journalism" or "literary nonfiction" became the preferred phrases. The simple definition of New Journalism is the use of fiction techniques in nonfiction reporting. It describes the work of such authors as Norman Mailer, Tom Wolfe, Truman Capote, Joan Didion, and Hunter Thompson. Their work was "new" because they departed from traditional forms of feature writing and used fiction techniques such as scene-by-scene development, detailed description, and extensive dialog. Their purpose was not merely to report the facts, but to achieve an emotional impact on the readers by re-creating the feel and mood of an event.[18]

Most of the best-known work by the New Journalists first appeared in magazines, notably *Esquire*, the *New Yorker, New York, Harper's,* and *Rolling Stone.* For example, William Shawn, editor of the *New Yorker,* supported and encouraged Capote in writing *In Cold Blood,* which originally appeared as a four-part series in September and October 1965. When the book came out in Februrary 1966, it became New Journalism's first widely acclaimed best-seller after its first printing of 100,000 copies sold out in a few weeks. Columbia Pictures later paid $1 million for film rights and, by 1983, the book had earned Capote an estimated $2 million in royalties on more than 3 million copies.

Esquire, under editor Harold Hayes, was probably the most influential magazine in developing the New Journalism. *Esquire* did its part to disseminate 1960s culture with an irreverent, skeptical style of writing about politics, pop culture, celebrities, and changing lifestyles. *Esquire* preserved its record of New Journalism reporting in its well-known 981-page anthology titled *Smiling through the Apocalypse: Esquire's History of the Sixties.*

New Directions and New Technology

The 1970s marked a period in which magazines were repositioning and refocusing their strengths. Television was by now an entrenched part of American life. Increasingly targeted magazines continued to refine and develop their niche positions, while entrepreneurial publishers sought out new audiences.

On the technology front, IBM introduced its first personal computer in 1982, and Apple introduced its Macintosh in 1984. Pagemaker design software became available in 1985, and Quark Xpress was introduced in 1987. Hundreds of magazines began doing their own production and design instead of contracting them to outside agencies. By 1988, it seemed that almost anyone with a computer could publish a magazine at home.

Starting in the mid-1990s—and continuing today—the biggest issue for magazines has been finding the right business model to make the Internet a profitable ally. The chief executive officer of Meredith Corporation—America's second-largest publishing company—has said, "The Internet is our friend. Once viewed as a threat, the Internet is a medium that magazines are using as a growth catalyst on many fronts."[19] Chapter 10 dealt with the effects of the Internet on magazine publishing in greater detail.

O: The Oprah Magazine, which premiered in May 2000, became one of the most successful magazine launches in history. After two press runs, the initial May-June issue sold out of 1.6 million copies on newsstands. Two months later, the magazine increased its frequency from bimonthly to monthly and raised its rate base from 500,000 to 900,000. By the end of June 2004, the average paid circulation had reached 2.6 million. According to publisher Jill Seelig, the magazine's success was due to the fact that "Women are looking for meaning in their lives. It's the right message at the right time."[20]

The turn of the century saw the baby boomers turn to leisure and hobby interests, while many young mothers were leaving their high-powered corporate jobs to raise their children. The magazine industry wasn't far behind these trends. "Most new magazines catered to home-based interests such as crafts, hobbies and food, reflecting the nesting inclinations of the baby boom generation," according to Veronis Suhler Stevenson's 2005 *Communications Industry Forecast.*

For over a decade, Samir Husni, a University of Mississippi journalism professor who is also known as "Mr. Magazine" (www.mrmagazine.com) has been tracking every new magazine published in America. Husni picked the "Hottest Magazine Launches of the Past 20 Years" for the *MIN Magazine 2005 Annual.* His list included these twenty-two winners:

Elle	1985
Midwest Living	1986
Men's Health	1986
Country	1987
Cooking Light	1987
Parenting	1987
Traditional Home	1989
Entertainment Weekly	1990
Wizard	1991
Martha Stewart Living	1991
Wired	1992
InStyle	1994

Country Weekly	1994
People en Espanol	1996
Maxim	1997
ESPN: The Magazine	1998
More	1998
CosmoGirl	1999
O: The Oprah Magazine	2000
Lucky	2000
Real Simple	2000
In Touch Weekly	2003

While the magazines on this list represent some of the biggest publishers on the planet, *Wizard: The Comics Magazine* is a comics aficionado title created by Garub Shamus with money borrowed from his friends. An unimposing, bespectacled geek who likes to be called "the Big Cheese" by his employees, Shamus has spawned an entertainment empire that now includes four magazines and a toy catalog. *Wizard: The Comics Magazine* is published in five languages in more than forty countries worldwide.

Two other magazine segments prospered during the early years of the twenty-first century. First, magazines targeting the Hispanic population grew more than any other category between 1996 and 2006, according to *The Standard Periodical Directory*. The number of Hispanic titles jumped from 124 in 1996 to 329 in 2006.[21] Second, celebrity magazines continued their hold on American culture. "Celebrity magazines make up an estimated 25 percent of newsstand sales, and the market for these magazines shows no signs of slowing down," according to the *Communications Industry Forecast*.[22]

In a sense, no "history of magazines" or "history of the magazine industry" can be written. There are only individual histories of individual magazines. Each magazine has its own founder, its own story, its own writers, and its own personality and attitude. All we can do is pull a few examples and a few statistics from this 260-year history that illustrate its richness and continuing hold on American creativity and imagination.

As former Time Inc., president Reg Brack, Jr., told a Magazine Publishers of America conference, "Magazines have been a major force shaping American society, expressing our hopes and our fears, informing and molding the way we think and act at crucial points in history. In sum, the magazine is here to stay, an American original, as integral to the national landscape as baseball, mom, and apple pie."[23]

 ## Questions for Further Thought

1. Are there any advantages to knowing the history of your favorite magazines?

2. What characteristics of magazines have given them an apparent advantage over newspapers in avoiding declining circulations and readerships?

3   How would you compare magazines with newspapers and television in influencing public opinion? Do they have more or less influence?

4   If you had unlimited money for magazine subscriptions, what five titles would you be most likely to subscribe to?

Shop Talk

Margaret Bourke-White (1904–1971): American photojournalist who became famous for her *Life* magazine photography, including the photo of Fort Peck Dam on the first issue on Nov. 23, 1936. She was the first Western photographer allowed into the Soviet Union in 1930 and the first female war correspondent allowed in combat zones during World War II.

Andrew Bradford (1686–1742): a printer and newspaper publisher who published the first magazine in America, *A Monthly View of the Political State of the British Colonies,* on February 13, 1741. He beat rival Benjamin Franklin who published his magazine three days later.

Frank Munsey (1854–1925): The founder of *Munsey's* magazine, which became the first low-price, mass-circulation magazine. He dropped the price from a quarter to a dime in 1893 (less than the cost of production), which resulted in an increase in circulation from 60,000 to 700,000 over the next seven years. A dramatic increase in advertisers made it a profitable magazine.

Gilbert Hovey Grosvenor (1875–1966): After becoming editor of the *National Geographic* in 1903, he led the magazine for the next fifty years in pioneering photojournalism. During those years, it earned many photojournalism "firsts" and consistently ranked among the top five circulation leaders.

John H. Johnson (1918–2005): The founder of Johnson Publishing Company and *Ebony* in 1945, which became the nation's leading magazine aimed at a predominantly African-American readership. Johnson was the first black person to appear on the *Forbes* 400 list, and had a fortune estimated at close to $600 million.

Henry Robinson Luce (1898–1967): co-founder of *Time* magazine in 1923 with his friend Briton Hadden (1898–1929), who died six years later. Luce went on to launch *Fortune* in 1932, *Life* in 1936, and *Sports Illustrated* in 1954. Today the Time Inc. division of Time Warner is the nation's largest consumer magazine publisher with more than 150 titles.

E. T. Meredith (1876–1928): The founder of Meredith Corporation in Des Moines, Iowa, which had become the nation's second-largest magazine publisher by 2005. In 1922, he started a magazine named *Fruit, Garden, and Home.* which became *Better Homes and Gardens* in 1924 and the company's leading magazine.

Condé Nast (1873–1942): He began his magazine empire when he purchased *Vogue* in 1909. In 1914, he introduced *Vanity Fair,* a magazine that quickly set publishing standards in arts, politics, sports, and society. In 1939, he launched *Glamour.*

DeWitt (1889–1981) and Lila Bell Wallace (1889–1984): founders of *Reader's Digest* in 1922, which pioneered the "digest" format of reprinting the best articles from other periodicals after condensing them into a short, readable format. Today *Reader's Digest* is the world's largest independently published magazine with forty-eight international editions read by an estimated 100 million people in nineteen languages and sixty countries.

Your Future in the Business-to-Business Media

You've probably never heard of these magazines: *American Window Cleaner, Balloons and Parties, Box Office, Coal People, Hard Hat News, Onion World, Portable Restroom Operator,* or *Wines and Vines.* All of these publications look for articles from freelance writers. Most people who want to write for magazines don't dream of someday writing for *Pet Product News* or the *Beverage Journal.* Bylines in *Rolling Stone, Maxim,* or *Cosmopolitan* are more likely to top their wish list than one in *Automotive News.* But it would be a mistake to overlook the possibilities of B-to-B publishing.

Who Are the Readers?

Everyone from accountants to zoologists read publications that help them do their jobs better. The business-to-business media includes thousands of magazines for every conceivable job and profession. The phrase *business-to-business media* describes those companies that produce magazines, websites, and trade shows serving people who work in specific jobs, careers, and professions. They are "businesses that serve businesses" by providing information that serves the professional needs of their readers and users.

Trade magazines is a more casual but frequently used term describing the print media produced by these companies.

Trade magazines originated in 1774—thirty-three years after the first American consumer magazines—when Jonathan Crouch launched *South-Carolina Price Current*, which informed customers of current prices of barley, wheat, beeswax, rice, and other staples of the day. Following its great success, other publishers launched similar magazines in large East Coast cities. The prices of commodities and costs of shipping them throughout the world offered needed information to merchants and manufacturers. These early publishers were founders of today's business-to-business press. Their mission of providing useful, exclusive, and timely information to a select group of merchants and manufacturers carved a new niche in American publishing. By 1900, nearly six hundred business magazines were being published. Chilton's *Motor Age* (1899) served the emerging auto industry, for example, while Fairchild's *Men's Wear* (1896) became an important influence in the men's clothing industry.[1]

Today's **business-to-business** publications focus on specific areas and tell readers how to improve their job performance, increase profits, or improve customer service. They also cover trends, mergers, hiring news, and other business news within their industries and professions.

"Our readers are reading for business information, for news they can use, for the latest trends and developments that will help their business. Their biggest foe is time pressure," said Aric Press, editor-in-chief of the *American Lawyer.*[2]

Just as **convergence** is affecting newspapers and television and radio stations, it's also affecting the business-to-business media. In addition to print magazines, many of these companies now produce **trade shows** and constantly updated websites. This trend forced the industry association American Business Press to change its name to American Business Media a few years ago. Founded in 1906, this association represents 230 companies that produce 1,750 print publications, 2,000 websites, and 850 trade shows each year. Some offer free magazine subscriptions. Advertisers are so eager to reach people in some industries that they're willing to pay the bill.

The average executive who reads B-to-B magazines spends 2.2 hours per month reading 4.6 titles, according to a recent study by Yankelovich Research for American Business Media. The same study found that almost 70 percent of executive- or professional-level subscribers read three or more titles per month.

In appearance, most of these magazines look just like any consumer magazine. Their frequent use of glossy covers, exciting graphics, and compelling four-color photography means that all of the production techniques are the same. Content includes news stories and analysis, profiles, trends and issues, how-to, book and product reviews, and even humor. For example, *Successful Farming* published a story about the author's visit to the National Liars Hall of Fame in Dannebrog, Nebraska.[3]

While most consumer magazines have websites that replicate their print content, B-to-B companies are more likely to update their content daily or weekly. Whitney Sielaff, publisher and editorial director for *National Jeweler*, said that his magazine was historically known as a newsmagazine in the jewelry business. "The Internet forced us to change it to a news-analysis magazine. We had to back that up with a hard news site that provides constantly updated news to our readers." The extension into various forms of content delivery means that the magazine staff "are not just writers for a magazine; we are content providers," said Sielaff. [4]

The most mistaken notion about trade magazines is that you have to be an expert or practitioner in the field to work for one of its magazines. Almost all trade journal editors and publishers say they have had better success hiring journalists and training them in the specialty than they have had hiring experts and training them in journalism. Experts are more likely to use technical jargon that even readers of a particular specialized magazine might not understand.

Sielaff said that when he hires writers or editors for *National Jeweler*, he looks primarily for a journalism degree and news-writing experience. "I want someone who knows how to turn around copy and meet deadlines. I want someone who can copy edit, who knows AP style and knows how to use a dictionary. I want people who are curious, interested, and willing to learn," he said.

"Surprisingly, I knew little about healthcare coming into my first, part-time position at *Modern Healthcare*," said Nicole Voges, special projects editor. "I took a copy-editing test and there were some words related to the industry where I had to pick the correct spelling, and the copy I edited was actual copy from the magazine, but otherwise, it's all been on-the-job learning."[5]

Rob Spiegel, a senior editor at *Electronic News*, said that B-to-B editors "always choose writing abilities over technical education. They are not interested in engineers who are not trained and adept at reporting." [6]

Another mistake is to assume that trade publications want only positive, gushy pieces about products or companies. Writers often have to walk the fine line between being an advocate for an industry and being objective about its products. Some of the best investigative journalism is done by B-to-B reporters who report on defective products, unethical business practices, or serious problems affecting their industries. For example, the cover story "The Workers' Compensation Crisis" in *Entrepreneur* magazine reported that work-related injuries cost U.S. businesses nearly $1 billion per week. [7]

How to Find a B-to-B Magazine

Unlike consumer magazines, which anyone can subscribe to or purchase, business press magazines are not readily available to consumers. Newsstands don't carry them; they're available by subscription only. The best online source for information is American Business Media's website: www.americanbusinessmedia.com. You can click on the "membership directory" link to browse through an alphabetical listing of these 230 companies, links to their websites, and names and addresses of the magazines they publish. Or you can search for specific magazines by category or geography. The sidebar at the end of this chapter contains information on a dozen of the largest companies that publish between thirty and three hundred B-to-B magazines each.

Career Opportunities and Advantages

The major reason the B-to-B media offer good career choices is that they publish twice as many magazines as the consumer press. While most consumer magazines are published in New York, business press publishers are scattered around the country in cities such as Atlanta, Cleveland, Chicago, Denver, Detroit, Houston, Kansas City, Seattle, and Washington, D.C. While New York is a wonderful place to build a magazine career, many people simply don't want to live there.

"The advantages to working at a B-to-B over working at a consumer magazine are numerous," said Voges, special projects editor at Crain's *Modern Healthcare* in Chicago and a 2003 college graduate. "Compensation is the first thing that comes to mind—because I've found that B-to-B's are almost always more willing to pay more for good people than consumer magazines are—because consumer magazines have people tripping over themselves to take jobs, lowering the salary range for most entry-level positions. Trade magazines are more lucrative because there is less competition."[8]

She said that another advantage is that staffs are smaller. "So the opportunity to help with projects outside the scope of your position might be more plentiful than at a large consumer magazine where your only job is as a fact-checker or copy editor."

Sielaff, of *National Jeweler*, has spent his fifteen-year career in the business-to-business media. He sees three advantages to a B-to-B career over a consumer magazine career: more opportunities to write, more influence on your audience, and more interaction with an educated professional audience.

First, he said, "If you really want to write, you can get that done easier in this field. The Web offers some good opportunities as well." Second, "You're catering to a higher level of educated audience. Most of those you're writing for are heads of companies or business owners and smart entrepreneurs. If you're writing for a newspaper, chances are you're out there talking to people on the street." And third, he said, "You can really have an effect. You are helping people improve in what they do on a daily basis. You can become an integral part of their work."[9]

Marketing Business Publications

Because business magazines and journals are targeted to very specific segments of a business or industry, it is often more efficient—and more *profitable*—to offer free controlled circulation. *Controlled* simply means that the publisher controls which specific individuals will receive the magazine so that advertisers are guaranteed to reach 100 percent of the audience they want to reach. With consumer magazines, advertisers want to reach people who *paid* for their subscriptions (to ensure that these individuals are reading the magazines).

Whether or not free controlled subscriptions can make a magazine profitable depends on the nature of the audience reached, how much they want or need this particular magazine, how important it is to advertisers to reach these particular individuals, and whether or not there are strong competitors.

Like paid magazines, controlled-circulation business-to-business magazines must also back up their audience guarantees, by joining an independent magazine auditing bureau, such as the Business Publications Audit, Inc. or Audit Bureau of Circulations. For example, if the reader's name was found in a business directory, the directory must be available to the auditor. And for the name to qualify, the directory cannot be more than three years old. Even with names found in new directories, they must be requalified every three years, either by getting these individuals to "direct request" the continuation of their free subscription or by adding their names again from updated directories.

The rules for qualified controlled subscriptions, direct-requested subscriptions, and renewals are very specific; requiring all magazines to use the same criteria for subscriptions levels the playing field.

Another essential criterion for controlled-circulation magazines is that to enjoy the savings of second-class postage at least 50 percent of the readers must have directly requested the magazine. Most controlled-circulation magazines also set a price for a paid subscription. This not only establishes a value to the readers who receive the magazine for free, but also generates additional revenue from readers who do not meet the specific criteria for a free subscription (like position or title).

Diane Brady, a former marketing executive for *Institutional Investor* magazine, offers a good example of how the magazine tried to attract both paid and controlled circulation. "Even though many readers would easily have paid $100 per year for a subscription, it was more important to the advertisers to reach 100 percent of audience segments like CEOs of companies with more than $100 million in sales."

But she also said that generating revenue from paid subscribers was a goal.

"So when we sent mailings to ask people to direct-request their subscriptions, we offered a paid subscription with an attractive premium."

If they didn't pay, they still received the magazine, however, as long as they met the qualification criteria. "Of course we were very careful with the wording of the offers to avoid as much confusion as possible, without losing the opportunity to generate paid subscriptions," said Brady.[10]

Building a Subscriber Base

Finding of the *names* of targeted audiences requires significant research and marketing efforts, since they may not be available in any directory. Brady tells of a creative promotion she used to obtain the names and mailing address of CEOs and some of their key direct assistants, whose names could not be found in directories:

> We called the general phone number for each targeted company and asked confirmation of the mailing address and—when we could get it—the name of the *assistant* to the CEO. Most companies won't readily give out the names of their senior executives. Then we sent each assistant a FedEx package containing a personal letter accompanied with a Tiffany pen as an "advance thank-you gift" for providing us with the names we needed for complimentary subscriptions to our very prestigious magazine.

Sponsored Subscriptions

Another way of generating highly desirable names for advertisers—along with incremental income—is sponsored subscriptions. Another example from Brady's experiences with *Institutional Investor* magazine: "We wanted to introduce the magazine to executives in the making—MBA students at the top ten business schools. First we had to convince schools like Harvard and Yale that sending this magazine to their students was a benefit," noted Brady. This took a great deal of time and personal correspondence.

> Even then, the schools would not give out their names, but finally agreed to the complimentary subscriptions if we sent the magazines to them for delivery.
> Once we could guarantee this very elite audience, we sold exclusive sponsorships—one per category, such as one investment banking firm, one money management firm, et cetera. Then we added a second cover to the magazine noting that this complimentary subscription was a gift from the sponsors (named on the cover).
> At the end of the academic year, we offered the students special discounts on paid subscriptions "to ensure continuing service." This program not only provided a new audience segment for advertisers, it also generated significant incremental revenues and new readers we would have had difficulty finding through traditional marketing efforts.

In summary, business magazines offer multiple opportunities for revenues and franchise extension: advertising revenues, paid subscribers, sponsored subscriptions, spin-off newsletters, paid and/or sponsored conferences, and industry shows and events. A magazine does not have to have a large circulation to achieve any or all of these opportunities. As with all magazines, the quality of editorial content is key.

Questions for Further Thought

1   Study the websites of the five magazines mentioned at the beginning of this chapter: *American Window Cleaner, Box Office, Coal People, Portable Restroom Operator,* and *Wines and Vines.* Compare the different types of audiences and editorial needs for each of these magazines.

2   Do a telephone interview with the editor or publisher of any of these magazines and write a profile of the magazine.

3   Develop one article idea for each of these magazines.

Shop Talk

Business-to-business media: A term describing companies that produce magazines, tabloid newspapers, newsletters, websites, and trade shows serving people who work in specific jobs, careers, and professions. Their main purpose is to provide information that serves the professional needs of their readers and users.

Controlled circulation: Free subscriptions offered by trade publishers to targeted readers with key management or decision-making responsibilities in their companies or organizations. Some publishing companies offer free subscriptions to these targeted readers and paid subscriptions to others.

Convergence: The trend toward one company owning a variety of media outlets and having their writers and editors produce content for all of these outlets. They may include newspapers, magazines, newsletters, websites, and television and radio stations.

Trade magazines: The print publications produced by companies that comprise the business-to-business media, which may in addition produce tabloid newspapers, newsletters, websites, conferences, and trade shows that serve their industries.

Trade shows: An event allowing a publication's advertisers to purchase exhibit space to show their products and services to an audience comprised of the publication's readers.

The Business-to-Business Media: Contact Information

American Business Media   www.americanbusinessmedia.com

Founded in 1906, this 230-member association of business media companies represents 1,750 print publications, 2,000 websites, and 850 trade shows and special events.

The following list represents twelve of the largest business media companies that publish the most magazines and periodicals.

Advanstar, Inc.	www.advanstar.com
Primedia Business Magazines	www.primediabusiness.com
CMP Media LLC	www.cmp.com
Crain Communications, Inc.	www.crain.com
IDG Publishing	www.idg.com
International Data Group	
The McGraw-Hill Companies	www.mcgraw-hill.com
PennWell Corporation	www.pennwell.com
Penton Media, Inc.	www.penton.com
Primedia Business Magazines	www.primediabusiness.com
Reed Business Information	www.reedbusiness.com
Thomson Media	www.thomsonmedia.com
VNU Business Media	www.vnubusinessmedia.com

How to Avoid "Shattered Glass" and Other Dangers

What do the *New Republic* and *BusinessWeek* magazines, along with the newspapers the *Washington Post, Boston Globe, New York Times, USA Today*, and *Arizona Republic* have in common? Since 1998, all have fired one of their writers because of charges of plagiarism or fabrication of stories. In some cases, these writers lifted parts of their stories from articles that appeared in other publications. One writer created entirely fictitious characters and events for his stories.

In 1997, Stephen Glass was a twenty-five-year-old rising star at the *New Republic*, a respected political commentary magazine. The *New Republic*'s editor, Charles Lane, developed suspicions about the accuracy of one of Glass's stories after receiving a tip from a writer at a competing magazine. One thing led to another, and over the next several months Lane discovered that Glass had fabricated some or all of twenty-seven published stories in the *New Republic*. Glass was fired, and his story was made into the 2003 movie *Shattered Glass*.

"Shattered glass" is a good metaphor for the moral and legal pitfalls that can wreck a journalism career. Magazines face the same legal and ethical risks as newspapers—plagiarism, libel, slander, invasion of privacy, editorial bias, and inaccuracy. In addition, magazines face a special temptation—advertiser influence on editorial content—that seems to plague them more frequently than it does newspapers.

The purpose of this chapter is to help you stay out of trouble with the law and with your readers. If you become a magazine editor or publisher, there are three things you don't want to do: publish an article that libels someone, publish an article that invades someone's privacy, or publish an article that violates the copyright laws. Doing any of these things can land your magazine in court. Other questionable publishing practices may not bring you to court, but will damage your magazine's reputation with its readers. This chapter will touch on all of these issues. It won't substitute for a good attorney, but it will help you recognize red flags and warning signs in editorial content.

Eleven Commandments for Journalists

1 Always write the truth, the whole truth, and nothing but the truth.

2 Do not embarrass a public or private figure unless it will benefit the public. Don't publish anything that could harm someone's reputation unless exposing this information will serve a greater public good.

3 Be honest about your intentions and let people know where and how their comments will be used. Do not quote from everyday conversations if people do not know those comments may be published.

4 Verify the accuracy of what people tell you in interviews. Verifying that they said it isn't enough. If the quoted material is false and could damage someone's reputation, the publication may face a libel suit.

5 If you have damaging but true information about someone, call and give him or her the opportunity to respond before you publish it.

6 Make sure you could defend anything you publish as *provably true* in a court of law.

7 Respect the privacy of people you write about. Don't write about their personal matters without their explicit permission.

8 Do not steal intellectual property that belongs to others. U.S. copyright law treats Internet material the same as it does printed books, magazines, and newspapers. Do not lift text, quotes, photos, or graphics off the Internet.

9 Do not lift quotes out of other stories and make it appear that you interviewed the quoted person yourself. Attribute the source of all direct quotes that you—as a writer—did not personally hear.

10 Obtain signed "model releases" from all people in photos that you publish. Get written permission for using photos from the photographers or copyright owners.

11 Print a retraction or correction of all mistakes on page one or two of the next issue.

Libel

In 2003, the former head football coach at the University of Alabama sued a *Sports Illustrated* writer and its parent company, Time Inc., for libel and $20 million in damages. The writer Don Yaeger used a single anonymous source who said that she and a friend were paid $500 for a one-night liaison with the fifty-seven-year-old married coach in a Pensacola, Florida, hotel room.[1]

Public figures have difficulty winning libel suits. A magazine can say almost anything it wants about a public figure as long as it isn't a deliberate lie. Reporting on the suit by the Alabama coach, Stefan Fatsis, of the *Wall Street Journal*, wrote, "To win his suit, [the coach] who was fired from his Alabama post three days before the SI article appeared, would have to show more than errors in the piece. A public figure alleging libel must prove that the news organization acted with 'actual malice,' which means publishing information known to be false or recklessly disregarding whether the information was false or not."[2] Two years later, the two sides reached an out-of-court settlement.

Public figures can include entertainers, sports celebrities, and local public officials. A person may be a public figure where one controversial issue is concerned but not in other parts of his or her life.

Satire is another defense against libel. Humor magazines such as *MAD* can poke deliberate fun at public figures with a certain degree of impunity. And *Hustler* can make mean-spirited jibes at senators and actors and presidents under the cloak of satire.

Private citizens, however, have a much lower legal standard for winning libel suits. A magazine can lose a libel suit brought by a private citizen simply because of a typographical error that prints a middle initial wrong. That can occur when an innocent person is wrongly identified for incriminating behavior. Private citizens must only prove "negligence," which happens when editors fail to do sufficient fact-checking or proofreading.

The law has three requirements for a successful libel suit. First, the editorial content has to *damage a person's reputation*. Any statement that might lower the public esteem with which a person is regarded or hurt that person's capacity to practice his profession must be considered potentially libelous.

Second, the offended person must be *identified*, but not necessarily by name. If the damaging article identifies someone with incriminating details, even if it does not publish the person's name, your magazine is still at risk for a libel suit. Those details might include, for example, the company an individual works for or the city in which he or she lives.

Third, the damaging material must be *published*. If it appears on a printed page or a website, then it's obviously published. However, an internal memo or e-mail with damaging statements could also be considered "publication" in a court of law.

How to Avoid Committing Libel

Here are seven ways that magazines and other publications can avoid libel lawsuits.

1   Don't publish libelous material. There is no need to publish libelous material—even if it's true—unless it serves a greater public good. Do not embarrass a public or private figure unless it will serve the public good in some way. Exposing a public official's embezzlement of public funds benefits the public, but exposing embarrassing details about his wife's activities does not.

2   Prove that the offending statement is true. Potentially libelous material must be *provably* true, meaning you need enough evidence to convince a jury of its truthfulness. That means in most cases at least two on-the-record sources who can verify the claim or other physical evidence.

3   Prove consent. That means that you can prove that the offended person consented to the publication of the story. Anything that a person says during an interview that he consented to give may be published, even if he later changes his mind.

4   Avoid anonymous sources. In the Alabama libel case mentioned earlier, the coach's lawyer wanted *Sports Illustrated* to identify its confidential source so that he could directly challenge her credibility. Although sometimes necessary, anonymous sources weaken the credibility of any story and create a weaker defense if the magazine ends up facing a libel charge.

5   Use "privilege." Anything reported from a court of law or legitimate meeting of a government body—such as a city council or the U.S. Senate—falls under the protection of "privilege." Public officials and judicial officers receive wide latitude to carry out their professional duties. You can generally report on anything said in these hearings or meetings without fear of legal repercussions.

6   Use the "fair comment" defense. Libel law allows writers to express their opinions about public figures and issues of public concern. A critic can say almost anything about a restaurant, book, movie, play, or musical performance. Many reviews and opinion columns fall under this provision. If an article is clearly labeled as opinion (such as a review, column, or editorial), a court is much less likely to consider anything the writer says as libelous.

7   Publish a retraction. If you discover you made a mistake, publish a prominent retraction in the next issue. A retraction does not give legal immunity to a magazine. It will, however, often calm the temper of offended persons and encourage them to refrain from legal revenge.

Invasion of Privacy

A young woman agreed to pose semi-nude for a photo in a student magazine. She later threatened to file an invasion of privacy lawsuit against the magazine, claiming that she changed her mind and asked the photographer not to use it. The photographer's mistake, in this case, was failing to obtain a signed model release from the young woman. Although this case never went to court, it was a situation of "his word against her word."

The right of privacy is the right to be left alone by the media or at least control the way you are portrayed to others. You can violate someone's right to privacy in four ways.

1   Publishing private facts. That means publishing embarrassing private facts about individuals when those facts do not serve the public interest and are not part of a legitimate news story. "Newsworthiness" is a legitimate defense in invasion of privacy lawsuits, but the vagueness of the term often makes it the center of court debate. Public figures who are frequently in the news have a more difficult time proving "invasion of privacy" than ordinary "anonymous" citizens.

2   Intruding into an individual sphere's of privacy. This means trespassing into a home or other area not open to the public. Technology has made it easier for journalists to "intrude" by recording conversations or shooting photos from great distances. Intrusion can also occur when a journalist disguises his professional identity in order to obtain a story.

3   Publishing offensive information about people when it portrays them in a false light before the public. In April 2005, for example, a Florida judge upheld an $18 million jury verdict against the *Pensacola News Journal* for harming a businessman by casting him in a "false light." The jury had ruled in favor of the man, who said the newspaper's use of the phrase "shot and killed" in a story falsely implied he had murdered his wife—although the article noted two sentences later that authorities had investigated and determined it was a hunting accident.

4   Appropriating a person's name, photo, or voice without permission for commercial purposes. Advertisers most frequently do this when they use a celebrity's name, voice, or photo to imply endorsement of their products. Florida's law says, for example, no one may "publish, print, display or otherwise publicly use" a person's name or likeness without consent "for purposes of trade or for any commercial or advertising purpose."

Copyright Law

As a magazine editor, you need to understand three aspects of copyright law. First, you need to know the applications of copyright ownership that allow you to purchase all or partial rights to articles that freelance writers submit to you. Second, you need to know how to protect your **intellectual property** against unauthorized use by others. Finally, so that you don't commit plagiarism, staff and freelance writers need to know what's legal to use and what they cannot use when they do research. The Copyright Act has specific criteria covering all three areas.

The purpose of the U.S. Copyright Act is to protect "original works of authorship." Congress purposely chose the broad phrase "works of authorship" to avoid having to rewrite the Copyright Act every time a new medium was developed. That means that the Copyright Act (Title 17, U.S. Code) protects Internet pages and articles, computer software, and multimedia CDs even though these items didn't exist at the time the law was passed in 1978.

The Internet hasn't changed the copyright laws. It has simply made plagiarism easier and more tempting (but also easier to detect). If you publish an article on the Internet, copyright law protects it as soon as it's published regardless of whether the copyright symbol appears or whether the copyright is registered. If someone else copies and publishes your Internet article elsewhere, you can sue for copyright infringement using the same 1978 copyright law.

Creative works by writers, musicians, artists, sculptors, and computer programmers are their intellectual property. The law says that they alone hold the right to reproduction, distribution, public performance, and public display of their work. That includes the right to sell part or all of their ownership. Theft is theft, whether it occurs in the intellectual or material domains of life.

Some writers mistakenly believe that they have to register their work with the U.S. Copyright Office to protect it. The law recognizes that you own the copyright to your original work as soon as you write it. Because of the 1978 revision of the copyright law, works of authorship are automatically protected from the moment of their creation for the duration of the author's life plus an additional seventy years after the author's death. Prior to that revision, registration was necessary for authors to protect their works. There are still some advantages to registering a copyright, and we'll get to those later.

The only two requirements that the law makes for copyright protection are, first, that the article or other intellectual property be "original" and, second, that it's in a "fixed and tangible form." That means it doesn't even have to be printed on paper. Courts have ruled that a copy stored in the random access memory of a computer is a copy for copyright purposes, even though it disappears when you turn off the computer.

The copyright symbol on a document, however, serves as a reminder that federal laws protect its author against unauthorized copying or distribution. It may help to include the copyright symbol on copies of articles or handouts given to others. That tells users that it's your original creation, and you don't intend for them to photocopy or give it to others.

If you use a copyright notice, place it in the upper-right corner of the first page and include the following three elements:

1   The symbol © (the letter *C* in a circle) or the word *copyright*. On many computer programs, you can put a *c* between two parentheses, which automatically converts to a copyright symbol after the next space.
2   The year of the first publication of the work.
3   The name of the copyright owner.

Your copyright notice will look like this: © 2005 David E. Sumner.

Buying and Selling Intellectual Property Rights

The U.S. copyright law gives copyright owners the rights to reproduction, distribution, and public performance or public display of their work. Copyright lawyers call these the "copyright bundle of rights." Selling an article to a publisher means relinquishing partial rights in exchange for payment. Generally speaking, the more writers get paid, the more rights to future use they relinquish.

So it's a tradeoff. In business dealings, the relationship between a writer and an editor resembles that of a merchant and a customer. The editor wants to buy as much editorial material as possible for the lowest possible price. The writer wants to receive as much money as possible for the least amount of material.

Most magazines are registered with the U.S. Copyright Office as single collective entities. The magazine's copyright gives it ownership to the collection of articles, images, and photos and the way they are presented. The magazine doesn't own the copyright on individual articles unless they were staff-written or the editors purchased "all rights" from a freelance writer. Magazines typically purchase one-time rights to each article from freelance writers. The writer retains the copyright ownership, which means that if you want to get permission to reprint an article, the magazine's editor will often refer you to the originating writer.

Most editors and writers need to understand only three kinds of rights: **first rights, all rights**, and **reprint rights**. When you submit a manuscript to a magazine for publication, you should indicate whether you're offering "first rights" or "reprint rights" in the upper-right corner of the first page. If an editor wants to purchase "all rights" or any other form of rights, he or she will let you know.

First Rights

Magazines typically purchase "first serial rights" or "first rights" from freelance writers. *Serial* is a librarian's term for any periodical published on a regular timetable, such as weekly, monthly, or quarterly. After the article is published, the writer retains the right to sell unlimited reprint rights to other publishers. Sometimes magazines purchase "first North American serial rights," which means they become the first North American publication to publish it. The writer can still sell "first rights" outside of North America at any subsequent time.

Reprint Rights

While the formal phrase is "second serial rights," it's usually called "reprint rights," and means exactly what it says. Most print and online publications purchase reprint rights if the original publication's readership doesn't overlap with their own. Only the most prestigious magazines insist on buying editorial material that has never appeared elsewhere. Usually payment for reprint rights varies from 10 to 50 percent of the magazine's payment schedule for first rights. One writer, however, sold an article for $250 to a regional magazine published in several large cities and later sold reprint rights for $500 to a magazine with an international circulation. The two publications' overlapping readership was small. There is no limit to the number of times you can sell reprint rights to the same article.

All Rights

When magazines purchase "all rights," the writer relinquishes any right to publish it again elsewhere. Magazine publishers typically buy all rights when they wish to publish portions in another magazine they own, plan anthologies of their best material in book form, or retain the article in their Internet archives. An increasing number of large magazine publishers want to purchase all rights because it gives them the freedom to use the material in a variety of print and electronic formats.

First rights, reprint rights, and all rights are the most frequent rights that new writers and editors encounter. There are a few other terms, however, that you will encounter in a publishing career.

Work Made for Hire

This legal phrase, which appears in the federal copyright code, refers to the creative work done by a writer (or any kind of artist) for an employer.

Articles written by full-time newspaper and magazine writers usually come under the "work made for hire" provisions. The employer owns all of the rights to their work unless the employer gives specific permission to the writer to sell elsewhere. So full-time writers for newspapers and magazines cannot sell reprint rights to other publications without their employer's permission.

Some publications will ask freelance writers to sign a "work made for hire" agreement. That means the same thing for the writer as agreeing to sell all rights. *Encyclopedia Britannica*, for example, asks all of its freelance writers to sign "work made for hire" agreements. That gives the book publisher the rights to use their material on its website, in CD-ROM editions, and in its annual yearbooks.

Simultaneous Rights

Also known as "one-time rights," simultaneous rights allow writers to sell the same article at the same time to several publishers. Syndicated newspaper columns are the best example of one-time or simultaneous rights. Most magazines do not publish syndicated material and insist that their columnists write for their magazine only. They may occasionally accept an article offered simultaneously to other publications when it contains timely material that quickly becomes outdated. Since the process of selling an article may require several months of review time, simultaneous rights allow writers to sell it to magazines that accept it most quickly. Press releases from companies or nonprofit organizations also fall under the "simultaneous rights" designation, and magazines occasionally use their material in writing their own stories.

Electronic Rights

These rights cover a broad range of electronic media from online magazines to CD-ROM anthologies. If you sell material to a Web publisher, make sure the agreement is clear about whether the rights include the website only or whether the publisher could use it in subsequent print media.

Advantages of Copyright Registration

Most individual magazine articles are never registered with the U.S. Copyright Office. It isn't necessary. Hardly any editor would ever think of stealing an article from a competing magazine or from a freelance writer. Saving a few hundred dollars on an article would never offset the risk of damaging the magazine's reputation among professional writers and the public.

Books, plays, songs, and screenplays are usually the only intellectual property for which copyright registration offers advantages. If your creative work can potentially earn a lot of money, registering it with the U.S. Copyright Office protects it in these ways:

- Registration establishes a public record of the copyright claim.
- Registration is necessary before you can file an infringement suit.
- Copyright registration within three months of publication permits the plaintiff to win up to $30,000 in statutory damages plus attorney's fees in court actions. Otherwise, the court can only award "actual damages."

You can find the necessary information and required forms at www.copyright.gov. Print and complete Form TX (used for a "nondramatic literary work") and return it to the U.S. Copyright Office in Washington, D.C., with a $30 registration fee. If you're going to spend $30, however, save it for your potentially best-selling book, Broadway play, revolutionary computer program, or hit song.

What Copyright Doesn't Protect

We know of one writer who sent a query to a newspaper's feature editor proposing an article about how people who have jobs that require them to work on the holidays, such as medical and law enforcement personnel, pilots, and flight attendants, celebrate Christmas. The writer never received a reply, but on Christmas Day the newspaper published a feature on that identical topic. Of course, the writer was angered, but he could do nothing. He later learned that this isn't an original idea, since many newspapers and magazines publish articles on this topic every Christmas. Even if it were original, he had no grounds for accusing the paper of copyright infringement. That's because you can't copyright an idea. At least six types of material are not protected by copyright. These include:

1. Unpublished works that have not been fixed in a "tangible form of expression." That could include speeches, conversations, or performances never written or recorded.
2. Titles, names, short phrases, and slogans; variations of typographic ornamentation; lists of ingredients or contents. That means you can't copyright titles of articles.
3. Works from the public domain with no original authorship. This category includes calendars, telephone directories, and lists taken from public documents. After a copyright expires (seventy years after the death of the author), it falls into the public domain.
4. Press releases. Companies and organizations sending out press releases want that information published. They put it in the public domain and allow writers to use anything they want from it.
5. Published works of the U.S. government or government employees.

6   Ideas, procedures, methods, processes, and concepts.

The last category is particularly important for writers. As we previously noted, you cannot copyright the idea for an article; you can only copyright the particular way in which the idea is expressed and written. That's one reason that competing magazines and newspapers are great sources for article ideas. There's nothing wrong with taking an idea from another magazine, using your own interviews and research, and writing an original article on the same topic.

Avoiding Plagiarism and Understanding "Fair Use"

Three prominent historians who have written dozens of books and often appeared on television talk shows were all charged with plagiarism between 2001 and 2004. All of them admitted to inadvertently quoting other authors' material in their books and failing to give proper credit and attribution. While none was taken to court, one of them made an out-of-court settlement with the author she had inadvertently quoted.

When plagiarism occurs unintentionally, it still violates copyright law and its consequences can be just as serious as intentional plagiarism. All three of these historians damaged their reputations—and received fewer invitations to appear on the television talk shows.

Jayson Blair's widely reported plagiarism at the *New York Times* in 2003 led to his dismissal and the resignations of two of his editors. These and other recent incidents of plagiarism serve to warn writers that plagiarism can ruin their careers, violate federal laws, and increase the public's mistrust of anything they write.

"Lifting" quotes is one of the most common forms of plagiarism. Beginning writers may be tempted to lift a quote used in another source and use it in their articles without giving proper attribution to the first writer. Since journalistic writers don't use footnotes, you have to give proper credit within the context of the article. If you choose to use a source from another magazine, you should attribute it this way:

"According to a *Newsweek* article, the secretary of state was quoted as saying. . . ."

"We're losing our ratings," the TV program's producer told *TV Guide*.

The latest edition of the *MLA Handbook for Writers of Research Papers*, published by the Modern Language Association, distinguishes between three types of plagiarism:

1   Repeating or paraphrasing a few words without giving credit.
2   Reproducing a particularly apt phrase.
3   Paraphrasing an argument or line of thinking.

In each case, the plagiarist misrepresents to readers the intellectual property of others as his or her own.

Fair Use

Section 107 of the U.S. copyright law covers "fair use." In general, fair use means that you can use brief quotes from other sources as long as you give proper credit. The law gives permission to build upon the work of others for "purposes such as criticism, comment, news reporting, teaching (including multiple copies for classroom use), scholarship, or research."

"The primary objective of copyright is not to reward the labor of authors," wrote Justice Sandra Day O'Connor in a 1991 Supreme Court decision, "but to 'promote the progress of science and useful arts.' To this end, copyright assures authors the right to their original expression, but encourages others to build freely upon the ideas and information conveyed by a work."[3]

The fair use provision doesn't say how many words or how much information you can borrow without permission from the author. Writers generally agree you should not exceed 250 words in any circumstance and sometimes even less. The law gives four general guidelines that determine whether fair use applies to the use of someone else's intellectual property:

1   The purpose and character of the use, including whether such use is of a commercial nature or is for nonprofit educational purposes.
2   The nature of the copyrighted work.
3   The amount and substantiality of the portion used in relation to the copyrighted work as a whole.
4   The effect of the use upon the potential market for or value of the copyrighted work.

Plaintiffs file many lawsuits each year over the meaning of "fair use." In general, the courts have ruled that the first criterion (a profit motive for its use) and the fourth (its damage to the creator's market sales) are most important. The courts have also ruled that educational use of copyrighted material is not automatically fair use.

Journalistic ethics boils down to common courtesy, common sense, and the Golden Rule. Do unto others as you would like for them to do unto you. Don't steal what belongs to someone else. Don't hurt others. And always tell the truth.

 Questions for Further Thought

1   Watch *Shattered Glass,* the movie about the *New Republic* writer who fabricated part or all of twenty-six stories. What issues does the movie raise for magazine journalists?

2   What are the advantages and disadvantages of using anonymous sources?

3   Why are "ideas" (for newspaper and magazine articles) not protected by copyright law?

Shop Talk

All rights: The publisher can publish the article in its magazine, put it on its website, and publish portions in another magazine it owns or in a subsequent book or CD-ROM containing a collection of articles. The writer gives up any right to sell or reuse the material.

Common knowledge: Information that's available from several published sources and, therefore, not protected by copyright. Common knowledge falls into many categories, such as art, geography, science, history, music, medicine, and technology.

Electronic rights: These rights cover a broad range of electronic media, from online magazines to CD-ROM anthologies.

First serial rights (first rights): Rights sold to a publisher giving it the first opportunity to publish the article. After the article is published, writers retain the right to sell unlimited reprint rights to other publishers.

Intellectual property: Any work by a writer, musician, artist, sculptor, or computer programmer capable of commercial use or distribution. Original creators hold legal rights to reproduction, distribution, public performance, and public display of their work. They also have the right to sell part or all of their ownership.

Public domain: Any intellectual property not protected by copyright law that anyone may use. Published material more than one hundred years old and anything published by the U.S. government is generally in the public domain.

Reprint rights or second serial rights: Reprint rights give a publication the opportunity to reprint previously published material. Most publications purchase reprint rights if the original publication's readership doesn't overlap with their own.

Subsidiary rights: Used in book publishing, subsidiary rights include all other rights such as movie or television rights, foreign editions, book club rights, audio book editions, or electronic rights.

Simultaneous rights or one-time rights: Simultaneous rights allow the writer to sell the same article at the same time to several publishers. Syndicated newspaper columns are the best example of use of simultaneous rights.

Work made for hire: The creative work done by a writer or artist in which the employer retains full copyright ownership to the work. Articles written by full-time newspaper and magazine employees usually fall under "work made for hire" provisions.

What Does the Future Hold?

In a recent issue, *MIN Magazine* listed "The Most Intriguing Media Issues for 2006." These included accountability, circulation audits, consumers' changing media habits, blogs, and the challenge of extending one's brand.

According to Roberta Garfield, SVP of print strategy at TargetCast, one of the most important issues facing magazines and their advertisers is "Accountability, accountability, and accountability."[1] *Accountability* is a watchword for measuring the ROI (return on investment) and ROO (return on objectives) across media. It has always been a part of the advertising process, but with advertisers under increased pressure to show that every dollar spent delivers results, marketing expenditures are being held to the same level of accountability as other investment spending is.

"Marketers are shifting from input-based to outcome-based plans and measurements," observed Randall Rothenberg, a director at Booz Allen Hamilton.[2]

There are four stages in the consumer's decision-making process that marketers look to measure:

1   Brand awareness.
2   Message association.

3   Brand favorability.
4   Purchase consideration.

"More and more, we are measuring advertising success based on return on objective (ROO)," said Renetta McCann, CEO America for Starcom Worldwide. [3]

Wantedness

Over the last few years, discussion has intensified over the concept of "wantedness," a means for measuring how much a consumer desires a magazine based on the price paid, the renewal rate, and other factors. The concept is an attempt to establish an additional means for advertisers to measure the value of their investment, and to evaluate one publication against another.

Chip Block, cofounder of the subscription agency USAPubs, challenges advertisers for pushing "wantedness." What, he asked, does a fuzzy notion of a magazine's general "wantedness" have to do with the impact and effectiveness of an ad in inducing a response from a consumer? "In the case of television and most other media, advertisers aren't concerned with how the people got to watching or reading or seeing whatever it happens to be," Block argued. "They are primarily concerned with how the sausage tastes."[4]

Sponsored Circulation

Based on a recent ABC analysis, *Capell's Circulation Report* notes the increased use of public place **sponsored circulation,** which means that a company or organization purchases bulk subscriptions for its customers. And as editor Dan Capell pointed out, "Under new ABC rules, this circulation will soon be categorized as nonpaid." Bard Davis, in *Circulation Management*, calculates that sponsored sales now account for more than 6 percent of total paid circulation for the 592 audited consumer magazines.[5]

Folio: The Magazine for Magazine Management notes that the new rules are putting the Audit Bureau of Circulations at odds with consumer magazines.

"I hate the new ABC rules," said Michael Sheehy, circulation director of Werner media. "They're terrible for publishers because our goal is to be able to put our product in as many hands as would want to read it and pay for it."[6]

"We're in a panic," declared circulation consultant Rebecca Sterner. "It's not clear what kind of sponsors are acceptable." [7]

Controlled Circulation

Scott Masterson, senior vice president and general manager of *Forbes* and president of *American Heritage*, expects to see more controlled circulation used by consumer and business magazines. "The challenge is reaching the right eyeballs," he said. "How you get there is less important."[8]

This means reaching a targeted group of readers that are crucial to a particular group of advertisers. In-flight magazines, for example, offer the best example of controlled circulation by consumer magazines. Affluent, well-educated airline travelers are very attractive to many advertisers.

Reducing Rate Bases

"With annual subscription renewal rates averaging about 46 percent, retaining current subscribers and attracting new ones is critical to the magazine industry's future health," according to Veronis Suhler Stevenson's *2005 Communications Industry Forecast*.[9]

In recent years, a total of fifty-seven ABC-audited magazines initiated **rate base reductions** and thirty-nine elected not to claim a rate base. This trend is a response to such conditions as postal rate hikes, increased audit bureau scrutiny of paid circulation, the trend toward counting nonpaid circulation when evaluating the quality of an audience, and the rising influence of media agencies.

Another factor is that every circulation unit delivered over rate base is a waste. A huge bonus over rate base does not equal good circulation economics.

"I'm amazed there haven't been more rate base reductions. I still anticipate an increase in the number of rate base reductions in light of the new ABC rules," said Capell.

According to *Cappell's Circulation Report*, the top five rate base reductions in the last five years shows how 10 million–circulation magazines can't survive in the market today. *TV Guide* slashed its rate base by two thirds, from 9 million to 3.3 million; *National Geographic* by 3.25 million; *Reader's Digest* by 3.3 million; and *Family Circle* by 800,000.

Technology

"Consumer magazine circulation will be most affected over the next twenty years by the evolution of print, electronic, and other alternative media," observed consultant Steve Strickman. "The continuing acceleration of technology should change the types of products we market—and the way we sell them." [10]

Publishing's Perfect Storm

Rarely do so many diverse circumstances converge to completely change any given industry. But for the publishing industry, which spends so much of its life analyzing others, it must be particularly galling to look inward at its own downward spiral. At this particular point in time, publishing finds itself in its own equivalent of the perfect storm.

So, what are the components of this perfect storm? According to publishing consultant Marc T. Liu, there are three colliding elements:

1   Technology. Cable and satellite delivery are competing with print publishers by supplying cable TV, broadband delivery of Web services, and so on that are head-on competitors for ad revenues.

The Web is supplying new delivery mechanisms that are much more timely than print, thus competing with print editorial. The Web is changing consumer expectations, thus making the traditional six-week delay for print consumers to receive their first issue unacceptable.

Tivo, Netflix, podcasting, cable, broadband, online radio, satellite radio—all are competing with print for a shrinking share of the magazine consumer's money and time.

"Pay particular attention to the explosion of wireless devices and DVRs, the growth of on-demand and the saturation of broadband," said Renetta McCann, CEO America for Starcom Worldwide, to a 2005 international conference of magazine publishers. "Ours is a 'my media' world, and we even design our own entertainment by virtue of our mp3 players, digital phones and personal digital assistants. We have a world of information at our fingertips," she told the World Magazine Conference in New York.

"I believe the success of magazines can and will be achieved. But it will pivot on three deliverables: engagement, connectivity, and accountability," she said.[11]

2   Changing marketing systems. The sell-through rate for newsstand sales has declined from 50 percent ten years ago to around 30 percent today. The single-copy distribution system is imploding under wholesaler consolidation. Twenty years ago, there were three hundred wholesalers; today, five major wholesalers remain. This consolidation has resulted in a lack of adequate wholesaler systems and controls.

The consolidation of the supermarket industry into the "big box" stores (Wal-Mart, Target, and the like) has created an oligopoly in the magazine industry. Wal-Mart now accounts for 15 percent of all single-copy magazine sales. Competition for this limited retail shelf space has allowed these majors to boost their percentage of the retail fees. As a result of this shift in the fees to retailers from whole-salers, virtually none of the remaining wholesalers is profitable.

"I think Wal-Mart . . . represents about 15 or 16 percent of our retail sales," said Nina Link, president of the Magazine Publishers of America. "They are a tough partner. They want the lowest price. They don't like when magazines test their prices at different levels. They have issues with some of our magazines, which they have either bannered or covered in some way. We certainly acknowl-edge that not every magazine should be everywhere, but we have asked them to have an open mind and to recognize that different communities do have different populations and that they should be willing to have magazines representative of the community inter-ests. And not just have a blanket policy with all stores. So we have concerns about some of their practices and we have spoken with them. But we also see what an important partner they can be, and we're working with them."[12]

The advent of state lotteries virtually eliminated the magazine sweepstake business. American Family Publishers and Publishers Clearing House used to sell $500 million in magazines *per year.* Today, American Family Publishers is bankrupt and Publishers Clearing House magazine sales are down to less than $80 million.

Changes in ABC rules have dramatically increased the paper-work required by the sales agents. This will substantially reduce this major source of magazine subscriptions in the years ahead.

3　Changing supplier profiles. After many years of declining profits, the printing, paper and fulfillment industries went through massive acquisition programs by the majors in an effort to reduce costs . So substantial has this effort been that only a few companies remain at the top of each of these industries. With this oligopolistic structure, comes the suppliers' ability to control production, supplies and ultimately pricing. As the dominant players pay down the debt taken on to complete the acquisitions, they are left with greater profits and even more power to control their respective industries.

The rising cost of energy is another issue for publishers. In recent years, oil has gone from $20 per barrel to over $70. Paper uses a tremendous amount of energy in the drying process. The cost of ink, also a petroleum-based product, has dramatically increased. And, one of the largest expenses for the post office is fuel. All of these energy increases are now being passed through directly to the publishers because of the oligopolistc supplier situation.

The post office faces declining mail volumes due to competi-tion from the Internet. Virtually any company with monthly billing is pushing aggressively to convert their customers to web billing and paying. When the mail volumes decline, the revenue shortfall is spread to the remaining customers. So as the Internet become more pervasive in our lives, the mail volumes continue to fall and the U.S. Postal Services continues to raise prices.

What's the Future of Magazine Publishing?

With the costs moving against them and outdated marketing systems in decline, publishers need to embrace the new technologies to cut costs and boost customer involvement.

Publishing consultant Marc T. Liu says, "Fulfillment practices should be brought up to Amazon.com standards. E-billing and renewal should be expanded. E-newsletters, blogs, streaming video and information services should be added to content. Interactive product offerings should be added where ever possible. For example, music magazines should integrate TV, radio, videos, MP3 downloads, cell phone access, concert involvement, etc. into their product offerings. Multi-media content should be added where ever appropriate."[13]

William Kerr, chairman and CEO of Meredith Corporation, believes that five themes will shape the magazine publishing business in years to come.[14]

1   This is the century of Asia-Pacific. Kerr said that while some growth potential still exists in the United States and Europe, "Companies must cast an eye eastward towards the burgeoning markets in countries such as China and India." He notes that his company recently entered into a licensing agreement with a Chinese company to publish a local version of *Better Homes and Gardens.*

2   The Internet is your friend. Magazine companies now use the Internet as a growth catalyst on many fronts, Kerr said. "For our editors, it allows us a more frequent dialogue with readers. For our marketers, it provides another source of potential revenue generation. For our circulation professionals, it provides a low-cost alternative to generating subscriptions. And it is growing at a phenomenal rate," he said.

3   Build brands—not just sell advertising. While "beautiful ads in beautiful magazines are still the lifeblood of our business," according to Kerr, they are no longer sufficient. He encourages magazine publishers to "exploit our powerful magazine brands across many platforms, such as books, special interest publications, online events, licensing, promotions, etc."

4   Focus on profitable circulation. "Given the recent circulation scandals that have rocked both the newspaper and magazine industries, the ability to offer advertisers a reliable and verifiable readership is essential," Kerr said. "In order for a magazine to remain viable, it

must be able to possess a profitable direct-to-publisher rate base." He said that Meredith relies on its 85 million–name database and solicitation materials that emphasize the editorial content of its magazines to attract subscribers.

5   Maintain integrity, integrity, integrity. "When it comes to integrity, there are no shortcuts," Kerr said. "We need to cherish the trust placed in us by our readers and advertisers. With so many information and entertainment choices out there, we as an industry must stress integrity in everything we do."

Questions for further thought

1   Do you think that "branding" of a magazine by selling items like mugs, caps, and T-shirts helps raise the magazine's popularity or sales?

2   What are the advantages to magazines of intentional rate base reductions?

3   Discuss how the "perfect storm" of new technology, market delivery systems, and increased paper and postal costs threatens the future of magazines?

4   What free magazines (controlled circulation) can you find given away in grocery stores and other public places in your area? What type of advertisers choose these magazines over newspapers or broadcast stations?

Shop Talk

Audit Bureau of Circulations: The industry association that monitors and verifies circulation figures of magazines for advertisers and marketers.

Branding: The process of creating name recognition for a magazine and extending its brand awareness in auxiliary products such a caps, mugs, T-shirts, and so on.

Rate base reduction: The intentional reduction of a magazine's circulation because the additional cost of acquiring and servicing marginal subscribers exceeds the revenue they bring in.

Sponsored circulation: Bulk subscriptions purchased by a company for its customers. For example, a bank may purchase copies of a finance magazine for its customers.

Top Twenty-Five U.S. Magazine Publishing Companies

Since this book is "a complete guide," we felt it should provide you with practical information on where to find information about magazine publishers and where to look for a job in the industry. Around a thousand new magazines are launched every year, and hundreds more are bought and sold by their corporate owners. Magazine ownership, therefore, changes constantly. This listing will give you basic information about America's twenty-five largest magazine publishing companies and the magazines they publish. This information is accurate at the time this book goes to press, but may not be later. Using the Web addresses, however, you should be able to find updated information on the companies. Most websites will also offer you further information on the magazines, their content, histories, current staff, writer's guidelines, media kits, and other details.

Although a company's headquarters may be in New York, that doesn't mean that all of its magazines are published there. Large companies often have regional offices in various cities around the nation. For example, several of Time Warner's magazines are published by its Southern Progress, Inc., subsidiary in Birmingham, Alabama. If you are interested in any particular magazine, make sure you find the specific publishing address for that magazine.

Author's note: Magazines are ranked by 2004 net revenues. Foreign-published magazines owned by American companies are not included in the listings. Source for revenue and rankings: AdAge.com, based on information obtained from Publishers Information Bureau and TNS Media. Source for magazine ownership: corporate websites. Thanks to Leslie I. Benson, a Ball State University graduate student, for her help in compiling this section.

1   Time Warner, Inc. (170 publications)
    Time Inc.
    www.timewarner.com and www.timeinc.com
    2004 Net Revenue (millions): $4,851
    2004 Top Magazine (in revenue): *People*

Magazines Owned

25 Beautiful Gardens	*25 Beautiful Homes*
25 Beautiful Kitchens	*4x4*
Aeroplane	*All You*
Amateur Gardening	*Amateur Photographer*
Ambientes	*Angler's Mail*
Audi Magazine	*BabyTalk*
Balance	*Bird Keeper*
BMX Business News	*Bride to Be*
Bullfinch Press	*Business 2.0*
Cage and Aviary Birds	*Caravan*
Center Street	*Chat*
Chilango	*Classic Boat*
Coastal Living	*Cooking Light*
Cottage Living	*Country Homes and Interiors*
Country Life	*Cycle Sport*
Cycling Weekly	*Decanter*
English Woman's Weekly	*Entertainment Weekly*
Essence	*Essentials*
European Boat Builder	*Eventing*
EXP	*Expansión*
Field and Stream	*Fortune*
Fortune Asia	*Fortune Europe*
FSB: Fortune Small Business	*Golf Magazine*
Golf Monthly	*Guitar*
Hair	*Health*
Hi-Fi News	*Homes and Gardens*
Horse	*Horse and Hound*
IPC	*Ideal Home*
InStyle	*InStyle (Australia)*
International Boat Industry	*Land Rover World*
Life	*Life and Style*

Livingetc
Manufactura
MiniWorld
Model Collector
Motor Boat and Yachting
Motor Caravan
NME
Nuts
Outdoor Life
Park Home and Holiday Caravan
People en Español
Popular Science
Practical Parenting
Progressive Farmer
Quién
Racecar Engineering
Ride BMX
Salt Water Sportsman
Shoot Monthly
Ski
Soaplife
Southern Living
Sports Illustrated
Stamp Magazine
Sunset Books
Targeted Media
The Field
The Railway Magazine
This Old House
Time
Time for Kids
TransWorld Business
TransWorld Skateboarding
TransWorld Surf
TV Easy
Uncut
Vuelo
Warner Books
Web User
What Camera
What's on TV
Woman
Woman's Own
Women and Golf

Loaded
MBR: Mountain Bike Rider
Mizz
Money
Motor Boats Monthly
MotorBoating
Now
Obras
Parenting
People
Pick Me Up
Practical Boat Owner
Prediction
Quad Off-Road Magazine
Quo
Real Simple
Rugby World
Ships Monthly
Shooting Times
Skiing
Southern Accents
Sporting Gun
Sports Illustrated for Kids
Sunset
SuperBike
Teen People
The Golf
The Shooting Gazette
This Old House Ventures
Time Atlantic
Time Pacific
TransWorld Motocross
TransWorld Snowboarding
TV and Satellite Week
TVTimes
VolksWorld
Wallpaper
Warner Faith
Wedding
What Digital Camera
Who
Woman and Home
Woman's Weekly
World Soccer

Yachting	*Yachting Monthly*
Yachting World	*Yachts*

2   Advance Publications, Inc. (61+ publications)
Owns Condé Nast Publications, Fairchild Publications, Inc., the
Golf Digest Companies, and Parade Publications. Also owns 25 daily
newspapers, American City Business Journals (40+ weekly papers).
www.advance.net
2004 net revenue (millions): $2,420
2004 top magazine (in revenue): *Parade*

Magazines Owned
Condé Nast Publications
www.condenast.com

Allure	*Architectural Digest*
Bon Appétit	*Brides*
Cargo	*Condé Nast Traveler*
Domino	*Glamour*
Gourmet	*GQ*
House and Garden	*Lucky*
Modern Bride	*Self*
Teen Vogue	*The New Yorker*
Vanity Fair	*Vogue*
Wired	

Fairchild Publications, Inc.
www.fairchildpub.com/index.cfm

Bride's	*Children's Business*
Daily News Record	*Details*
Elegant Bride	*Fairchild Bridal Connection*
Footwear News	*Home Furnishing News*
InFurniture	*Jane*
Menswear	*Supermarket News*
Vitals Man	*Vitals Woman*
W	*W Jewelry*
Your Prom	

Women's Wear Daily
www.WWDMediaWorldWide.com

Beauty Biz	*Beauty Report International* (published in English, German, and French)
Fairchild 100	*FLASH*

WWD.com

WWD: The Magazine (regional editions in Los Angeles, Atlanta, Dallas, and Chicago)

WWDAccessories

WWDBook Division

WWDClassifieds

WWDCEO Summits

WWDCustom Publishing and Advertorials

WWD/DNR Specialty Store Newsletter

WWDInnerwear

WWDLuxury

WWDMagic

WWDSwim

Golf Digest Companies
www.mediabrains.com/client/golfdig/bg1/search.asp

Golf Digest

Gold for Women

Golf World

Golf World Business

Parade Publications
www.parade.com
Parade Magazine

3 Hearst Corporate Communications (21 publications)
www.hearstcorp.com
2004 net revenue (in millions): $1,837
2004 top magazine (in revenue): *Good Housekeeping*

Magazines Owned

Cosmopolitan

CosmoGIRL!

Country Living

Country Living Gardener

Esquire

Good Housekeeping

Harper's Bazaar

House Beautiful

Marie Claire

O: The Oprah Magazine

Popular Mechanics

Quick and Simple

Redbook

Seventeen

SHOP Etc.

SmartMoney

Teen

Town and Country

Town and Country Travel

Veranda

Weekend

4 Meredith Corporation (25 publications)
www.meredith.com
2004 net revenue (millions): $1,534
2004 top magazine (in revenue): *Better Homes and Gardens*

Magazines Owned
Subscription Magazines

American Baby

Better Homes and Gardens

Child
Family Circle
Ladies' Home Journal
More
Successful Farming
WOOD
American Patchwork and Quilting
Creative Home
Diabetic Living
Garden, Deck, and Landscape
Paint Décor
Scrapbooks, Etc.

Country Home
Fitness
Midwest Living
Parents
Traditional Home
Special-Interest Publications
Country Gardens
Decorating
Do It Yourself
Garden Ideas and Outdoor Living
Renovation Style

5 Prism Business Media (formerly Primedia Business
   Magazines and Media) (71 publications)
   www.primediabusiness.com
   2004 net revenue (millions): $1,206
   2004 top magazine (in revenue): *Motor Trend*

Magazines Owned

Access Control and Security Systems
American Printer
American Trucker
Association Meetings
Broadcast Engineering
Cement Americas
Club Industry's Fitness Business Pro
Corn and Soybean Digest
Delta Farm Press
Electrical Construction
   and Maintenance
Electrical Wholesaling
Farm Industry News
Fire Chief
Government Security
Hay and Forage Grower
Live Design
Millimeter
MIX
Modern Uniforms
Music Education Technology
National Real Estate Investor
Paper, Film, and Foil Converter
Profitable Embroiderer

American City and County
American School and University
Apply
BEEF
Bulk Transporter
Chief Marketer 360°
Concrete Products
Corporate Meetings and Incentives
DIRECT
Electrical Marketing

Electronic Musician
Financial and Insurance Meetings
Fleet Owner
Grounds Maintenance
HomeCare
Medical Meetings
Mine and Quarry Trader
Mobile Radio Technology
Multichannel Merchant
National Hog Farmer
Operations and Fulfillment
Power Electronics Technology
PROMO

Radio Magazine
Registered Rep.
Remix
Retail Traffic
Rock Products
Southeast Farm Press
Special Events Magazine
Telephony
Transmission and Distribution World
Video Systems
Ward's Dealer Business
Wearables Business
Wireless Review

Refrigerated Transporter
Religious Conference Manager
Rental Equipment Register
RF Design
Sound and Video Contractor
Southwest Farm Press
Stitches Magazine
Trailer/Body Builders
Trusts and Estates
Ward's Auto World
Waste Age
Western Farm Press

6   The Reader's Digest Association, Inc. (20 publications)
www.rd.com
2004 net revenue (millions): $917
2004 top magazine (in revenue): *Reader's Digest*

Magazines Owned
American Woodworker
Reader's Digest
Reader's Digest Selecciones

Family Handyman
Reader's Digest Large Print
RD Specials

Reiman Media Group
www.reimanpub.com
Backyard Living
Cooking for 2
Country Discoveries
Farm and Ranch Living
Reminisce
Quick Cooking

Birds and Blooms
Country
Country Woman
Light and Tasty
Taste of Home

7   International Data Group (259 publications)
www.idg.com
2004 net revenue (millions): $755
2004 top magazine (in revenue): *PC World*

Magazines Owned
(U.S. only; all other IDG magazines in other countries)
*Access Learning: Cable in
    the Classroom*
CIO Magazine

Bio-IT World

ClubLife

Code Vault
CSO Magazine
Network World
Star Wars Insider
Video Event

Computerworld
GamePro
PC World
Taste for Life

8   The McGraw-Hill Companies (6 publications)
www.mcgraw-hill.com
2004 net revenue (millions): $687
2004 top magazine (in revenue): *BusinessWeek*

Magazines Owned
Aviation Week Group
www.aviationnow.com
Aviation Week and Space Technology
Overhaul and Maintenance

BusinessWeek Group
BusinessWeek

McGraw-Hill Construction
Architectural Record
Engineering News-Record

Platts
Power Magazine

9   Reed Business (part of Reed Elsevier) (150 publications)
www.reedbusiness.com
2004 net revenue (millions): $594
2004 top magazine (in revenue): *EDN*

Magazines Owned
Reed Business

Building and Construction
Building Design and Construction
Consulting-Specifying Engineer
GIANTS
Interior Design
Professional Remodeler

Construction Equipment
Custom Builder
HousingZone.com
Professional Builder

Design
Design News
Medical Design Technology   *Product Design and Development*

Electronics
ECN   *ECN Asia*
EDN   *EDN Asia*
EDN China   *EDN Europe*
EDN Japan   *EITD (Electronic Industry*
                                         Telephone Directory)
Electronic Business   *Electronic Business Japan*
Electronic News   *Electronics Manufacturing Asia*
Electronics Manufacturing China   *In-Stat*
Microprocessor Report   *Semiconductor International*
Semiconductor Packaging   *Test and Measurement World*
Wireless Design and Development   *Wireless Design and Development*
Asia

Entertainment
411 Publishing   *Daily Variety*
DVD Exclusive   *MarketCast*
Variety   *Variety.com*
Video Business   *VLife*

Gifts and Furnishings
Casual Living   *Furniture Today*
Fusion   *Garden Décor*
Gifts and Decorative Accessories   *Home Accents Today*
Home Textiles Today   *Israel Diamonds*
JCK (Jewelers' Circular Keystone) *JCK Luxury*
JCK Trends   *Kids Today*
Leather Today   *New York Diamonds*
Playthings   *SoHo Today*
TWICE (This Week in Consumer Electronics)

Hospitality
Chain Leader   *Foodservice Equipment and Supplies*
HOTELS   *HOTELS' Investment Outlook*
Restaurants and Institutions

Manufacturing
Asia Food Journal   *Control Engineering China*
InMFG (formerly Industrial   *Kellysearch*
Product Bulletin)

Media
Tradeshow Week   *TrendWatch Graphic Arts*

Printing
AF Lewis   *Converting Magazine*
Graphic Arts Blue Books   *Graphic Arts Monthly*
Packaging Digest   *Printmarketplace.com*

Publishing
Críticas   *Library Hotline*
Library Journal   *netConnect*
Publishers Weekly   *School Library Journal*

Process
Chemical Equipment   *Control Engineering*
Control Engineering Europe   *Food Manufacturing*
IAN Inside Products   *Pharmaceutical Processing*
Powder/Bulk Solids   *Production Technology News*

Reed Construction Data
Buildcore Suite of Products   *BuildingTeam Summit*
California Builder and Engineer   *CanaData Construction Forecasting*
CanaData Construction Starts   *Capital Asset Management*
(AssetObjects)
Construction   *Construction Bulletin*
Construction Digest   *Construction News*
Constructioneer   *CSI's MANU-SPEC*
CSI's SPEC-DATA   *Daily Commercial News*
Dixie Contractor   *First Source CAD*
Green Sheet   *Greensheet Logger*
Health Market Data   *Hospitality Profiles*
iMedia   *Journal of Commerce*
KeyPRODUCTS   *Manufacturer Catalogs*
Market Link   *Michigan Contractor and Builder*
Midwest Contractor   *New England Construction*
Pacific Builder and Engineer   *Plans Direct CD-ROM*
Plans Direct Print   *Reed Bulletin (Canada)*
Reed Bulletin   *Reed Clark Reports*
Reed Connect   *Reed DailyCards*
Reed Design Registry   *Reed First Source*
Reed First Source Suite of Products *Reed Market Fundamentals*
Reed Private Plan Rooms   *Reed StartsOnline*
ReedFirstSource.com   *Rocky Mountain Construction*
RSMeans Cost Books   *RSMeans CustomCost Estimator*

RSMeans Insurance Services *RSMeans Reference Books*
RSMeans Research Services *RSMeans Seminars/Training*
Texas Contractor *Western Builder*

Science and Medical
BioScience Technology *Drug Discovery and Development*
GandP *Laboratory Equipment*
RandD Research and Development *Scientific Computing*
Surgical Products

Supply Chain
Industrial Distribution *Logistics Management*
Manufacturing Business Technology *Material Handling Product News*
  (formerly MSI)
Modern Materials Handling *Purchasing*
Supply Chain Management Review *Industrial Maintenance*
    and Plant Operation

Plant Engineering

Telecommunications
BandC (formerly Broadcasting *CED*
  and Cable)
Multichannel News *Wireless Week*

10 Hachette Filipacchi Media U.S. (24 publications)
    www.hfmus.com
    2004 net revenue (millions): $552
    2004 top magazine (in revenue): *Woman's Day*

    Magazines Owned
    American Photo *Boating*
    Car and Driver *Cycle World*
    ELLE *ELLE DECOR*
    ELLEgirl *Flying*
    For Me *Home*
    Metropolitan Home *Mobile Entertainment*
    Popular Photography and Imaging *Premiere*
    Road and Track *Road and Track Speed*
    Sound and Vision *Woman's Day*

    Woman's Day Special-Interest Publications
    Decorating Ideas *Gardening and Outdoor Living*
    Holiday Cookies *Holiday Cooking*
    Home Remodeling *Weekend Decorating*

11 American Media, Inc. (15 publications)
www.nationalenquirer.com
2004 net revenue (millions): $537
2004 top magazine (in revenue): *Shape*

Magazines Owned
Celebrity Living Weekly   *Country Weekly*
Fit Pregnancy   *Flex*
iShape   *Looking Good Now*
Men's Fitness   *MPH*
Muscle and Fitness   *Muscle and Fitness Hers*
National Enquirer   *Natural Health*
Shape   *Star*
Weekly World News

12 Rodale (9 publications)
www.rodale.com
2004 net revenue (millions): $421
2004 top magazine (in revenue): *Men's Health*

Magazines Owned
Backpacker   *Best Life*
Bicycling   *Men's Health*
Mountain Bike   *Organic Gardening*
Prevention   *Runner's World*
Women's Health

13 Forbes, Inc. (6 publications)
www.forbesinc.com/index.shtml
2004 net revenue (millions): $370
2004 top magazine (in revenue): *Forbes*

Magazines Owned
American Heritage   *American Legacy*
Forbes   *Forbes Asia*
Forbes FYI   *Invention and Technology*

14 The Washington Post Co. (2 publications)
Also owns numerous newspapers and Kaplan, Inc.
www.washpostco.com
2004 net revenue (millions): $366
2004 top magazine (in revenue): *Newsweek*

Magazines Owned
Arthur Frommer's Business Travel
Newsweek

15 Walt Disney Co.
http://corporate.disney.go.com
2004 net revenue (millions): $357
2004 top magazine (in revenue): *ESPN: The Magazine*
Magazines Owned
Disney Adventures
ESPN: The Magazine
Family Fun

16 United Business Media (63 publications)
www.unitedbusinessmedia.com
2004 net revenue (millions): $354
2004 top magazine (in revenue): *Information Week*

Magazines Owned

Abstracts in Hematology and Oncology

Acumen Information

Applied Neurology

Bass Player

Business Communications Review

C/C++ Users Journal

Consultant for Pediatricians

Diagnostic Imaging Europe

Dr. Dobb's Journal

DV Magazine

Electronics Supply and Manufacturing Magazine

EQ

Game Developer

Government Video

Headache and Pain

Information Week

Intelligent Enterprise

IT Architect

The Journal of Musculoskeletal Medicine

Keyboard

MSDN Magazine

Oncology

Optimize

Pro Sound News

Psychiatric Times

Abstracts in Respiratory Infections

The AIDS Reader

Bank Systems and Technology

BioMechanics

Cancer Management: A Multidisciplinary Approach

Consultant

Diagnostic Imaging

Digital Cinematography

Drug Benefit Trends

EE Times

Embedded Systems Design

Frets

Government Enterprise

Guitar Player

Infections in Medicine

Insurance and Technology

Issues in Urology

The Journal of Critical Illness

The Journal of Respiratory Diseases

Media Line

Network Computing

Oncology News International

Planet Analog

Psychiatric Issues in Emergency Care Settings

Rental and Staging Systems

Residential Systems	*Secure Enterprise*
Software Development	*Storage Pipeline*
Sys Admin	*Systems Contractor News*
TechNet Magazine	*Technology and Learning*
Televisions Broadcast	*Videography*
Wall Street and Technology	*Xtreme Video Magazine*

17 Gemstar-TV Guide International, Inc. (2 publications)
www.gemstartvguide.com
2004 net revenue (millions): $321
2004 top magazine (in revenue): *TV Guide*
Magazines Owned
TV Guide Magazine
TV Guide Online

18 Dennis Publishing, Ltd. (29 publications)
www.dennispublishing.com
2004 net revenue (millions): $316
2004 top magazine (in revenue): *Maxim*

Magazines Owned
(U.S. only; all other magazines in other countries)
Blender
Maxim
Men's Fitness
Stuff
The Week

19 VNU Business Media (53 publications)
www.vnubusinessmedia.com
2004 net revenue (millions): $299
2004 top magazine (in revenue): *Adweek*

Magazines Owned

Adweek	*Adweek's Best Spots*
Adweek's Marketing y Medios	*American Artist*
Amusement Business	*Architectural Lighting*
Architecture	*Back Stage*
Back Stage West	*Billboard*
Billboard Radio Monitor	*The Bookseller*
Brandweek	*Bulletin d'Information*
Commercial Property News	*Contract*
Convenience Store News	*Couture International Jeweler*
Display and Design Ideas	*Editor and Publisher*

EMB (Embroidery/Monogram *Eurotec*
Business Magazine)
Europa Star China *Europa Star Espana*
Europa Star Europe *Europa Star International*
Europa Star USA and Canada *Film Journal International*
The Gourmet Retailer *The Hollywood Reporter*
Hospitality Design *Impressions*
Incentive *Info Express*
Kirkus Reviews *Kitchen + Bath Business*
Mediaweek *Meeting News*
Multi-Housing News *National Jeweler*
PDN (Photo District News) *Potentials*
Presentations *Progressive Grocer*
Ross Reports Television and Film *Sales and Marketing Management*
SGB (Sporting Goods Business) *Successful Meetings*
Training *Watercolor*
Watson Guptill Publications

20 American Express Publishing Corporation
www.amexpub.com
Travel + Leisure
2004 net revenue (millions): $286
2004 top magazine (in revenue): *Travel + Leisure*

Magazines Owned
Departures *Executive Travel Magazine*
Food and Wine *SkyGuide*
Travel + Leisure *Travel + Leisure Family*
Travel + Leisure Golf

21 National Geographic Society
www.nationalgeographic.com
2004 net revenue (millions): $256
2004 top magazine (in revenue): *National Geographic*
Magazines Owned
National Geographic
National Geographic Adventure
National Geographic Explorer Magazine
National Geographic for Kids
National Geographic Traveler
National Geographic World

22 IAC/InterActiveCorp
http://iac.com

2004 net revenue (millions): $252
2004 top magazine (in revenue): *Entertainment*

Magazines Owned
IAC Businesses:

Ask Jeeves, Inc.	*Citysearch*
Cornerstone Brands, Inc.	*Domania*
Entertainment Publications	*Evite*
GetSmart	*Gifts.com*
HSN	*HSE24*
iNest	*Interval International*
LendingTree	*Match.com*
PRC	*RealEstate.com*
ReserveAmerica	*ServiceMagic*

23 Crain Communications, Inc. (24 magazines; 6 newspapers)
Also owns 6 city publications.
www.crain.com
2004 net revenue (millions): $252
2004 top magazine (in revenue): *Automotive News*

Magazines Owned

Advertising Age	*American Coin-Op*
American Drycleaner	*American Laundry News*
Automobilewoche	*Automotive News*
Automotive News Europe	*AutoWeek*
BtoB	*Business Insurance*
Creativity	*European Rubber Journal*
InvestmentNews	*Modern Healthcare*
Modern Physician	*Pensions and Investments*
Plastics News	*RCR Wireless News*
Rubber and Plastics News	*TelevisionWeek*
Tire Business	*Urethanes Technology*
Waste News	*Workforce Management*

24 Zuckerman Media Properties (1 publication)
www.usnews.com
U.S. News and World Report
2004 net revenue (millions): $236
2004 top magazine (in revenue): *U.S. News and World Report*

Magazines Owned
U.S. News and World Report

25 Ziff Davis Media Inc. (8 publications)
    www.ziffdavis.com
    2004 net revenue (millions): $205
    2004 top magazine (in revenue): *PC Magazine*

Magazines Owned

Baseline	*CIO Insight*
Computer Gaming World	*Electronic Gaming Monthly*
ExtremeTech	*eWeek*
Official U.S. Playstation Magazine	*PC Magazine*

Suggested Reading

Abrahamson, David. *Magazine-Made America: The Cultural Transformation of the Postwar Periodical.* Cresskill, NJ: Hampton Press, 1996.

Angeletti, Norberto, and Alberto Oliva. *Magazines That Make History: Their Origins, Development, and Influence.* Gainesville: University Press of Florida, 2004.

Bacon's Magazine Directory. Chicago: Bacon's Media, annual.

Gale Directory of Publications and Broadcast Media. Detroit, MI: Gale Publications, annual.

Husni, Samir. *Launch Your Own Magazine: A Guide for Succeeding in Today's Marketplace.* Nashville, TN: Hamblett House, 1998.

Johnson, Sammye, and Patricia Prijatel. *The Magazine from Cover to Cover.* New York: McGraw-Hill, 2003.

Kobak, James B. *How to Start a Magazine and Publish It Profitably.* New York: M. Evans and Company, 2002.

Magazine Publishers of America. *The Magazine Handbook 2005–2006.* Annual updates available at *www.magazine.org*.

Mogel, Leonard. *The Magazine: Everything You Need to Make It in the Magazine Business,* 3rd ed. Pittsburgh: Graphic Arts Technical Foundation, 1998.

Patterson, Benton Rain, and Coleman E. P. Patterson. *The Editor in Chief: A Management Guide for Magazine Editors,* 2nd ed. Ames, IA: Blackwell Professional Publishing, 2003.

Sumner, David E. "American Newsmagazines." In *Encyclopedia of International Media and Communication.* San Diego, CA: Academic Press, Reed-Elsevier, 2003.

———. "American Magazines in the 20th Century." In *The Age of Mass Communication,* ed. William David Sloan. Northport, AL: Vision Press, 1998.

Sumner, David E., and Holly G. Miller. *Feature and Magazine Writing.* Ames, IA: Blackwell Professional Publishing, 2005.

Tebbel, John, and Mary Ellen Zuckerman. *The Magazine in America, 1741–1990.* New York: Columbia University Press, 1991.

Veronis Suhler Stevenson. *Communications Industry Forecast 2005–2009,* 19th ed. New York: Veronis Suhler Stevenson, 2005.

Magazine Associations

American Business Media (business-to-business magazines)
www.americanbusinessmedia.org

675 Third Avenue
New York, NY 10017–5704
Tel: 212–661–6360

American Jewish Press Association (Jewish magazines)
www.ajpa.org

1255 New Hampshire Avenue, NW, #702
Washington, D.C. 20036
Tel: 202–250–6144

Associated Church Press (Protestant magazines)
www.theacp.org

1410 Vernon Street
Stoughton, WI 53589–2248
Tel: 608–877–0011

Catholic Press Association (Catholic magazines)
www.catholicpress.org

3555 Veterans Memorial Highway, Unit O
Ronkonkoma, NY 11779
Tel: 631–471–4730

Evangelical Press Association
http://www.epassoc.org
P.O. Box 28129
Crystal, MN 55428
Tel: 763–535–4793

International Association of Business Communicators (corporate magazines)
www.iabc.com

One Hallidie Plaza, Suite 600
San Francisco, CA 94102
Tel: 415–544–4700

Magazine Publishers of America (consumer magazines)
www.magazine.org

810 Seventh Avenue, 24th Floor
New York, NY 10019
Tel: 212–872–3700

Society of National Association Publications (association magazines)
www.snaponline.org

8405 Greensboro Drive, #800
McLean, VA 22102
Tel: 703–506–3285

Notes

Chapter 1

1   Compaine, Benjamin M. *Who Owns the Media? Concentration of Ownership in the Mass Communications Industry*. White Plains, NY: Knowledge Industry Publications, Inc., 1982, 169.

2   These figures are documented in studies reported in *The Magazine Handbook 2005* published by the Magazine Publishers of America and available in pdf format at *www.magazine.org*.

3   Scott Crystal interview with David E. Sumner, New York City, 2 Aug. 2005.

4   Catherine Black as quoted on "Your World with Neil Cavuto," Fox Television News, May 9, 2005.

5   Reader Experience Study, Northwestern University Media Management Center. Published by Magazine Publishers of America (*www.magazine.org*), accessed 5/31/05.

6   Ted Spiker e-mail to David E. Sumner, 30 Jan. 2006.

7   *The Magazine Handbook 2005–2006*. Magazine Publishers of America. Available at *www.magazine.org*.

8   Victor Navasky interview with David E. Sumner, New York City, 1 Aug. 2005.

9   Christopher Collins, "How The Economist Made a Million," *Magazine World* published by the Federation of the International Periodical Press, London. (May 2005), 12.

10 Veronis, Suhler Stevenson, *Communications Industry Forecast 2005–2009*, 19th ed. (New York: Veronis Suhler Steven, 2005), 423.

11 Compaine, Benjamin M. *Who Owns the Media?*, 144.

12 Scott Crystal interview with David E. Sumner, New York City, 2 Aug. 2005.

13 Bill Mickey, "Tracking Web-Based Subscriptions," *FOLIO: The Magazine for Magazine Management*, 5 Dec. 2005 (*www.foliomag.com*) accessed 4/3/06).

14 Nina Link interview with David E. Sumner, New York City, 1 Aug. 2005.

Chapter 2

1 Richard Stolley telephone interview with David E. Sumner, 17 Feb. 2005.

2 Joe Treen e-mail to David E. Sumner, 1 Feb. 2006.

3 Nicoel Voges e-mail to David E. Sumner, 30 Jan. 2006.

4 John Mack Carter e-mail to Sherrill Rhoades, Feb. 2006.

5 Jacqueline Leo, interview with David E. Sumner, Pleasantville, New York, 4 Aug. 2005.

6 David E. Sumner, "Teaching Standards in Feature and Magazine Writing Classes," presented at the annual convention of the Association for Education in Journalism and Mass Communication, San Antonio, Texas, August 2005.

Chapter 3

1 James B. Kobak, *How to Start a Magazine and Publish It Profitably* (New York: M. Evans and Company, 2002), 149.

2 Kobak, *How to Start a Magazine*, 44.

3 Ibid.

4 Samir Husni, *Launch Your Own Magazine* (Nashville: Hamblett House, Inc. 1998), 42.

5 Joshua Goodman, David Heckerman and Robert Routhwaite, "Stopping Spam," *Scientific American* (April 2005), 42–49.

Chapter 4

1 James B. Kobak, *How to Start a Magazine and Publish It Profitably* (New York: M. Evans and Company, 2002).

2 Richard Stolley telephone interview with David E. Sumner, 17 Feb. 2005.

3 Walter Bernard interview with David E. Sumner, New York City, 2 Aug. 2005.

4   Angelo Gandino telephone interview with Sherrill Rhoades, Feb. 2006.

5   James B. Kobak, *How to Start a Magazine and Publish It Profitably* (New York: M. Evans and Company, 2002).

6   Quoted in *Magazine Publishing* by Sammye Johnson and Patricia Prijatel (Lincolnwood, IL: NTC Contemporary, 2000), 223.

7   Association for Education in Journalism and Mass Communication, 2005 Magazine Division Student Competition. Quoted from judges' comments accessible at *www.aejmcmagazine.org*.

8   Benton Rain Patterson and Coleman E.P. Patterson, *The Editor in Chief: A Management Guide for Magazine Editors*, 2nd edition. (Ames, IA: Blackwell Professional, 2003), 101–102.

Chapter 5

1   Kate White, "How to Create Covers That Sell," *Magazine World* Published by Federation of the International Periodical Press (August 2005) 20–21.

2   "Got it Covered," *Network Computing* 10, 22 (1 November 1999), 1.

3   James B. Kobak, *How to Start a Magazine and Publish It Profitably* (New York: M. Evans and Company, 2002), 184.

4   David E. Sumner, "Sixty-Four Years of Life: What Did Its 2,128 Covers Cover? *Journal of Magazine and New Media Research*, Fall 2002.

5   Kate White, "How to Create Covers That Sell," 20–21.

6   Quoted in *Magazine Publishing* by Sammye Johnson and Patricia Prijatel (Lincolnwood, IL: NTC Contemporary, 2000), 240.

7   Quoted in Ina Saltz, "How to play the cover game now," *Folio* (March 2004), 31.

8   J.C. Suares interview with David E. Sumner, New York City, 5 Aug. 2005.

9   Kate White, "How to Create Covers That Sell," 20–21.

Chapter 6

1   James B. Kobak, *How To Start a Magazine and Publish It Profitably* (New York: M. Evans and Company, 2002), 178.

2   Samir Husni, *Launch Your Own Magazine: A Guide for Succeeding in Today's Marketplace* (Nashville: Hamblett House, Inc., 1998), 25.

3   Stewart Ramser telephone interview with David E. Sumner, 28 Jan. 2006.

4   Richard Stolley telephone interview with David E. Sumner, 25 July 2005.

5   Nina Link interview with David E. Sumner, New York City, 1 Aug. 2005.

6   Scott Crystal interview with David E. Sumner, New York City, 3 Aug. 2005.

7   *Magazines 2005–2006, Engagement and Results*, 26 Sept. 2005.

8 Yankelovich Omniplus, Feb. 2004. Information provided courtesy of John Squires of Time Inc.

9 Personal interview, John Squires interview with David E. Sumner, New York City, 5 Aug. 2005.

10 Ibid.

11 Ibid.

12 David E. Sumner, "Who Pays for Magazines—Advertisers or Magazines," *Advertising Research Journal*, Nov.-Dec. 2001.

13 Joe Mandese, "Paid Product Placement Surges In Magazines, Newspapers, Other Media," *Media Daily New* (26 July 2005), 61.

14 Teresa Ennis, editor. "Marketers and Magazines: Seven Big-Name Advertisers Talk about What They Need from Print." *Folio* (1 April 2000), 32–46.

15 Ibid.

Chapter 7

1 With credit to James Kobak in *How to Start a Magazine and Publish It Profitability* for these three basic concepts.

2 David Ball e-mail to Sherrill Rhoades, Feb. 2006.

3 Quoted in Charles P. Daly, Patrick Henry and Ellen Ryder, *The Magazine Publishing Industry* (New York: Allyn and Bacon, 1997), 94. This book contains a highly recommended chapter on "Circulation Principles."

4 Veronis Suhler Stevenson, *Communications Industry Forecast 2005–2009* (New York: Veronis Suhler Stevenson, 2005), 423.

5 Ned Desmond interview with David E. Sumner, New York City, 5 Aug. 2005.

6 Susan Allyn e-mail to Shirrel Rhoades, Feb. 2006.

7 Bob Cohn interview with Shirrel Rhoades, New York City, March 2006.

8 Vince Dema e-mail to Shirrel Rhoades, Feb. 2006.

9 Lawrence Freeman e-mail to Shirrel Rhoades, Feb. 2006.

10 Charles Block, "Wooing New Readers—Publishers Team with Businesses to Promote Publications," *American Demographics* (1 Jan. 2002).

11 Junius R. Clark III interview with Shirrel Rhoades, New York City, July 2005.

12 Steve Aster e-mail to Shirrel Rhoades, Feb. 2006.

13 Jim Sokolowski e-mail to Shirrel Rhoades, Feb. 2006.

14 Leonard Mogel, *The Magazine: Everything You Need to Know to Make It in the Magazine Business,* 4th ed. (Pittsburgh, Graphic Arts Technical Foundation, 1998), 88.

15 Jim Meneough interview with Shirrel Rhoades, New York City, Oct. 2005.

16 Daly, Henry and Ryder, *The Magazine Publishing Industry* (Allyn and Bacon, 1997), 107.

17 Shirrel Rhoades e-mail to David E. Sumner, April 2006.

18 "What About the Future?" *Circulation Management* (Sept. 2005), 33.

19 Ibid.

20 Quoted in *Launch Your Own Magazine* by Samir Husni (Nashville: Hamblett House, 1998), 121.

Chapter 8

1 James Kobak, "The Unchanging Principles of a Good Launch," *Folio: The Magazine for Magazine Management* (1 April 2004). Accessed at *www.foliomag.com*.

2 Dale Buss, "Ten Reasons New Magazines Fail," *Folio: The Magazine for Magazine Management* (February 2004), 42.

3 Ted Spiker e-mail to David E. Sumner, 30 Jan. 2006.

4 Diane Brady interview with Sherrill Rhoades, Key West, Florida, Jan. 2006.

5 James Kobak, "The Unchanging Principles of a Good Launch."

Chapter 9

1 Stewart Ramser telephone interview with David E. Sumner, 21 Jan. 2006.

2 Paul Hale e-mail to Sherrill Rhoades, Feb. 2006.

3 Leonard Mogel, *The Magazine: Everything You Need to Know to Make It in the Magazine Business*, 4th ed. (Pittsburgh: Graphic Arts Technical Foundation, 1998), 126.

4 Ibid.

Chapter 10

1 Tim Berners-Lee to Alt.hypertext newsgroup. 6 Aug. 1991. Archived at: *http://groups.google.com/groups?selm=6487%40cernvax.cern.ch* (accessed 20 Sept. 2002).

2 Nina Link interview with David E. Sumner, New York City, Aug. 1, 2005.

3 Bert Langford, "Six Ways Technology is Changing Publishing," *Folio: The Magazine for Magazine Management* (1 July 2005). Accessed at *www.foliomag.com*.

4 Laura Petreca, "Four Hurdles for Disney's Iger," *USA Today* (3 Oct. 2005), 1B.

5   William T. Kerr, "Five Themes That Will Shape Our Business," *Magazine World* published by the Federation of the International Periodical Press, London. (October 2005, 21).

6   R. J. Lehmann, "Is Your Web Site Stealing Your Readers," *Folio: The Magazine for Magazine Management* (15 September 2000), 35.

7   *Communications Industry Forecast 2005–2009, 19th edition.* Published by Veronis Suhler Stevenson, 2005.

8   Michael E. Holmes, Robert A. Papper, Mark N. Popovich and Michael Bloxham. *Middletown Media Studies: Concurrent Media Exposure* (Muncie: Ball State University, Center for Media Design, Fall 2005), 27.

9   *Magazine Dimensions 2005* (New York: Media Dynamics, Inc. 2005), 97.

10 *Communications Industry Forecast 2005–2009, 19th edition.* Published by Veronis Suhler Stevenson, 2005, 421.

11 Nina Link interview with David E. Sumner, New York City, 1 Aug. 2005.

12 Guy Consterdine, ed. *Routes to Success for Consumer Magazine Website* (London: Federation of the International Periodical Press, May 2005).

13 Ned Desmond interview with David E. Sumner, New York City, 5 Aug. 2005.

14 Chris Haines interview with David E. Sumner, New York City, 14 June 2002.

15 Ibid.

16 Bill Mickey, "The New Republic Boosts Subs and Service Through the Web," *Folio: The Magazine for Magazine Management* 3 Aug. 2005.

17 Chris Haines telephone interview with David E. Sumner, 27 May 2004.

18 Josha Macht telephone interview with David E. Sumner, 27 May 2004.

Chapter 11

1   "Daughter of 'Deep Throat' concedes finances were a motive," The Associated Press, (5 June 2005). Accessed on Lexis-Nexis, 8 April 2006.

2   "Publishing," *Encyclopedia Britannica, 15th ed. v. 26* (Chicago: Encyclopedia Britannica, Inc., 1995), 421.

3   Sammye Johnson and Patricia Prijatel, *Magazine Publishing* (Lincolnwood, IL: NTC/Contemporary Publishing, 2000), 48.

4   Andrew Bradford, "The Plan of the Undertaking," *The American Magazine or a Monthly View of the Political State of the British Colonies* (January 1741); i. Cited in Johnson and Prijatel, *Magazine Publishing*, 49.

5   "Publishing," *Encyclopedia Britannica, 15th ed. v. 26* (Chicago: Encyclopedia Britannica, Inc., 1995), 441.

6   Frank Luther Mott, *A History of American Magazines 1741–1890* (Cambridge: Harvard University Press, 1966), 30.

7   John Tebbel and Mary Ellen Zuckerman, *The Magazine in America 1741–1990* (New York: Columbia University Press, 1991), 11, 57.

8   Norberto Angeletti and Alberto Oliva, *Magazines That Make History: Their Origins, Development and Influence* (Gainesville, University Press of Florida, 2004).

9   Angelitti and Oliva, 290.

10   Jacqueline Leo interview with David E. Sumner, Pleasantville, New York, 4 Aug. 2005.

11   Richard Stolley telephone interview with David E. Sumner, 17 Feb. 2005.

12   Joe Treen e-mail to David E. Sumner, 1 Feb. 2006.

13   "Condé Nast Publications," *International Directory of Company Histories, v. 13* (Farmington Hills, MI: St. James Press, 1996), 177.

14   John H. Johnson (with Lerone Bennett, Jr.) *Succeeding Against the Odds* (New York: Time-Warner Books, 1989), 159.

15   David Abrahamson, *Magazine-Made America: The Cultural Transformation of the Postwar Periodical* (Cresskill, NJ: Hampton Press, 1996), 27.

16   John T. Cabell, "The birth of cross-border publishing." *FIPP Magazine World* (London: Federation of the International Periodical Press), December 2004, 14–15.

17   Arif Durrani, "The golden age of international licensing," *FIPP Magazine World* (London: Federation of the International Periodical Press), December 2004, 18–19.

18   David E. Sumner, "Modern Magazines, 1900-Present," in William David Sloan, ed. *The Age of Mass Communication* (Tuscaloosa, AL: Vision Press, 1996), 431.

19   William T. Kerr, "Five Themes That Will Shape Our Business," *FIPP Magazine World* (London: Federation of the International Periodical Press), October 2005, 21.

20   Sarah Gonsen, "The Incredible, Sellable O," *Folio: The Magazine for Magazine Management* (February 2001), 26.

21   Nat Ives, "Hispanic titles lead growth among periodicals," *Advertising Age* (17 Jan. 2006).

22   Veronis Suhler Stevenson, *Communications Industry Forecast 2005–2009* (New York: Veronis Suhler Stevenson, 2005), 423.

23   Reginald Brack, Jr., American Magazine Conference, Oct. 2005, New York City. Accessed at *www.magazine.org*, 16 Jan. 2006.

Chapter 12

1   David P. Forsyth and Warren Berger, "Trading Places" [a history of the business press], *Folio* (March 1991), 79–90.

2   Aric Press e-mail to David E. Sumner, 23 Aug. 2004.

3   Roger Welsch, "Musings from the mud porch," *Successful Farming* (April 2004), 65.

4   Whitney Sielaff telephone interview with David E. Sumner, 2 Aug. 2004.

5   Nicole Voges e-mail to David E. Sumner, 29 Jan. 2006.

6   Rob Spiegel, "Writing for trade and business publications," *2004 Writer's Market Online* (Cincinnati: F&W Publishing, 2004), 60.

7   Joshua Kurlantzick, "The workers' compensation crisis: Can it be fixed?" *Entrepreneur* (January 2004), 57.

8   Nicole Voges e-mail to David E. Sumner, 29 Jan. 2006.

9   Whitney Sielaff telephone interview with David E. Sumner, 2 Aug. 2004.

10   Shirrell Rhoades interview with Diane Brady, Key West, Fla., Jan. 2006.

Chapter 13

1   Stefan Fatsis, "A Coach's lawsuit poses challenge for Time Inc." *Wall Street Journal* (13 July 2005), 1A.

2   Ibid.

3   Justice Sandra Day O'Connor (Feist Publications, Inc. v. Rural Telephone Service Co., 499 US Code 340, 349 (1991).

4   Justice Sandra Day O'Connor (Feist Publications, Inc. v. Rural Telephone Service Co., 499 US Code 340, 349 (1991).

Chapter 14

1   "Most Intriguing Media Issues for 2006," *MIN Magazine Annual 2005.*

2   *Accountability: A Guide to Measuring ROI and ROO Across Media,* New York: Magazine Publishers of America, 2005.

3   Ibid.

4   *Circulation Management,* July 1, 2002.

5   "Circulation Levels Remain Surprisingly High," *Circulation Management,* November 2005.

6   "Making Sense of the Auditing Rules," *Folio: The Magazine for Magazine Management,* October 2005.

7   Ibid.

8   Scott Masterson interview with Shirrell Rhoades, New York City, July 2005.

9   Veronis Suhler Stevenson, *Communications Industry Forecast 2005–2009, 19th ed.* (New York: Veronis Suhler Stevenson, 2005), 421.

10   "What About the Future?" *Circulation Management,* September 2005.

11 Renetta McCann, "Screens reign supreme," *FIPP Magazine World* (August 2005), 28–29.

12 Nine Link interview with David E. Sumner, New York City, 1 Aug. 2005.

13 Marc T. Liu e-mail to Shirrel Rhoades, 8 April 2006.

14 William T. Kerr, "Five themes that will shape our business," *FIPP Magazine World* (October 2005), 21.

Index

Media Industries

General Editor
David Sumner

The Media Industries series offers comprehensive, classroom friendly textbooks designed to meet the needs of instructors teaching introductory media courses. Each book provides a concise, practical guide to all aspects of a major industry. These volumes are an ideal reference source for anyone contemplating a career in the media.

To order other books in this series, please contact our Customer Service Department:

(800) 770-LANG (within the U.S.)
(212) 647-7706 (outside the U.S.)
(212) 647-7707 FAX

Or order online at www.peterlang.com